THE

HEAVENLY FATHER.

Lectures on Modern Atheism.

BY

ERNEST NAVILLE,

CORRESPONDING MEMBER OF THE INSTITUTE OF FRANCE (ACADEMY OF THE MORAL AND POLITICAL SCIENCES), LATE PROFESSOR OF PHILOSOPHY IN THE UNIVERSITY OF GENEVA.

TRANSLATED FROM THE FRENCH

BY HENRY DOWNTON, M.A.,

ENGLISH CHAPLAIN AT GENEVA.

—"To this deplorable error I desire to oppose faith in GOD as it has been given to the world by the Gospel—faith in the HEAVENLY FATHER."

Author's Letter to Professor Faraday (v. p. 193).

BOSTON:
WILLIAM V. SPENCER.
1867.

CAMBRIDGE:
PRESS OF JOHN WILSON AND SON.

PREFACE.

THESE Lectures, in their original form, were delivered at Geneva, and afterwards at Lausanne, before two auditories which together numbered about two thousand five hundred men. A Swiss Review published considerable portions of them, which had been taken down in short-hand, and on reading these portions, several persons, belonging to different countries, conceived the idea of translating the work when completed by the Author, and corrected for publication. Proof-sheets were accordingly sent to the translators as they came from the press: and thus this volume will appear pretty nearly at the same time in several of the languages of Europe.

The hearty kindness with which my fellow-countrymen received my words has been to me both a delight and an encouragement. The expressions of sympathy which have reached me from abroad allow me to hope that these pages, notwithstanding the deficiencies and imperfections of which I am keenly sensible, reflect some few of the rays of the truth which God has deposited on the earth, thereby to unite in the same faith and hope men of every tongue and every nation.

ERNEST NAVILLE.

GENEVA, *May*, 1865.

NOTE BY THE TRANSLATOR.

THE appearance of this translation so long after that of the original work is in contradiction to the foregoing statement of the Author, that it would appear at nearly the same time with it. The delay has been due to causes beyond the translator's control — in part to the difficulty of revising the press at so great a distance from the place of publication, the translator being resident at Geneva. This latter circumstance causes an exception in another particular as regards this translation, the proposal to translate the Lectures having been made to the Author, and kindly accepted by him, during the course of their delivery at Geneva.

The mere statement by the Author of the numbers, large as they were, of those who formed the auditories, can give but a small idea of the enthusiasm with which they were received by the crowds which thronged to hear them, and which were composed of all classes of persons, from the most distinguished savant tó the intelligent artisan.

It is not to be expected that the Lectures when read, even in the original, and still less in a translation, can produce the vivid impression which they made on those, who, with the translator, had the privilege of hearing them delivered,—the Author having few rivals, on the Continent or elsewhere, in the graces of polished eloquence; but the subjects treated are, it is to be feared, of increasing importance, not abroad only, but in England; and in fact one Lecture, the fourth, is in a large measure occupied with forms of atheism which owe their chief support to English authors. In that Lecture the Author shows that the spiritual origin of man cannot "be put out of sight beneath details of physiology and researches of natural history," and that these not only "cannot settle," but "cannot so much as touch the question."

The same Lecture is occupied in part by a practical refutation of the prejudice against religion drawn from the irreligious character of many men of science. The Author's subject has led him in the present work to confine his illustrations on this head to the question of natural religion: but the translator will avow that a main motive with him to undertake the labor of this translation has been the wish to prove, in the instance of the distinguished Author himself, that men of incontestable eminence as metaphysical philosophers may hold and profess boldly their faith in doctrines, which many who affect to guide the religious opinions of our youth would teach them to despise as the heritage of narrow minds, and to cast away as incompatible with the highest intellectual cultivation. Such doctrines are those of the fall and ruin of man by nature, the necessity for Divine agency in his recovery, his need of propitiation by the sacrifice of the God-Man — *l'Homme-Dieu*. These truths are explicitly stated by the Author in his former course of lectures — *La Vie Éternelle*,* in which, while discoursing eloquently on that eternal life which is the portion of the righteous, he does not

* A translation of this work, by an English lady, has been published by Mr. Dalton, 28, Cockspur street.

shrink from declaring his belief in its awful counterpart, the eternal condemnation of the wicked.

"The offence of the Cross" has not "ceased," and many finding that these are the opinions of this Author, will perhaps lay down his book as unworthy of their attention: yet the editor, biographer, and expositor of the great French thinker, Maine de Biran, will not need introduction to the intellectual magnates of our own or of any country. The translator will be thankful, if some of those,—the youth more especially,—of his own country, who have been dazzled by the glare of false science, shall find in this work a help to the reassuring of their faith, while they learn in a fresh example that there are men quite competent to deal with the profoundest problems which can exercise our thoughts, who at the same time have come to a conviction,—compatible as they believe with principles of the clearest reason,—of the truth of those very doctrines which form the substance of evangelical Christianity. In saying this, the translator is far from claiming the Author as belonging to the same school of theology with himself: but differing with him on some important points, he has yet believed that this volume is calculated to be of much use in the present condition of religious thought in England, and in this hope and prayer he commends it to the blessing of Him, whose being and attributes, as our God and Father in Jesus Christ, are therein asserted and defended.

GENEVA, *November*, 1865.

CONTENTS.

LECTURE I.

OUR IDEA OF GOD.

(At Geneva, 17th Nov. 1863.—At Lausanne, 11th Jan. 1864.)

GENTLEMEN,

Some five-and-twenty or thirty years ago, a German writer published a piece of verse which began in this way: "Our hearts are oppressed with the emotions of a pious sadness, at the thought of the ancient Jehovah who is preparing to die." The verses were a dirge upon the death of the living God; and the author, like a well educated son of the nineteenth century, bestowed a few poetic tears upon the obsequies of the Eternal.

I was young when these strange words met my eyes, and they produced in me a kind of painful bewilderment, which has, I think, for ever engraven them in my memory. Since then, I have had occasion to learn by many tokens that this fact was not at all an exceptional one, but that men of influence, famous schools, important tendencies of the modern mind, are agreed in proclaiming that the time of religion is over, of religion in all its forms, of religion in the largest sense of the word. Beneath the social disturbances of the day, beneath the discussions of science, beneath the anxiety of some and the sadness of others, beneath the ironical and more or less insulting joy of a few, we read at the foundation of many intellectual manifestations of our time these gloomy words: "Henceforth no more God for humanity!" What may well send a shudder of fright through society — more than threatening war, more than possible revolution, more than the plots which may be hatching in the dark against the security of persons or of property — is, the number, the importance, and the extent of the efforts which are making in our days to extinguish in men's souls their faith in the living God.

This fear, Gentlemen, I should wish to communicate to you, but I should wish also to confine it within its just limits. Religion (I take this term in its most general acceptation) is not, as many say that it is, either dead or dying. I want no other proof of this than the pains which so many people are taking to kill it. It is often those who say that it is dead, or falling rapidly into dissolution, who apply themselves to this work. They are too generous, no doubt, to make a violent attack upon a corpse; and it is easy to understand, judging by the intensity of their exertions, that in their own opinion they have something else to do than to give a finishing stroke to the dying.

Present circumstances are serious, not for religion itself, which cannot be imperilled, but for minds which run the risk of losing their balance and their support. Let it be observed, however, that when it is said that we are living in extraordinary times, that we are passing through an unequalled crisis, that the like of what we see was never seen before, and so on, we must always regard conclusions of this nature with distrust. Our personal interest in the circumstances which immediately surround us produces on them for us the magnifying effect of a microscope: and our principal reason for thinking that our epoch is more extraordinary than others, is for the most part that we are living in our own epoch, and have not lived in others. A mind attentive to this fact, and so placed upon its guard against all tendency to exaggeration, will easily perceive that religious thought has in former times passed through shocks as profound and as dangerous as those of which we are witnesses. Still the crisis is a real one. Taking into account its extent in our days, we may say that it is new for the generation to which we belong; and it is worthy of close consideration. To-day, as an introduction to this grave subject, I should wish first to determine as precisely as possible what is our idea of God; to inquire next from what sources we derive it; and lastly to point out, as clearly as I may, the limits and the nature of the discussion to which I invite you.

In asking what sense we must give to the word "God," I am not going to propose to you a metaphysical definition, or any system of my own: I am inquiring what is in fact the idea of God in the bosom of modern society, in the souls which live by this idea, in the hearts of which it constitutes the joy, in the consciences of which it is the support.

When our thoughts rise above nature and humanity to that invisible Being whom we speak of as God, what is it which passes in our souls?

They fear, they hope, they pray, they offer thanksgiving. If a man finds himself in one of those desperate positions in which all human help fails, he turns towards Heaven, and says, My God! If we are witnesses of one of those instances of revolting injustice which stir the conscience in its profoundest depths, and which could not on earth meet with adequate punishment, we think within ourselves, — There is a Judge on high! If we are reproved by our own conscience, the voice of that conscience, which disturbs and sometimes torments us, reminds us that though we may be shut out from all human view, there is no less an Eye which sees us, and a just award awaiting us. Thus it is (I am seeking to establish facts) that the thought of God operates, so to speak, in the souls of those who believe in Him. If you look for the meaning common to all these manifestations of man's heart, what do you find? Fear, hope, thanksgiving, prayer. To whom is all this addressed? To a Power intelligent and free, which knows us, and is able to act upon our destinies. This is the idea which is found at the basis of all religions; not only of the religion of the only God, but of the most degraded forms of idolatrous worship.

All religion rests upon the sentiment of one or more invisible Powers, superior to nature and to humanity.

When philosophical curiosity is awakened, it disengages from the general sentiment of power the definite idea of the cause which becomes the explanation of the phenomena. The reason of man, by virtue of its very constitution, finds a need of conceiving of an absolute cause which escapes by its eternity the lapse of time, and by its infinite character the bounds of limited existences; a principle, the necessary being of which depends on no other; in a word a unique cause, establishing by its unity the universal harmony. So, when reason meets with the idea of the sole and Almighty Creator, it attaches itself to it as the only thought which accounts to it for the world and for itself.

The Creator is, first of all, He whose glory the heavens declare, while the earth makes known the work of His hands. He is the Mighty One and the Wise, whose will has given being to nature, and who directs at once the chorus of stars in the depths of the heavens, and the drop of vital moisture in the herb which we tread under foot.

If, after having looked around, we turn our regard in upon ourselves, we then discover other heavens, spiritual heavens, in which shine, like stars of the first magnitude, those objects which cause the heart of man to beat, so long as he is not self-degraded: truth, goodness, beauty. Now we feel that we are made for this higher world. Material enjoyments may enchain our will; we may, in the indulgence of unworthy passions, pursue what in its essence is only evil, error, and deformity; but, if all the rays of our true nature are not extinguished, a voice issues from the depth of our souls and protests against our debasement. Our aspirations toward these spiritual excellences are unlimited. Our thought sets out on its course: have we solved one question? immediately new questions arise, which press, no less than the former, for an answer. Our conscience speaks: have we come in a certain degree to realize what is right and good? immediately conscience demands of us still more. Is our feeling for beauty awakened? Well, sirs, when an artist is satisfied with the work of his hands, do you not know at once what to think of him? Do you not know that that man will never do any thing great, who does not see shining in his horizon an ideal which stamps as imperfect all that he has been able to realize? The voice which urges us on through life from the cradle to the grave, and which, without allowing us a moment's pause, is ever crying — Forward! forward! this voice is not more imperious than the noble instinct which, in the view of beauty, of truth, of good, is also saying to us — Forward! forward! and, with the American poet, *Excelsior!* higher, ever higher! Many of you know that instinct familiar to the *climbers of the Alps*,* as they are called, who, arrived at one summit, have no rest so long as there remains a loftier height in view. Such is our destiny; but the last peak is veiled in shining clouds which conceal it from our sight. Perfection, — this is the point to which our nature aspires; but it is the ladder of Jacob: we see the foot which rests upon the earth; the summit hides itself from our feeble view amidst the splendors of the infinite.

These objects of our highest desires — beauty in its supreme manifestation, absolute holiness, infinite truth — are united in one and the same thought — God! The attributes of the spiritual are never in us but as borrowed attributes; they

* Aux *grimpeurs des Alpes.*

dwell naturally in Him who is their source. God is the truth, not only because He knows all things, but because He is the very object of our thoughts; because, when we study the universe, we do but spell out some few of the laws which He has imposed on things; because, to know truth is never any thing else than to know the creation or the Creator, the world or its eternal Cause. God it is who must be Himself the satisfaction of that craving of the conscience which urges us towards holiness. If we had arrived at the highest degree of virtue, what should we have done? We should have realized the plan which He has proposed to spiritual creatures in their freedom, at the same time that He is directing the stars in their courses by that other word which they accomplish without having heard it. God is the eternal source of beauty. He it is who has shed grace upon our valleys, and majesty upon our mountains; and He, again, it is (I quote St. Augustine) who acts within the souls of artists, those great artists, who, urged unceasingly towards the regions of the ideal, feel themselves drawn onwards towards a divine world.

God then above all is He who *is*, — the Absolute, the Infinite, the Eternal, — in the ever mysterious depths of His own essence. In His relation to the world, He is the cause; in His relation to the lofty aspirations of the soul, He is the ideal. He is the ideal, because being the absolute cause, He is the unique source, at the same time that He is the object, of our aspirations: He is the absolute cause, because being He who *is*, in His supreme unity, nothing could have existence except by the act of His power. We are able already to recognize here, in passing, the source at which are fed the most serious aberrations of religious thought. Are truth, holiness, beauty considered separately from the real and infinite Spirit in which is found their reason for existing? We see thus appear philosophies noble in their commencement, but which soon descend a fatal slope. The divine, so-called, is spoken of still; but the divine is an abstraction, and apart from God has no real existence. If truth, beauty, holiness are not the attributes of an eternal mind, but the simple expression of the tendencies of our soul, man may render at first a sort of worship to these lofty manifestations of his own nature; but logic, inexorable logic, forces him soon to dismiss the divine to the region of chimeras. These rays are extinguished together with their luminous centre; the soul loses the secret of its destinies, and, in the measureless grief which possesses it, it proclaims at length that all is vanity. We shall have, in the sequel, to be witnesses together of this sorrowful spectacle.

Such is the basis of our idea of God: we must now discover its summit. Before the thought of this Sovereign Being, by whose Will are all things, and who is without cause and without beginning, our soul is overwhelmed. We are so feeble! the thought of absolute power crushes us. Creatures of a day, how should we understand the Eternal? Frail as we are, and evil, we tremble at the idea of holiness. But milder accents, as you know, have been heard upon the earth: This Sovereign God—He loves us. In proportion as this idea gains possession of our understanding, in the same proportion our soul has glimpses of the paths of peace. He loves us, and we take courage. He hears us, and prayer rises to Him with the hope of being heard. He governs all, and we confide in His Providence. When your gaze is directed towards the depths of the sky, does it never happen to you to remain in a manner terrified, as you contemplate those worlds which without end are added to other worlds? As you fix your thoughts upon the immeasurable abysses of the firmament, — as you say to yourselves that how far soever you put back the boundary of the skies, if the universe ended there, then the universe, with its suns and its groups of stars, would still be but a solitary lamp, shining as a point in the midst of the limitless darkness, — have you never experienced a sort of mysterious fright and giddiness? At such a time turn your eyes upon nearer objects. He who has made the heavens with their immensity, is He who makes the corn to spring forth for your sustenance, who clothes the fields with the flowers which rejoice your sight, who gives you the fresh breath of morning, and the calm of a lovely evening: it is He, without whose permission nothing occurs, who watches over you and over those you love. Possess yourselves thoroughly with this thought of love, then lift once more your eyes to the sky, and from every star, and from the worlds which are lost in the furthest depths of space, shall fall upon your brow, no longer clouded, a ray of love and of peace. Then with a feeling of sweet affiance you will adopt as your own those words of an ancient prophet: "Whither shall I go from

Thy Spirit, or whither shall I flee from Thy Presence? If I ascend up into heaven, Thou art there: if I make my bed in hell, behold, Thou art there. If I take the wings of the morning, and dwell in the uttermost parts of the sea; even there shall Thy hand lead me, and Thy right hand shall hold me:"* then you will understand those grand and sweet words of Saint Augustine, some of the most beautiful that ever fell from the lips of a man: "Are you afraid of God? Run to His arms!"

Thus our idea of God is completed,—the idea of Him whom, in a feeling of filial confidence, we name the Father, and whom we call the *Heavenly* Father, while we adore that absolute holiness, of which the pure brightness of the firmament is for us the visible and magnificent symbol. Goodness is the secret of the universe; goodness it is which has directed power, and placed wisdom at its service.

My object is not to teach this idea, but to defend it: it is not, I say, to teach it, for we all possess it. There is no one here who has not received his portion of the sacred deposit. This sacred idea may be veiled by our sorrows, per-

* Psalm cxxxix. 7–10.

verted by our errors, obscured by our faults; but, however thick be the layer of ashes heaped together in the depth of our souls — look closely: the sacred spark is not extinguished, and a favorable breath may still rekindle the flame.

We have considered the essential elements of which our idea of God is composed. And whence comes this idea? What is its historical origin? I do not ask what is the historical origin of religion, for religion does not take its rise in history; it is met with everywhere and always in humanity. Those who deny this are compelled to "search in the darkness for some obscure example known only to themselves, as if all natural inclinations were destroyed by the corruption of a people, and as if, as soon as there are any monsters, the species were no longer any thing." * The consciousness of a world superior to the domain of experience is one of the attributes characteristic of our nature. "If there had ever been, or if there still anywhere existed, a people entirely destitute of religion, it would be in consequence of an exceptional downfall which would be tantamount to a lapse into animality." † I am

* J. J. Rousseau.

† *Les Origines Indo-Européennes*, by Adolphe Pictet, ii. 651.

not therefore inquiring after the origin of the idea and sentiment of the Deity, in a general sense, but after the origin of the idea of the only and Almighty Creator as we possess it. In fact, if religion is universal, distinct knowledge of the Creator is not so.

Our own past strikes its roots into the historic soil which, in the matter of creeds, is known by the name of paganism or idolatry. At first sight what do we find in the opinions of that ancient world? No trace of the divine unity. Adoration is dispersed over a thousand different beings. Not only are the heavenly bodies adored and the powers of nature, but men, animals, and inanimate objects. The feeling of the holiness of God is not less wanting, it would seem, than the idea of His unity. Religion serves as a pretext for the unchaining of human passions. This is the case unfortunately with religion in general, and the true religion is no exception to the rule: but what characterizes paganism is that in its case religion, by its own proper nature, favors the development of immorality. Celebrated shrines become the dens of a prostitution which forms part of the homage rendered to the gods; the religious rites of ancient Asia, and those of

Greece which fell under their influence, are notorious for their lewdness. The temples of false deities, too often defiled by debauchery, are too often also dishonored by frightful sacrifices. The ancient civilization of Mexico was elegant and even refined in some respects; but the altars were stained, every year, with the blood of thousands of human beings; and the votaries of this sanguinary worship devoured, in solemn banquets, the quivering limbs of the victims. Let us not look for examples too far removed from the civilization which has produced our own. In the Greek and Roman world, the stories of the gods were not very edifying, as every one knows: the worship of Bacchus gave no encouragement to temperance, and the festivals of Venus were not a school of chastity. It would be easy, by bringing together facts of this sort, to form a picture full of sombre coloring, and to conclude that our idea of God, the idea of the only and holy God, does not proceed from the impure sources of idolatry. The proceeding would be brief and convenient; but such an estimation of the facts, false because incomplete, would destroy the value of the conclusion. In pagan antiquity, in fact, the abominations of which I have just reminded you did not by themselves make up religious tradition. Side by side with a current of darkness and impurity, we meet with a current of pure ideas and of strong gleams of the day.

Almost all the pagans seem to have had a glimpse of the Divine unity over the multiplicity of their idols, and of the rays of the Divine holiness across the saturnalia of their Olympi. It was a Greek who wrote these words: "Nothing is accomplished on the earth without Thee, O God, save the deeds which the wicked perpetrate in their folly." * It was in a theatre at Athens that the chorus of a tragedy sang, more than two thousand years ago: "May destiny aid me to preserve unsullied the purity of my words and of all my actions, according to those sublime laws which, brought forth in the celestial heights, have Heaven alone for their father, to which the race of mortal men did not give birth, and which oblivion shall never entomb. In them is a supreme God, and one who waxes not old." † It would be easy to multiply quotations of this order, and to show you in the documents of Grecian and Roman civilization numerous traces of the knowledge of the

* Cleanthes, *Hymn to Jupiter*. † Sophocles. *Œdipus R.*

only and holy God. Listen now to a voice which has come forth actually from the recesses of the sepulchre: it reaches us from ancient Egypt.

In Egypt, as you know, the degradation of the religious idea was in popular practice complete. But, under the confused accents of superstition, the science of our age is succeeding in catching from afar the vibrations of a sublime utterance. In the coffins of a large number of mummies have been discovered rolls of papyrus containing a sacred text which is called the *Book of the Dead*. Here is the translation of some fragments which appear to date from a very remote epoch. It is God who speaks: "I am the Most Holy, the Creator of all that replenishes the earth, and of the earth itself, the habitation of mortals. I am the Prince of the infinite ages. I am the great and mighty God, the Most High, shining in the midst of the careering stars and of the armies which praise me above thy head. . . . It is I who chastise and who judge the evil-doers, and the persecutors of godly men. I discover and confound the liars . . . I am the all-seeing Judge and Avenger . . . the guardian of my laws in the land of righteousness." *

* *Handbuch der gesammten ägyptischen Alterthumskunde*, von Dr. Max Uhlemann. Leipzig, 1857.

These words are found mingled, in the text from which I extract them, with allusions to inferior deities; and it must be acknowledged that the translation of the ancient documents of Egypt is still uncertain enough. Still this uncertainty does not appear to extend to the general sense and bearing of the recent discoveries of our savants. Myself a simple learner from the masters of the science, I can only point out to you the result of their studies. Now, this is what the masters tell us as to the actual state of mythological studies. Traces are found almost everywhere, in the midst of idolatrous superstitions, of a religion comparatively pure, and often stamped with a lofty morality. Paganism is not a simple fact: it offers to view in the same bed two currents, the one pure and the other impure. What is the relation between these two currents? A passage in a writer of the Latin Church throws a vivid light upon their actual relation in practical life. It is thus that Lactantius expresses himself: "When man (the pagan) finds himself in adversity, then it is that he has recourse to God (to the only God). If the horrors of war threaten him, if there appear a contagious disease, a drought, a tempest, then he has recourse to God.

. . . If he is overtaken by a storm at sea, and is in danger of perishing, immediately he calls upon God; if he finds himself in any urgent peril, he has recourse to God. . . . Thus men bethink themselves of God when they are in trouble; but as soon as the danger is past, and they are no longer in any fear, we see them return with joy to the temples of the false gods, make to them libations, and offer sacrifices to them." * This is a striking picture of the workings of man's heart in all ages; for, as our author observes, "God is never so much forgotten of men as when they are quietly enjoying the favors and blessings which He sends them." † As regards our special object, this page reveals in a very instructive manner the religious condition of heathen antiquity. The thought of the sovereign God was stifled without being extinguished; it awoke beneath the pressure of anguish; but ordinary life, the life of every day, belonged to the easy worship of idols.

It may now be asked what is the historical relation between the two currents of paganism of which we have just established the actual relation in practical life. Did humanity begin with a

* *Institutions divines*, ii. 1. † Id.

coarse fetichism, and thence rise by slow degrees to higher conceptions? Do the traces of a comparatively pure monotheism first show themselves in the most recent periods of idolatry? Contemporary science inclines more and more to answer in the negative. It is in the most ancient historical ground (allow me these geological terms) that the laborious investigators of the past meet with the most elevated ideas of religion. Cut to the ground a young and vigorous beech-tree, and come back a few years afterwards: in place of the tree cut down you will find coppice-wood; the sap which nourished a single trunk has been divided amongst a multitude of shoots. This comparison expresses well enough the opinion which tends to prevail amongst our savants on the subject of the historical development of religions. The idea of the only God is at the root,—it is primitive; polytheism is derivative. A forgotten, and as it were slumbering, monotheism exists beneath the worship of idols; it is the concealed trunk which supports them, but the idols have absorbed all the sap. The ancient God (allow me once more a comparison) is like a sovereign confined in the interior of his palace: he is but seldom thought of, and only on great occasions; his ministers alone act, entertain requests, and receive the real homage.

The proposition of the historical priority of monotheism is very important, and is not universally admitted. It will therefore be necessary to show you, by a few quotations at least, that I am not speaking rashly. One of the most accredited mythologists of our time, Professor Grimm, of Berlin, writes as follows: "The monotheistic form appears to be the more ancient, and that out of which antiquity in its infancy formed polytheism. . . . All mythologies lead us to this conclusion." * Among the French savants devoted to the study of ancient Egypt, the Vicomte de Rongé stands in the foremost rank. This is what he tells us: "In Egypt the supreme God was called the one God, living indeed, He who made all that exists, who created other beings. He is the Generator existing alone who made the heaven and created the earth." The writer informs us that these ideas are often found reproduced "in writings the date of which is anterior to Moses, and many of which formed part of the most ancient sacred hymns;" then he comes to

* *Deutsche Mythol.* Third edition, page LXIV.

this conclusion: "Egypt, in possession of an admirable fund of doctrines respecting the essence of God, and the immortality of the soul, did not for all that defile herself the less by the most degrading superstitions; we have in her, sufficiently summed up, the religious history of all antiquity." * As regards the civilization which flourished in India, M. Adolphe Pictet, in his learned researches on the subject of the primitive Aryas, arrives, in what concerns the religious idea, at the following conclusion: "To sum up: primitive monotheism of a character more or less vague, passing gradually into a polytheism still simple, such appears to have been the religion of the ancient Aryas." † One of our fellow-countrymen, who cultivates with equal modesty and perseverance the study of religious antiquities, has procured the greater part of the recent works published on these subjects in France, Germany, and England. He has read them, pen in hand, and, at my urgent request, he has kindly allowed me to look over his notes which have been long accumulating. I find the following sentence in the manuscripts which he has shown me: "The

* *Annales de philosophie chrétienne*, t. 59, p. 228.*r.*

† *Les Origines Indo-Européennes*, ii. 720.

general impression of all the most distinguished mythologists of the present day is, that monotheism is at the foundation of all pagan mythology."

The savants, I repeat, do not unanimously accept these conclusions : savants, like other men, are rarely unanimous. It is enough for my purpose to have shown that it is not merely the grand tradition guaranteed by the Christian faith, but also the most distinctly marked current of contemporary science, which tells us that God shone upon the cradle of our species. The august Form was veiled, and idolatry with its train of shameful rites shows itself in history as the result of a fall which calls for a restoration, rather than as the point of departure of a continued progress.

The august Form was veiled. Who has lifted the veil? Not the priests of the idols. We meet in the history of paganism with movements of reformation, or, at the very least, of religious transformation: Buddhism is a memorable example of this; but it is not a return towards the pure traditions of India or of Egypt which has caused us to know the God whom we adore. Has the veil been lifted by reflection, that is to say by the labors of philosophers?

Philosophy has rendered splendid services to the world. It has combated the abominations of idolatry; it has recognized in nature the proofs of an intelligent design; it has discerned in the reason the deeply felt need of unity; it has indicated in the conscience the sense of good, and shown its characteristics; it has contemplated the radiant image of the supreme beauty — still it is not philosophy which has restored for humanity the idea of God. Its lights mingled with darkness remained widely scattered, and without any focus powerful enough to give them strength for enlightening the world. To seek God, and consequently to know Him already in a certain measure; but to remain always before the altar of a God glimpsed only by an *élite* of sages, and continuing for the multitudes the unknown God: such was the wisdom of the ancients. It prepared the soil; but it did not deposit in it the germ from which the idea of the Creator was to spring forth living and strong, to overshadow with its branches all the nations of the earth. And when this idea appeared in all its splendor, and began the conquest of the universe, the ancient philosophy, which had separated itself from heathen forms of worship, and had covered them with its contempt, contracted an alliance with its old adversaries. It accepted the wildest interpretations of the common superstitions, in order to be able to league itself with the crowd in one and the same conflict with the new power which had just appeared in the world. And this sums up in brief compass the whole history of philosophy in the first period of our era.

The monotheism of the moderns does not proceed historically from paganism; it was prepared by the ancient philosophy, without being produced by it. Whence comes it then? On this head there exists no serious difference of opinion. Our knowledge of God is the result of a traditional idea, handed down from generation to generation in a well-defined current of history. Much obscurity still rests upon man's earliest religious history, but the truth which I am pointing out to you is solidly and clearly established. Pass, in thought, over the terrestrial globe. All the superstitions of which history preserves the remembrance are practised at this day, either in Asia or in Africa, or in the isles of the Ocean. The most ridiculous and ferocious rites are practised still in the light of the same sun which gilds, as he sets, the spires and domes of our churches. At this very day, there are nations upon the earth which prostrate themselves before animals, or which adore sacred trees. At this very day, perhaps at this hour in which I am addressing you, human victims are bound by the priests of idols; before you have left this room, their blood will have defiled the altars of false deities. At this very day, numerous nations, which have neither wanted time for self-development, nor any of the resources of civilization, nor clever poets, nor profound philosophers, belong to the religion of the Brahmins, or are instructed in the legends which serve as a mask to the pernicious doctrines of Buddha. Where do we meet with the clear idea of the Creator? In a unique tradition which proceeds from the Jews, which Christians have diffused, and which Mahomet corrupted. God is known, with that solid and general knowledge which founds a settled doctrine and a form of worship, under the influence of this tradition and nowhere else. We assert this as a simple fact of contemporary history; and there is scarcely any fact in history better established.

The light comes to us from the Gospel. This

light did not appear as a sudden and absolutely new illumination. It had cast pale gleams on the soul of the heathen in their search after the unknown God; it had shone apart upon that strange and glorious people which bears the name of Israel. Israel had preserved the primitive light encompassed by temporary safe-guards. It was the flame of a lamp, too feeble to live in the open air, and which remained shut up in a vase, until the moment when it should have become strong enough to shine forth from its shattered envelope upon the world. The worship of Jehovah is a local worship; but this worship, localized for a time, is addressed to the only and sovereign God. To every nation which says to Israel as Athaliah to Joash:

> I have my God to serve — serve thou thine own,*

Israel replies with Joash:

> Nay, Madam, but my God is God alone;
> Him must thou fear: thy God is nought — a dream! †

Israel does not affirm merely that the God of Israel is the only true God, but affirms moreover

* J'ai mon Dieu que je sers, vous servirez le vôtre.

† Il faut craindre le mien;
Lui seul est Dieu, Madame, et le vôtre n'est rien.

that the time will come when all the earth will acknowledge Him for the only and universal Lord. A grand thought, a grand hope, is in the soul of this people, and assures it that all nations shall one day look to Jerusalem. Its prophets threaten, warn, denounce chastisements, predict terrible catastrophes; but in the midst of their severer utterances breaks forth ever and again the song of future triumph:

> Uplift, Jerusalem, thy queenly brow:
> Light of the nations, and their glory, thou! *

Thus is preserved in the ancient world the knowledge of God amongst an exceptional people, amidst the darkness of idolatry and the glimmerings of an imperfect wisdom. And not only is it preserved, but it shines with a brightness more and more vivid and pure. The conception of sovereignty which constitutes its foundation, is crowned as it advances by the conception of love. At length He appears by whom the universal Father was to be known of all.

Have you not remarked the surprising simplicity with which Jesus speaks of His work? He

* Lève, Jérusalem, lève ta tête altière!
Les peuples à l'envi marchent à ta lumière.

speaks of the universe and of the future as a lawful proprietor speaks of his property. The field in which the Word shall be sown is the world. He introduces that worship in spirit and in truth before which all barriers shall fall. He knows that humanity belongs to Him; and when He foretells His peaceful conquest, one knows not which predominates in His words, simplicity or grandeur. Now this predicted work has been done, is being done, and will be done. No one entertains any serious doubt of this. The idea of God, as it exists amongst Christian peoples, bears on its brow the certain sign of victory.

In many respects, we are passing through the world in times which are not extraordinary, and among things little worthy of lasting record. Still great events are being accomplished before our eyes. The ancient East is shaken to its foundations. The work of foreign missions is taken up again with fresh energy. Ships, as they leave the shores of Europe, carry with them, — together with those who travel for purposes of commerce, or from curiosity, or as soldiers, — those new crusaders who exclaim: God wills it! and are ready to march to their death in order to proclaim the God of life to nations plunged in darkness. The advances of industry, the developments of commerce, the calculations of ambition, all conspire to diffuse spiritual light over the globe. These are noble spectacles, revealing clearly the traces of a superior design, which the mighty of this world are accomplishing, even by the craft and violence of their policy: they are the manifest instruments of a Will to which oftentimes they are insensible. The knowledge of God is extending; and while it is extending, it is enriching itself with its own conquests. Just as it absorbed the living sap of the doctrines of the Greeks, so it is strengthening itself with the doctrines of the ancient East and of old Egypt, which an indefatigable science is bringing again to light. Christian thought is growing, not by receiving any foreign impulse from without, but like a vigorous tree, whose roots traverse new layers of a fertile soil. All truth comes naturally to the centre of truth as to its rallying-point; and to the universal prayer must be gathered all the pure accents gone astray in the superstitious invocations which rise from the banks of the Ganges or from the burning regions of Africa. The day will come, when our planet, in its revolutions about the sun, shall receive on no point of its surface the rays of the orb of day, without sending back, over the ruins of idol-temples for ever overthrown, a song of thanksgiving to the God of Abraham, Isaac, and Jacob, become through Jesus Christ the God of all mankind.

We know now whence comes our idea of God: it is Christian in its origin. It proceeds from this source, not only for those who call themselves Christians, but for all those who, in the bosom of modern society, believe sincerely and seriously in God. But little study and reflection is required for the acknowledgment that the doctrines of our deists are the product of a reason which has been *evangelized* without their own knowledge. They have not invented, but have received the thought, which constitutes the support of their life. A mind of ordinary cultivation is free henceforward from all danger of falling into the artless error of J. J. Rousseau, when he pretended that even though he had been born in a desert island and had never known a human being, he would have been able to draw up the confession of faith of the *Vicaire Savoyard*. The habit of historical research has dispelled these illusions. A French writer, distinguished for solid erudition, wrote not long ago: "The civilized world has received from Judea the foundations of its faith. It has learned of it these two things which pagan antiquity never knew — holiness and charity; for all holiness is derived from belief in a personal, spiritual God, Creator of the universe; and all charity from the doctrine of human brotherhood!" * Religion, in its most general sense, is found wherever there are men; but distinct knowledge of the Heavenly Father is the fruit of that word which comes to us from the borders of the Jordan, — a word in which all the true elements of ancient wisdom are found to have mutually drawn together, and strengthened each other. In the very heart of our civilization, those men of mind who succeed in freeing themselves in good earnest from the influence of this word come, oftener than not, to throw off all belief in the real and true God, if they have strength of mind enough properly to understand themselves.

How is it that the full idea of the Creator, — an idea which true philosophers have sought after in all periods of history, and of which they

* *Etudes Orientales*, par Adolphe Franck, p. 427.

have had, so to speak, glimpses and presentiments, — how is it that this idea is a living one only under the influence of the tradition which, proceeding originally from Abraham and Moses, has been continued by Jesus Christ? It is not impossible to point out the spiritual causes of this great historical phenomenon. Faith in God, in order to maintain itself in presence of the difficulties which rise in our minds, and — to come at once to the core of the question — the idea of the love of God, in order to maintain itself in presence of evil and of the power of evil on the earth, has need of resources which the Christian belief alone possesses. The knowledge of the Heavenly Father is essentially connected with the Gospel: this is the historical fact. This fact is accounted for by the existence of an organic bond between all the great Christian doctrines: this is my deliberate conviction. I frankly declare here my own opinions: to do so is for me a matter almost of honor and good faith; but I declare them, without desiring to lay any stress upon them in these lectures. My present object is to consider the idea of God by itself. I isolate it for my own purposes from Christian truth taken as a whole, but without making the separation in my thoughts. The thesis which I propose to maintain is common to all Christians, that is quite clear; but further; in a perfectly general sense, and in a merely abstract point of view, it is a proposition maintained equally by the disciples of Mahomet; it is maintained by J. J. Rousseau and the spiritualist philosophers who reproduce his thoughts. It is clear in fact that just as Jesus Christ is the corner-stone of all Christian doctrine, so God is the foundation common to all religions.

Before concluding this lecture I desire to answer a question which may have suggested itself to some amongst you. What are we about when we take up a Christian idea in order to defend it by reasoning? Are we occupied about religion or philosophy? Are we treading upon the ground of faith, or on the ground of reason? Are we in the domain of tradition, or in that of free inquiry? I have no great love, Gentlemen, for hedges and enclosures. I know very well, better, perhaps, than many amongst you, because I have longer reflected on the subject, what are the differences which separate studies specially religious, from philosophical inquiries. But when the question relates to God, to the universal cause, we find ourselves at the common root of religion and philosophy, and distinctions, which exist elsewhere, disappear. Besides, these distinctions are never so absolute as they are thought to be. You will understand this if you pay attention to these two considerations: there is no such thing as pure thought disengaged from every traditional element: there is no such thing as tradition received in a manner purely passive, and disengaged from all exercise of the reflective faculties.

You think you are employed about philosophy when you shut yourself up in your own individual thoughts. A mistake! The most powerful genius of modern times failed in this enterprise. Descartes conceived the project of forgetting all that he had known, and of producing a system of doctrine which should come forth from his brain as Minerva sprang all armed from the brain of Jupiter. Now-a-days a mere schoolboy, if he has been well taught, ought to be able to prove that Descartes was mistaken, because the current of tradition entered his mind together with the words of the language. It is not so easy as we may suppose to break the ties by which God has bound us all together in mutual dependence.

Man speaks, he only thinks by means of speech, and speech is a river which takes its rise in the very beginnings of history, and brings down to the existing generation the tribute of all the waters of the past. No one can isolate himself from the current, and place himself outside the intellectual society of his fellows. We have more light than we had on this subject, and the attempt of Descartes, which was of old the happy audacity of genius, could in our days be nothing but the foolish presumption of ignorance.

As for the purely passive reception of tradition, this may be conceived when only unimportant legends are in question, or doctrines which occupy the mind only as matters of curiosity; but when life is at stake, and the interests of our whole existence, the mind labors upon the ideas which it receives. Religion is only living in any soul when all the faculties have come into exercise; and faith, by its own proper nature, seeks to understand. The distinction between traditional data therefore and pure philosophy is far from being so real or so extensive as it is commonly thought to be. But for lack of time, I might undertake to prove to you more at length that the labor of individual thought upon the common tradition is the absolute and permanent law of development for the human mind.

We have to steer between two extreme and contrary pretensions. What shall we say to those theologians who deny all power to man's reason, and consider the understanding as a receiver which does nothing but receive the liquid which is poured into it? to those theologians who, not content with despising Aristotle and Plato, think themselves obliged to vilify Socrates and calumniate Regulus? We will tell them that they depart from the grand Christian tradition, of which they believe themselves *par excellence* the representatives. We will add that they outrage their Master by seeming to believe that in order to exalt Him it is necessary to calumniate humanity. Again, what shall we say to those philosophers, who do not wish for truth except when they have succeeded in educing it by themselves? to those philosophers who draw a little circle about their own personal thought, and say: If truth discovers itself outside this circle we have no wish to see it; and who boast that they only are free, because they have abandoned the common beliefs? We will tell them that they are deceiving themselves by taking for their own personal thought the *débris* of the tradition of the human race. We will add that their pretended independence is a veritable slavery. A strange sort of liberty that, which should forbid those who affect it to accept a faith which appeared to them to be true, because they were not the inventors of it. Listen to this wise reflection of a contemporary writer: "Philosophy allows us to range ourselves on the side of Platonism: why should it not also allow us to range ourselves on the side of the Christian faith, if there it is that we find wisdom and immutable truth? The choice ought to seem as free and as worthy of respect on the one side as on the other; and philosophy which claims liberty for itself, is least of all warranted in refusing it to others." * To be free, is to look for truth wherever it may be found, and it is to obey truth wherever we meet with it. When the question therefore relates to God, or to the soul and its eternal destinies,— to the man who asks me, Are you occupied with religion or philosophy? I have only one answer to give: I am a man, and I am seeking truth.

A final consideration will perhaps put these

* Barthélemy St. Hilaire, in the *Séances et travaux de l'Académie des sciences morales et politiques*, LXX., p. 134.

thoughts in a more striking light. If you think the most important of the discussions of our day to be that between natural and revealed religion, between deism and the Gospel, you have not well discerned the signs of the times. The fundamental discussion is now between men who believe in God, in the soul, and in truth, and men, who, denying truth, deny at the same time the soul and God. When these high problems are in question, periodicals and other publications, which have the widest circulation, and which gain admission into every household, bring us too often the works of writers without convictions, eager to spread amongst others the doubt which has devoured their own beliefs. They have received entire, and without losing an obole of it, the heritage of the Greek Sophists. They involve in fact in the same proscription Socrates and Jesus Christ, Paul of Tarsus and Plato of Athens: they have no more respect for the opinions of Descartes and Leibnitz than for those of Pascal and Bossuet. The great question of the day is to know whether our desire of truth is a chimæra; whether our effort to reach the divine world is a spring into the empty void. When the question relates to God, inasmuch as He is the basis of reason no less than the object of faith, all the barriers which exist elsewhere disappear: to defend faith is to defend reason; to defend reason is to defend faith. The unbridled audacity of those who deny fundamental truths is bringing ancient adversaries, for a moment at least, to fight beneath the same flag. What they would rob us of, is not merely this or that article of a definite creed, but all faith whatever in Divine Providence, every hope which goes beyond the tomb, every look directed towards a world superior to our present destinies. But take courage. This flame lighted on the earth, and which is evermore directed towards heaven, has passed safely through rougher storms than those which now threaten it; it has shone brightly in thicker darkness than that in which men are laboring so hard to enshroud it. It is not going to be extinguished, be very sure, before the affected indifference of a few wits of our day, and the haughty disdain of a few contemporary journalists.

In a word, Gentlemen, — to take the idea of God as it has been handed down to us, and to study its relation to the reason, the heart, and the conscience of man, — this is my proposed method of proceeding. To show you that this idea is truth, because it satisfies the conscience, the heart, and the reason — this is the object I have in view. Of this object I am sure you feel the importance: nevertheless, and that we may be more alive to it still, I propose to you to sound with me the abysses of sorrow and darkness which are involved in those terrible words — "without God in the world."

LECTURE II.

LIFE WITHOUT GOD.

(At Geneva, 20th Nov. 1863. — At Lausanne, 13th Jan. 1864.)

GENTLEMEN,

I propose to examine to-day what are the consequences for human life of the total suppression of the idea of God. This suppression is the result of atheism properly so called: it is also the result of scepticism raised into a system. The soul which doubts, but which seeks, regrets, hopes, is not wholly separated from God. It gives Him a large share in its life, inasmuch as the desire which it feels to meet with Him, and the sadness which it experiences at not contemplating Him in a full light, become the principal facts of its existence. But doubt adopted as a doctrine realizes in its own way, equally with atheism properly so called, life without God, the mournful subject of our present study.

Having God, the spiritual life has a firm base and an invincible hope. The vapors of earth may indeed for a moment obscure the sky. One while fogs hang about the ground; another while clouds send forth the thunder-bolt; but, above the regions of darkness and of tempest, the eye of faith contemplates the eternal azure in its unchanging calm. Life has its sorrows for all; but it is not only endurable, it is blessed, when in view of the instability of all things, in view of evil, of injustice, and of suffering, there can breathe from the depths of the soul to the eternal, the Holy One, the Comforter, those words of patience in life and of joy in death: *My God!* Take God away, and life is decapitated. Even this comparison is not sufficient; life, rather, becomes like to a man who should have lost at once both his head and his heart. The immense subject which opens before us falls into an easy and natural division: we will fix our attention successively upon the individual and upon society.

PART I.

THE INDIVIDUAL.

MAN thinks, he feels, and he wills: these are the three great functions of the spiritual life. Let us inquire what, without God, would become, first, of thought, which is the instrument of all knowledge; next, of the conscience, which is the law of the will; then of the heart, which is the organ of the feelings. We will begin with thought.

Let us go back to the origin of modern philosophy. The labors of Descartes will make us acquainted, under the form clearest for us, with a current of lofty thoughts which does honor to ancient civilization, and which has come down to us through the writings of Plato and St. Augustine. We have seen that Descartes deceived himself, when he thought to separate himself altogether from tradition, and forgot the while how intimately men's minds are bound together in a common possession of truth. He was mistaken, because he confounded the idea, natural to the human mind, of an infinite reason, with the full idea of the Creator; so attributing to the efforts of his own philosophy that gift of truth which he had received from the Christian tradition. But, having so far recognized his error, listen now to this great man, and judge if he were again mistaken in those thoughts of his which I am about to reproduce to you.

Descartes strives hard to doubt of all things, persuaded that truth will resist his efforts, and come forth triumphant from the trial. He doubts of what he has heard in the schools: his masters may have led him into error. He doubts of the evidence of his senses: his senses deceive him in the visions of the night; what if he were always dreaming, and if his waking hours were but another sleep with other dreams! He will doubt even of the certainty of reason: what if the reason were a warped and broken instrument? Reason is only worth what its cause may be worth. If man is the child of chance, his thoughts may be vain. If man is the creature of a wicked and cunning being, the light of reason may be only an *ignis fatuus* kindled by a malicious and mocking spirit. Here is a soul plunged in the lowest abysses of doubt; but it is a manly soul which seeks in doubt a trial for truth, and not a comfortable pillow on which slothfully to repose. How does Descartes upraise himself? By a thought known to every one, and which was already found in St. Augustine: "*Cogito, ergo sum.* I think, therefore I am." Deceive me who will; if I am deceived, I exist. Here is a certainty protected from all assault: I am. But what a poor certainty is this! What does it avail me to have rescued my existence from the abysses of universal doubt, if above the deep waters which have swallowed up all belief floats only this naked and mortifying truth: 'I am; but I exist only perhaps to be the sport of errors without end. The first step therefore taken by the philosopher would be a fruitless one if it were not followed by a second. An eye is open, and says: I see; but it must have a warrant that the light by which it sees is not a fantastic brightness. No, replies Descartes; reason sees a true light; and this is how he proves it: I am, I know myself; that is certain. I know myself as a limited and imperfect being; that again is certain. I conceive then infinity and perfection; that is not less certain; for I should not have the idea of a limit if I did not conceive of infinity, and the word *imperfect* would have no meaning for me, if I could not imagine perfection, of which imperfection is but the negation. Starting from this point, the philosopher proves by a series of reasonings that the conception of perfection by our minds demonstrates the real existence of that perfection: God is. He adds, that the existence of God is more certain than the most certain of all the theorems of geometry. You will observe, Gentlemen, that the man who speaks in this way is one of the greatest geometricians that ever lived. He has found God, he has found the light. Reason does not deceive, when it is faithful to its own laws: the senses do not deceive, when they are exercised according to the rules of the understanding. Error is a malady; it is not the radical condition of our nature; it is not without limits and without remedy, for the final cause of our being is God, that is to say truth and goodness.

From everlasting God was true,
For ever good and just will be,

says one of our old psalms. Faith in the veracity of God—such is the ground of the assurance of believers; such is also the foundation on which has been raised the greatest of modern philoso phies. Without the knowledge of God and faith in his goodness, man remains plunged in irremediable doubt, possessing only this single, poor, and frightful certainty: I am; and I exist perhaps only to be eternally deceived.

But, it has been said, and it needed no great cleverness to say it — What a strange way is this of reasoning! Here is a man who first proves that God is, by means of his reason; and then proves that his reason is good because God is. His reason demonstrates God to him, and God demonstrates his reason to him: it is an argument of which any schoolboy can at once see the fallacy; it is manifestly a vicious circle. This has been said again and again by persons who have neglected a sufficiently simple consideration. The error is apparently a gross one; is it not likely that the argument has been misunderstood? Ought we not to look very closely at it, before declaring that one of the most lucid minds that have ever appeared in the world left at the basis of his doctrine a fault of logic which any schoolboy can discover? Self-sufficient levity of spirit is not the best means of penetrating the thought of leading minds; and it very often happens to us to fail of understanding because we have failed in respect.

Let us examine with serious attention, not the very words of Descartes, as an historian might do, but the course of thought of which Descartes is one of the most illustrious representatives.

To recognize in the reason traces of God, and to show that in faith in God consists the only warrant of the reason, is not to argue in a vicious circle, because, in this way of proceeding, what we are employed in is not reasoning, but analysis; we are establishing a fact in order to ascertain what that fact implies and supposes. This fact is the natural faith which man has in his own reason, when his reason reveals to him the immediate light of evidence, or the mediate light of certainty. Now, when man confides in his reason, it is not in his individual reason that he confides, for he has no doubt that what is evident for him is so also for others. If, tossed by a tempest, he were thrown upon an island of savages, he would not think that those savages, when they came to reflect, would be able to discover that the axioms of our geometry are false, or to make elements of logic which would contradict our own. We believe in a general reason, everywhere and always the same, and in which the reason of each individual participates. We believe therefore that there is a principle of truth which exists in itself, a reason which is eternal and everywhere present; in other words, we believe in God considered as the source of the universal intelligence. To believe in one's reason, is to believe in God, in this sense: the fact of the confidence which we place in our own faculty of thought, supposes a concealed faith in eternal truth. This is the analysis of which I was speaking. It is a circle if you please, but it is a circle of light, outside of which there is, as we shall see by and by, nothing but darkness and hard contradictions.

You deny the existence of God. On what ground do you rest this denial? On the ground of your reason. You believe then that your reason is good, you believe it very good, since you do not hesitate to trust it, while you undertake to prove false the fundamental instincts of human nature. But you would not venture to say that this reason which you believe in with a faith so firm is your own separate reason merely, your personal and exclusive property. You believe in the universal reason; you believe in God, considered at least as the source of the understanding. The man therefore who denies God, affirms Him in a certain sense at the same time that he denies Him. He denies Him in his words, in the external form of his thought; he affirms Him in reality, as the Supreme Intelligence, by the very trust which he places in his own thought. Our understanding is only the reflected ray of the Divine verity. Therefore it is that Descartes, as soon as he has laid the first foundations of his system, interrupts the chain of his reasonings to trace these lines: "Here I think it highly meet to pause for a while in contemplation of this all-perfect God, to ponder deliberately his marvellous attributes, to consider, admire, and adore the incomparable beauty of that immense light, at least so far as the strength of my mind, which remains in a manner dazzled by it, shall allow me to do so."* Thus it is that while descending into the depths of the understanding, the philosopher who is supposed to be absorbed in pure abstractions, discovers all at once a sublime brightness, and exclaims with the ancient patriarch: "The LORD is in this place, and I knew it not!"† God is everywhere; He is in the heights of heaven, He

* *Méditation troisième*, at the end. † Gen. xxviii. 16.

is in the depths of thought. Remember those celebrated words of Lord Chancellor Bacon: "A little knowledge inclineth the mind to atheism, but a further acquaintance therewith bringeth it back to religion."

God is not demonstrated, in the ordinary sense which we attach to the word demonstrate;* He is pointed out† as the source of all light. The attempt to demonstrate God as anything else is demonstrated, by descending, that is, from higher principles until the object in view is arrived at—this attempt implies a contradiction. God is in fact the first principle, the foundation of all principles, the principle beyond which there is nothing. We may describe the process by which the human mind rises to this supreme idea; but to wish to demonstrate God by mounting higher than Himself in order to look for a point of departure—this is literally to wish to light up the sun. If the sun of intelligences is extinguished, reason sets out on its way vaguely enlightened still with the remains of the light which it has reflected; but it is not long ere it is stumbling in darkness. Then it is that—be not deceived about it!—the doubts which Descartes called up by an act of

* *Démontrer.* † "*On le montre.*"

his own will do in good earnest invade the soul. We possess a natural certainty, which does not suppose a clear view of God; we reason without thinking distinctly of the principles on which we reason, just as, when we are in a hurry, we take the shortest cut without thinking of the axiom of geometry which prescribes the straight line. But if we pass from the natural order of our thoughts into the domain of science, if we ask — what is it which guarantees to me the value of my reason? then the question is put, and many perish in the passage which separates natural faith from the domain of science, — that dangerous passage where doubt spreads out its perfidious fogs and its deceitful marshes. The moment the question is started of the worth of reason, and all the schools of scepticism do start it, our answer must be — *God;* and we must find light in this answer, or see thought invaded in its totality by an irremediable doubt. Then men come to ask themselves if all be not a lie; and they speak of the universal vanity, without making the reserve of Ecclesiastes.* There are more souls ill of this

* "Vanity of vanities; all is vanity.... Let us hear the conclusion of the whole matter: Fear God, and keep his commandments: for this is the whole duty of man." (Eccles. i. and xii.)

malady than are supposed to be so. Many begin by setting up proudly against God what they call the rights of reason, and by and by we see this reason, which has revolted against its Principle, vacillate, doubt of itself, and at last, losing itself in a bitter irony, wrap itself, with all beside, in the shroud of a universal scorn.

Without God reason is extinguished. What, in like case, will happen to the conscience? The conscience is a reality. I will say willingly in the style of the prophets: Let my tongue cleave to the roof of my mouth, ere I deny conscience, and disparage the sacred name of duty! Yes, conscience is a reality; but God is in it: He it is who gives to it its necessary basis and its indispensable support. The conscience is the august voice of the Master of the universe. God has given us the light of the understanding that we may see and comprehend some portions of the works which He has created without us: a work there is for which He would have us to be fellow-workers with Him. The heaven of stars is a spectacle for the eyes of the body, a grander spectacle still for the contemplation of the mind which has understood their wondrous mechanism. We admire them; but if the stars failed to attract our admiration, no one of them on that account would cease to trace its orbit. There is another heaven, a heaven of loving stars and free, the sight of which is one day to fill us with rapture, and the realization of which is to be the work of our love and of our will. Before we contemplate it we must make it; this is our high and awful privilege. The plan of the spiritual heavens is deposited in the soul, and the utterances of the conscience reveal it to the will. It is a law of justice and of love. This law is evermore violated, because it is proposed to liberty, and liberty rebels: it subsists evermore, because it is the work of the Almighty. Humanity, in its strange destiny, has never ceased to outrage the rule which it acknowledges, and to pronounce upon its own acts a ceaseless condemnation. The laws which are investigated by the physical sciences are the plan of the Creator realized in nature: the law proposed to liberty is the plan of the Creator to be realized by the community of minds. Such is the explanation of the conscience: God is its solid foundation.

Duty and God, morality and religion, are inseparable principles; all the efforts of a false philosophy have never succeeded, and never will succeed, in disjoining them. Men will never be prevented from believing that God is holy, and that His will is binding upon them: they will never be prevented from believing that holiness is divine, and that the will of God reveals itself in the admonitions of the conscience. Therefore the progress of religion and the progress of morality are closely united; the morality of a people depends above all on the idea which it forms to itself of God. The conscience, in fact, at the same time that it is real and permanent in its bases, is variable in the degrees of its light. It is enlightened or obscured, according as the man's religious conceptions are pure or corrupted; and, on the other hand, when the religious worship is degraded beyond a certain limit by error and the passions, the conscience protests, and by its protest purifies the religious conceptions. It has often been said, that in the onward march of humanity, morality is separated from faith, and comes at last to rest upon its own bases. It is a notion of the eighteenth century, which, although its root has been cut, is still throwing out shoots in our time. The attempt has been made to support this theory by the great name of Socrates. It is affirmed that the sage of Athens, breaking the bond which connects the earth with heaven, separated duty from its primitive source. Listen: Placed in the alternative of either renouncing his mission or dying, it is thus that Socrates addresses his judges: "Athenians, I honor you and I love you, but I will obey the Deity rather than you. My whole occupation is to persuade you, young and old, that before the care of the body and of riches, before every other care, is that of the soul and of its improvement. Know that this it is which the Deity prescribes to me, and I am persuaded that there can be nothing more advantageous to the republic than my zeal to fulfil the behest of the Deity." * Does the man who speaks in this way appear to you to have wished to break the link which connects morality with religion? He separates himself from the established religion; he pursues with his biting raillery shameful objects of worship; his conscience protests. But, while it protests, it attaches itself immediately to a higher and holier idea of that God, of whose perfections the sage of Athens had succeeded in obtaining a glimpse.

God then is the explanation of the conscience: He is moreover its support. It has need in sooth

* Apology.

to be supported,—that voice which speaks within us; because it is unceasingly contradicted and denied. The spectacle which the world presents is not an edifying one; the facts which are taking place on the earth are not all of a nature to maintain the steadfastness of the moral feeling. Let us imagine an example, a striking example, such as it would be easy to find realized on a small scale in more commonplace events. A peaceable population, menaced in its most sacred rights, has taken up arms in the simplest and most legitimate self-defence. I do not allow my thoughts to rest upon the soldiers who are advancing to oppress it—mere instruments as they are in the hands of their leaders—but upon the leaders themselves. One of these, without the least necessity, with a calculating coolness, to which he sacrifices all the feelings of a man, or under the sway of one of those ferocious instincts which at times gain the mastery over the soul, gives up a town, a village, to all the horrors of slaughter, pillage, and fire. The blood of the victims will scarcely, perhaps, have grown cold, the last gleams of the fire will not yet be extinct, when this man shall be receiving the praises of his superiors. Men will laud the bravery and daring of his exploit; his sovereign will place upon his breast a brilliant cross, the august sign of the world's redemption; he will return to his country amidst the acclamations of the multitude, and drink in with delight the shouts of triumph which greet him as he moves on his way. For such things as these, is there to be no penalty but troublesome recollections which may sometimes be banished, and a few timid protests soon hushed by the loud voice of success? Verily there are perpetrated beneath the sun acts which cry aloud for vengeance. Have you never felt it—that mighty cry—rising from your own bosom, at the sight of some odious crime, or on reading such and such a page of history? And it must be so; it must be that the cry for vengeance will rise, until the soul has learnt to transform imprecation into prayer, and the desire for justice into supplication for the guilty. But if, in the presence of crime, we were forced to believe that there will never be either vengeance or pardon, the mainspring of the moral life would be broken, and humanity would at length exclaim, like Brutus in the plains of Philippi:—"Virtue! thou art but a name!"

The conscience is a reality; but its voice is

troublesome, and the captious arguments which go to deny its value find support in the evil tendencies of our nature. If it has no faith in eternal justice it runs the risk of being blunted by contact with the world. So doubt takes place, doubt still deeper and more agonizing than that which bears upon the processes of the understanding. The questions which arise are such as these:—"This voice of duty—whence comes it? and what would it have? May not conscience be a prejudice, the result of education and of habit? It has little power, it seems, for it is braved with impunity. Many say that it is a factitious power from which one comes at last to deliver one's self by resisting it. Am I not the dupe of an illusion? I am losing joys which others allow themselves. Barriers encompass me on every hand, for there are for me prohibited actions, unwholesome beauties, culpable feelings. Others are free, and make a larger use of life in all directions. What if I too made trial of liberty!" Here lies the temptation. When the soul aspires to become larger than conscience and more tolerant than duty, it is not far from a fall. The honest woman will be tempted to repine at the liberty of the courtesan, and the man who is bound by his word will become capable of looking with envy on the liberty of the liar. Then come terrible experiences which teach at length that the unbinding of the passions is the hardest of slaveries, and that, in the struggle between inclination and duty, it is liberty which oppresses and law which sets free. Happy then is he who, feeling himself to be sinking in gloomy waters, cries to that God who is able to rescue him from the abyss, and strengthens his shaken conscience by replacing it on its solid foundation. "God speaks and reigns. All rebellion is transient in its nature; justice will at length be done. Justice may be slow in the eyes of the creature of a day, seeing that He who shall dispense it has eternity at his disposal." But if God be not a refuge for us from men and from the world, if, when we see all that is passing around us, we cannot cast a look beyond and above the earth, men may lose their faith in duty. And this faith is lost in fact. If there are not dead consciences, there are consciences at any rate singularly sunk in sleep. There are men for whom goodness, truth, justice, honor, seem to be a coinage of which they make use because it is current, but without for themselves attaching to it any value. These pieces of money have no longer in their eyes any visible impression, because the conception of the almighty and just God is the impression which determines duty and guarantees its value.

When the necessary alliance of moral order with religious thought is denied, the reality of conscience is opposed to what are called theological hypotheses always open to discussion. It is seen well enough that men may doubt of God, but it is supposed to be impossible to doubt of conscience. This is an illusion of generous minds. Those who would keep this illusion must not open the pages of the history of philosophy where the negation of duty does not occupy less space than the negation of God; they must not cast their eyes too much about them; they must also take care not to open the most widely circulated books, and the most fashionable periodicals: otherwise, as we shall see, they would not be long in finding out that this morality which they would fain have superior to all attacks, is perhaps what of all things is most attacked now-a-days, and that that conscience which it is impossible to deny is in fact the object of denials the most audacious on the part of a few of the present favorites of fame. The voice of duty is heard no doubt even when God does not come distinctly into mind;

but when the questions are clearly put, if God is denied, conscience grows dim, and comes at last to be extinguished. This obscuration does not take place all at once: the potter's wheel goes on turning for a while, says an old Hindoo poem, after that the foot of the artisan is withdrawn from it. But the darkening takes place gradually with time: such at least is the general rule. There are exceptional men who seem to escape this law, and to bear in their bosom a God veiled from their own consciousness. Such men may be found, and even in considerable numbers, in a time like ours, when doubt is, in many cases, a prejudice which current opinion deposits on the surface of minds without penetrating them deeply. There are men all whose convictions have fallen into ruins, while their conscience continues standing like an isolated column, sole remaining witness of a demolished building. The meeting with these heroes of virtue inspires a mingled feeling of astonishment and respect. They are verily miracles of that divine goodness of which they are unable to pronounce the name. If there is a man on earth who ought to fall on both knees and shed burning tears of gratitude, it is the man who believes himself an atheist, and who has received from Providence so keen a taste for what is noble and pure, so strong an aversion for evil, that his sense of duty remains firm even when it has lost all its supports. But the exception does not make the rule; and that which is realized in the case of a few is not realized long, and for all. You know those crusts of snow which are formed over the *crevasses* of our glaciers. These slight bridges are able to bear one person who remains suspended over the abyss, but let several attempt to pass together,—the frail support gives way, and the rash adventurers fall together into the gulf. Such is the destiny of those schools of philosophy in which the notion of God disappears, and of those civilizations in which the sense of God is extinguished; they fall into dark regions where the light of goodness shines no longer.

After the mind and conscience, it remains for us to speak of the heart. Man, an intelligent and free being, has in his reason an instrument of knowledge, and in his conscience a rule for his will. But man is not sufficient for himself, and cannot live upon his own resources. If you inquire what the word heart expresses, in its most general acceptation, you will find that it always expresses a tendency of the soul to look, out of itself, in things or persons, for the support and nourishment of its individual life. Does the question concern the relations of man with his fellows? The heart is the organ of communication of one soul with another, for receiving, or for giving, or for giving and receiving at the same time, in the enjoyment of the blessing of a mutual affection. The heart is in each of us what those marks are upon the scattered stones of a building in course of construction which indicate that they are to be united one to another. The philosopher suffices for himself, the stoics used to say; the heart is the negation of this haughty maxim. From the heart proceeds love, that son of abundance and of poverty, to speak with Plato, that needy one ever on the search for his lost heritage. Love has wings, said again the wisdom of the Greeks, wings which essay to carry him ever higher. Let us extricate the thought which is involved in these graceful figures: Our desires have no limits, and indefinite desires can be satisfied only by meeting with an infinite Being who can be an inexhaustible source of happiness, an eternal object of love. "Our heart is made for love," said Saint Augustine, the great Christian disciple of Plato: "therefore it is unquiet till it finds repose in God." From this unrest proceed all our miseries. Men do not always succeed in contenting themselves with a petty prosaic happiness, a dull and paltry well-being, and in stifling the while the grand instincts of our nature. If then the heart lives, and fails of its due object; if it does not meet with the supreme term of its repose, its indefinite aspirations attach themselves to objects which cannot satisfy them, and thence arise stupendous aberrations. With some, it is the pursuit of sensual gratifications; they rush with a kind of fury into the passions of their lower nature. With others it is the ardent pursuit of riches, power, fame,—feelings which are always crying more: More! and never: Enough. And the after-taste from the fruitless search after happiness in the paths of ambition and vanity is not less bitter perhaps than the after-taste from sensual enjoyments. Listen to the confession of a man whose works, full as they are of beauties, are disfigured by so many impure allusions, that the author appears to have indulged, more than most others, in the giddy follies and culpable pleasures of life:

If, tired of mocking dreams, my restless heart
  Returns to take its fill of waking joy,

Full soon I loathe the pleasures which impart
No true delight, but kill me, while they cloy.*

Here are the accents of a true confession. These are moreover truths of daily experience. I have seen—and which of you could not render similar testimony?—I have seen the sick man, deprived of all the ordinary avocations and amusements of life, and with pain for his constant companion, I have seen him find joy in the thought of his God, and feeding, without satiety, on this bread of contentment. I have seen the face of the blind lighted up by a living faith, and radiant with a light of peace, for him sweeter and brighter than the rays of the sun. But where God is wanting, and all connection is broken with the source of joy, there you shall see the richest of the rich, the most prosperous among the ambitious, the man of fame whose renown is most widely extended,—you shall see these men carrying the heavy burden of discontent. Their brow, unillumined by the celestial ray, is furrowed by the lines of sadness. If you meet them in a moment of candor, these rich, ambitious, and famous

* Si mon cœur, fatigué du rêve qui l'obsède,
A la réalité revient pour s'assouvir,
Au fond des vains plaisirs que j'appelle à mon aide,
Je trouve un tel dégoût que je me sens mourir.

men will tell you with a sigh: "All this does not satisfy; we are but pursuing chimeras." Still they continue to run after these chimeras. They cry Vanity! Vanity! and they do not cease to pursue vanity. They flee from themselves: if they retired within themselves, they would find there ennui, inexorable ennui, which is but the sense of that place which God should fill left void in the depth of the soul. For the deceived heart, life becomes a bitter comedy. Those who do not succeed in blinding themselves by the dust of thoughtless folly, end oftentimes by wrapping themselves in disdain as with a cloak; they seek a sad and solitary satisfaction in the greatness of their contempt for life. But neither does this satisfy: disdain is not a beverage, and contempt is not food.

Such are the destinies of the heart, to which God is wanting. But I hope, Gentlemen, that you have here some remonstrances to offer. I have just spoken of the pleasures of sense, of pride, of vanity, and I have made no allusion to those affections in which the heart manifests its highest qualities. Shall we forget the joys of pure love? the domestic hearth? friendship? country? Do not fear that, having given myself up to a fit of misanthropy, I am come hither to blaspheme the true happinesses of life. But do the affections of earth offer us sufficient guarantees? We have need of the infinite to answer to the immensity of our desires; in the presence of those we love, have we no need of the Eternal that we may lean our hearts on Him? Will not all human love become a source of torment, if we have no faith in the love of Him who will stamp holy affections with the seal of His own eternity?

A single question will suffice to enlighten us on this head. Do you know the feeling of anxiety? We all know it, though in different degrees. Epidemical disease may appear. The cholera has started on its course; it has left the interior of Asia, and is approaching. The report is current that neighboring cities have begun to feel its ravages. Those we love—in a month, in a week, where will they be? War is declared. We hear of preparations for death; the sovereigns of Europe apply themselves to calculations which seem to portend torrents of blood. If war breaks out, that brother, that son, who will have to take up arms, that daughter who will one day perhaps find herself at the mercy of an unbridled soldiery ——. But let us not look for examples so far away. Have you no dear one in a distant land of whom you are expecting tidings? And those who are near you! To-morrow, to-day, now perhaps, while you are listening to me, a fatal malady is discovering its first symptoms——. Have you received the hard lessons of death? If you see children playing, full of ruddy and joyous health, does it happen to none of you to think of another child, once the joy of your fireside, now lying beneath the sod? Does it never happen to you, by a sinister presentiment, to see features you love to gaze on convulsed with agony or pale in death? And yet you must either see the death of your beloved ones, or they must lay you in the earth; for every life ends with the tomb, and we do but walk over graves. When the soul has been thus wounded by anxiety, for this poisoned wound there is one remedy, but only one: "God reigns!" Nothing happens without the permission of His goodness. And of all those who are dear to us, we can say: "Father, to Thy hands I commit them." If we are without this trust, we shall only escape torment by levity. Without God our mind is sick; our conscience and our heart are sick also, and in a way more grievous still.

PART II.

SOCIETY.

WE have just studied what life without God would be for the individual. Let us now direct our attention to those collections of human beings which form societies. We shall not speak here of the relations of civil with ecclesiastical authorities,—a complex question, the solution of which must vary with times, places, and circumstances. Let us only remark that the distinction between the temporal and spiritual order of things is one of the foundations of modern civilization. This distinction is based upon those great words which, eighteen hundred years ago, separated the domain of God from the domain of Cæsar. Religion considered as a function of civil life; dogma supported by the word of a monarch or the vote of a body politic; the formula of that dogma imposed forcibly by a government on the lips of the governed—these are *débris* of paganism which have been struggling for centuries against the restraints of Christian thought.* The religious convictions of individuals do not belong to the State; religious sentiments are not amenable to human tribunals; and it would be hard to say whether it is the spiritual or the temporal order of things which suffers most from the confusion of these distinct domains. Religion should have its own proper life, and its special representatives; civil life ought to be set free from all tyranny exercised in the name of dogma; but religion is not the less on that account, by the influence which it exerts over the consciences of men, the necessary bond and strength of human society.

* Christian States have given the force of law to institutions, such, for instance, as monogamy, which date their origin from the Gospel records. Here we have the normal development of civilization: religious faith enlightens the general conscience, and reveals to it the true conditions of social progress. In this order of things, it is not a question of *beliefs*, but of *acts* imposed in the name of the interests of society. The state may take account of the religious beliefs of its subjects, and enter into such relations as may seem to it convenient with the ecclesiastical authorities: this is the basis of the system of concordats, a system which has nothing in it contrary to first principles, so long as liberty is maintained. But the establishment of *national* religions, decreed by the temporal power and varying in different states, manifestly supposes a foundation of scepticism. For the idea of truth, one and universal in itself, is substituted the idea of decisions obligatory for those only who are under the jurisdiction of a definite political body. If the State, without pretending to

"You would sooner build a city in the air," said Plutarch, "than cause a State to subsist without religion." Some have contested in modern times this opinion of ancient wisdom. The philosophy of the last century, as we have said already, wished to separate duty from the idea of God. It pretended to give as the only foundation for society a civil morality, the rules and sanction of which were to be found upon earth. The men of blood who for a short time governed France, gave once as the order of the day — *Terror and all the virtues:* this was a terrible application of this theory. Virtue rested on a decree of political

decree dogma, receives it from the hands of the Church, and imposes it upon its subjects, it seems at first that the temporal power has placed itself at the service of the Church, but that the idea of truth is preserved. But when the question is studied more closely, it is seen that this is not the case, and that the state usurps in fact, in this combination, the attributes of the spiritual power. In fact, before protecting *the true religion*, it is necessary to ascertain which it is; and in order to ascertain the true religion, the political power must constitute itself judge of religious truth. So we come back, by a *détour*, to the conception of national religions. The Emperor of Russia and the Emperor of Austria will inquire respectively which is the only true religion, to the exclusive maintenance of which they are to consecrate their temporal power. To the same question they will give two different replies; and each nation will have its own form of worship, just as each nation has its own ruler.

power, and, for want of the judgment of God, the guillotine was the sanction of its precepts. Healthier views begin now to prevail in the schools of philosophy. One of the members of the *Institut de France*, M. Franck, has lately published a volume on the history of ancient civilization,* with the express intention of showing that the conception which a people has of God is the true root of its social organization. According to the worth of the religious idea is that of the civil constitution. Before M. Franck, twenty years ago, a man of the very highest distinction as a public lecturer, indicated this movement of modern thought. M. Edgard Quinet, in his Lyons course, taught that the religious idea is the very substance of civilization, and the generating principle of political constitutions. He announced "a history of civilization by the monuments of human thought," and added: "Religion above all is the pillar of fire which goes before the nations in their march across the ages; it shall serve us as a guide." † Benjamin Constant exhibits in the variation of his opinions the transition from the

* *Etudes orientales*, 1861.

† *Unité morale des peuples modernes*, — a lecture delivered at Lyons, 10 April, 1839. This lecture is inserted after the *Génie des Religions* in the complete works of the author.

stand-point of the last century to that of the present. He had at first conceived of his work upon religion as a monument raised to atheism, he ends by seeking in religious sentiments the condition necessary to the existence of civilized societies.* Here is a real progress; and this progress brings us back to the thought above quoted from Plutarch. In fact, take away the idea of God, and the first consequence will be that you will sacrifice all the conquests of modern civilization; the next, that you will soon have rendered impossible the existence of any society whatever. I am going to ask your close attention to these two points successively.

History does not offer to our view an uninterrupted progress, as certain optimists suppose; still less does it present the spectacle of an ever-increasing deterioration, as misanthropes affirm; and lastly, it is not true, as we hear it said sometimes, that all epochs are alike, as good one as another. There are times better than those which follow them; and there are epochs less degraded than those which precede them. Human societies fall and rise again; their march exhibits windings

* Franck, *Philosophie du droit ecclésiastique*, pages 117 and 118.

and retrograde steps, because that march is under the influence of created liberty; but when their destinies are regarded at one view, it is clearly seen that they are advancing to a determined end, because while man is in restless agitation, God is leading him on. The conquests of modern civilization are great and sacred realities. What are these conquests? Let us not stay at the surface of things, but go to the foundation. Societies fallen into a condition of barbarism have for their motto the famous saying of a Gallic chief: Woe to the vanquished! In institutions, as in manners, the triumph of force characterizes barbarous times. The right of the strongest is the twofold negation of justice and of love; and what characterizes civilization, issuing from the barbarous condition, the fragments of which it so long trails after it, is the establishment of that justice which founds States, and, upon the basis of justice, the development of the benevolence which renders communities happy. These are the two essential conditions of social progress. These conditions are necessary even to the progress of industry and of material welfare.

Modern civilization,—that, namely, which we so designate, while we relegate, so to speak, into the past the contemporaneous societies of the vast East, — modern civilization possesses a power unknown to antiquity. Justice has a foundation in the conscience, benevolence has natural roots in the heart; but a moment has been when justice and love appeared in the world with new brightness, like rays disengaged from clouds. Modern civilization was then deposited on the earth in a powerful germ, of which nothing was any more to arrest the growth. That moment was when the idea of God appeared in its fulness: modern civilization was born of the Gospel. The knowledge of God strengthens justice, and the thought of the common Father develops benevolence. These theses are well known; let us confine ourselves to a few rapid illustrations.

There exists an institution in which has been embodied the negation of social justice — Slavery. Slavery is at length disappearing before our eyes from the bosom of Christendom; and its final retreat is doing honor to Russia, and bathing America in blood. This is perhaps the greatest of the events which the annals of history will inscribe on the page of the nineteenth century. Now slavery was, in the past, an almost universal institution. The finest intellects of Greece devoted a portion of their labors to its justification. Rome, at the most brilliant period of its civilization, caused slaves to kill one another, in savage spectacles intended to delight the populace, or during sumptuous banquets for the amusement of wealthy debauchees!* How has slavery disappeared little by little! How has man been rediscovered beneath that living *thing* of which was made, one while an instrument of labor, and another while the sport of execrable passions? Inquire into this history. You will find the reason and the heart making their protests heard in antiquity, but without becoming efficacious. One day all is changed, and the foundations of slavery begin to shake. At that memorable epoch you will meet with a written document, the first in which is shown in its germ the great social fact which was about to have birth. It is not an emperor's decree, it is not the vote of a body politic, it is a letter a few lines long written by a prisoner to one of his friends. The substance of this letter was: "I send thee back thy slave; but in the name of God I beg of thee to receive him as thy brother; think of the common Master who

* Schmidt, *Essai historique sur la Société civile dans le monde romain.* Bk. I. ch. 3.

is in heaven." This letter was addressed—"To Philemon;" the name of the writer was Paul. It is the first charter of slave emancipation. Ponder this fact, Gentlemen: contemplate the ancient institution of slavery shaken to its foundations, without being the object of any direct attack, by the breath of a new spirit. You will then understand how historians can tell us that the relations of states, belligerent rights, civil laws, political institutions, all these things of which the Gospel has never spoken, have been, and are being still, every day transformed by the slow action of the Gospel. God has appeared; justice is marching in His train.

Justice is the foundation of society; but without the spirit of love, justice remains crippled, and never reaches its perfection. Justice maintains the rights of each; love seeks to realize the communication of advantages among all. Justice overthrows the artificial barriers raised between men by force and guile; love softens natural inequalities and causes them to turn to the general good. Need I tell you that the knowledge of God is a light of which the brightest ray is love to men? Benevolence, that feeling natural to our hearts, is strengthened, extended, transfigured, by becoming charity; — charity, that union of the soul with the Heavenly Father, which descends again to earth in loving communion between all His children. The soul separated from God may be conscious of strong affections: but study well the character of a virtue which is nourished from purely human sources; you will see that it may for the most part be expressed in these terms — "To love one's friends heartily, and to hate one's enemies with a generous hatred; to esteem the honest and to despise the vicious." But that virtue which loves the vicious while it hates the vice, that virtue which will avenge itself only by overcoming evil with good, that virtue which, while it draws closer the bonds of private affections, makes a friend of every man, that virtue which we call divine, by a natural impulse of our heart — what is the source from which it flows? The following fact will sufficiently answer the question. On the façade of one the hospitals of the Christian world, are read these Latin words, the brief energy of which our language cannot render: *Deo in pauperibus*, "This edifice is consecrated to God in the person of the poor." Here is the secret of charity: it discerns the Divine image deposited in every human soul.

But do not mistake here: we cannot love, with a love natural and direct, the rags of squalid poverty, the brands of vice, the languors and sores of sickness; but let God manifest Himself, and our eyes are opened. The beauty of souls breaks forth to our view beneath the wasting of the haggard frame, and from under the filth of vice. We love those immortal creatures fallen and degraded; a sacred desire possesses us to restore them to their true destination. Has an artist discovered in a mass of rubbish, under vulgar appearances, a product of the marvellous chisel of the Greeks? He sets himself, with a zeal full of respect, to free the noble statue from the impurities which defile it. Every soul of man is the work of art Divine, and every charitable heart is an artist who desires to labor at its restoration. Henceforward we can understand that love of suffering and of poverty, that passion for the galleys and the hospital, which have at times thrown Christians into extravagances which our age has no reason to dread. God in the poor man, God in the sick man, God in the vicious man and the criminal; this, I repeat, is the grand secret of charity. Charity passes from the heart of men and from individual practice into social customs and institutions. Charity it is which, by degrees, takes from law its needless rigors, and from justice its useless tortures; which substitutes the prison in which it is sought to reform the guilty for the galley, which completes the corruption of the criminal ; it is charity that opens public asylums for all forms of suffering; and that will realize, up to the limits of what is possible, all the hopes of philanthropy. If God ceases to be present to the mind and conscience of men, justice and love lose their power. Without the powerful action of justice and of love, society would descend again, by the ways of corruption, towards the struggles of barbarism. Observe, study well, all that is going on around us. Does our civilization appear to you sufficiently solid to give you the idea that it can henceforth dispense with the foundations on which it has reposed hitherto?

The sentiments of justice and of benevolence which form the double basis of the progress of society, suppose a more general sentiment which is their common support — the sentiment of humanity. The idea that man has a value in himself, that he is, in virtue of his quality as man, independently of the places which he inhabits and of the position which he occupies in the world, an object of justice and of love;—this idea includes in itself all the moral part of civilization. Social progress is only the recognition, ever more and more explicit, of the value of one soul, of the rights of one conscience. Now, the idea of humanity has the closest possible connection with the knowledge of God, considered as the Father of the human race. Ancient wisdom, superior to the worship of idols, had gained a glimpse of the fact that the philosopher is a citizen of the universe; and that famous line of Terence: "I am a man, and I reckon nothing human foreign to me," excited, it is said, the applause of the Roman spectators. But these were mere gleams, extinguished soon by the general current of thought. It was the pale dawn of the idea of humanity. Whence came the day?

I will limit the question by defining it. The idea of humanity is the idea of the worth and consequently of the rights of each individual man. It is the idea of liberty; not of liberty interpreted by passion and selfishness as the inauguration of the license which violates right, but of liberty interpreted by reason and conscience as the limit which the action of each man encounters in the right of his neighbor. We are not speaking here of the equality of political rights, which is not always a guarantee of veritable liberty. We are speaking of a social condition such that man, in the exercise of his faculties, in the manifestation of his thoughts, in his efforts for the causes which he loves, so long as he does not violate the rights of others, does not meet with an arbitrary power to arrest him. Still farther to limit our subject, we shall speak of the most important manifestation of that liberty — liberty of conscience, of which religious liberty is the most ordinary and most complete manifestation. This is only one of the points of the subject, but it is a point which in reality supposes and includes all the rest. This liberty — whence does it come?

It does not come from paganism. Paganism, with its national religions, could only produce fanaticism or doubt. Each people having its own particular religion, to exterminate the foreigner was to serve the cause of the gods of the country. A war-cry descended from the Olympus of each several nation — that Olympus which the gods quitted, in case of need, to take part in the quarrels of men. Did reason perceive the nothingness of these national divinities? Then scepticism appeared. The idea of the supreme

God being unsettled with all, and wholly obscured for the crowd, when men ceased to believe in the gods of the nation, they lost all belief whatsoever. For this cause doubt prevailed so widely at the decline of the ancient world. Those pantheons in which all religions were received, welcomed, protected, are the ever-memorable temples of scepticism. Now you know what voice made itself heard, when the ancient civilization was enfeebled by the spirit of doubt: "Henceforth there is neither Greek nor barbarian, bond nor free. Ye are all brethren, and for all there is one God, and one truth:" here behold the root of scepticism severed. And the same voice added: "This only God is the lawful Owner of His creatures; and when you presume to do violence to the consciences which belong to Him, you know not by what spirit you are animated:" here behold the fountain of fanaticism dried up. God is acknowledged; He is the Master of souls: faith founds liberty.

The Witness to universal truth appears before Rome as represented by a deputy of Cæsar. He is a fanatic, says the Roman; then he goes his way, and leaves Him to be put to death. But ere long, a dull hoarse murmur of the nations, extending through all the length and breadth of the mighty empire, gives token that He who was dead is alive again, and is speaking to the general conscience. Then Rome starts from her sleep ; Rome; the politic tolerant Rome, sheds rivers of blood. Her tolerance allowed men to believe everything, but on condition that they believed seriously in nothing. Rome was directed by the sure instinct of despotism. She did not fear the gods of the Pantheon, because she could always place above them the statue of the Emperor : whereas what was now in question was, while leaving to Cæsar the things which were Cæsar's, to place a Sovereign above the Emperor, and to raise a legislation above the legislation of the empire. Therefore the Roman city determined to give a death-blow to Christianity, — to the idea of universal truth, because if that idea gained entrance into the understanding, the cause of the liberty of souls was gained. So it was that indifference became ferocious, and that doubt led back to fanaticism.

I have told you whence liberty does not come; but whence comes it? Whence comes liberty? Ask any scholar of the Lyceums of France; he will answer you, without hesitation: Liberty comes from the French revolution! — No doubt, whispers an older comrade in his ear; but do not forget the philosophy of the eighteenth century which developed the principles which the revolution put in practice. — That is all very well, a Protestant will say; but let us consider the grand fact of the Reformation: it is from the sixteenth century that liberty has its date. — Well and good, adds an historian; but do you not know that the Germans were they who poured a generous and free blood into the impoverished blood of the men who had been fashioned by the slavery of the empire? I contest nothing, and I am not sufficiently well-informed to pronounce with confidence upon the action of all these historic causes.* But this I venture to affirm, — that if any one thinks to fix definitely the hour when liberty was born in history, he is mistaken: for it has no other date than that of the human conscience, and I will say with M. Lamartine:

> Give me the freedom which that hour had birth,
> With the free soul, when first in conscious worth
> The just man braved the stronger! *

Liberty had birth the first time that, urged by his fellow men to acts which wounded his conscience,

* La liberté que j' aime est née avec notre âme
Le jour où le plus juste a bravé le plus fort.

a man, relying upon God, felt himself stronger than the world. That Socrates had not studied, I fancy, in the school of the Encyclopedists, and was no German either, that I know of, who said to the judges of Athens, with death in prospect: "It is better to obey God than men." And when those words were repeated by the Apostles of the universal truth, the death of Socrates, that noble death which has justly gained for him the admiration of the universe, was reproduced in thousands and thousands of instances. Children, women, young girls, old men, perished in tortures to attest the rights of conscience; and the blood of martyrs, that seed of Christians, as a father of the Church called it,* was not less a seed of liberty. Liberty was not born in history; but if you wish to fix a date to its grandest outburst, you have it here; there is no other which can be compared with it.

Some of you are thinking perhaps, without saying so, that I am maintaining a hard paradox. To look for the source of liberty of conscience in religion, is not this to forget that the Christian Church has often marked its passage in history by a long track of blood rendered visible by the

* Tertullian.

funereal light of the stake? I forget nothing, Sirs, and I beg of you not to forget anything either. There are three remarks which I commend to your attention.

It must not be forgotten that the Gospel first obtained extensive success when Roman society was in the lowest state of corruption, and that its representatives were but too much affected by the evils which it was their mission to combat.

It must not be forgotten that there came afterwards hordes of barbarians who in a certain sense renovated the worn-out society, but who poured over the new leaven a coarse paste hard to penetrate.

It must not be forgotten, lastly, that if a cause might legitimately be condemned for the faults of its defenders, there are none, no, not a single one, which could remain erect before the tribunal which so should give judgment. Every cause in this world is more or less compromised by its representatives; but there are bad principles, which produce evil by their own development, and there are good principles which man abuses, but which by their very nature always end by raising a protest against the abuse. It is in the light of this indisputable truth that we are about to enter upon a discussion of which you will appreciate the full importance.

Sceptical writers affirm that toleration has its origin in the weakening of faith; and, drawing the consequence of their affirmation, they recommend the diffusion of the spirit of doubt as the best means of promoting liberty of conscience. We have here the old argument which would suppress the use to get rid of the abuse. Persecutions are made in the name of religion; let us get rid of faith, and we shall have peace. Prisons have been built and the stake has been set up in the name of God: let us get rid of God, and we shall have toleration. Observe well the bearing of this mode of argument. Let us get rid of fire, and we shall have no more conflagrations; let us get rid of water, and no more people will be drowned. No doubt, — but humanity will perish of drought and of cold.

Let us examine this subject seriously: it is well worth our while. If toleration proceeds from the enfeebling of religious belief, we ought among various nations to meet with toleration in an inverse proportion to the degree of their faith. This is a question then of history. Let us study facts. Recollecting first of all that ancient Rome did not draw forth a germ of liberty from its scepticism, let us throw a glance over existing communities.

Sweden is far behind England in regard to liberty of conscience. Is it that religious convictions are weaker in England than in Sweden? Has the religious liberty which Great Britain practises sprung from indifference? Is it not rather that that land produces an energetic race, and that it has been so often drenched with the blood of the followers of different forms of worship, that that blood cried at length to heaven, and that the conscience of the people heard it? There is more religious liberty in France than in Spain. Is it the case that the true cause of the intolerance of the Spanish people is a more lively and more general faith than that of the French? That is not so certain.

Switzerland is one of the countries in which is enjoyed the greatest liberty of opinion. Is Switzerland a land of indifference? Was not the comparative firmness of its citizens' convictions remarked during the conflicts of the last century? Do not the United States bear in large characters upon their banner this inscription: LIBERTY OF CONSCIENCE? America is not distinguished as a country without religion; on the contrary, it is blamed for the excursiveness of its faith, for the multiplicity and sometimes for the extravagance of its sects. Was it a sceptic that taught the inhabitants of the New World to respect religious convictions? Assuredly not! William Penn was shut up in the Tower of London for the crime of free thought. Set free from prison, he crossed the ocean. While intolerance was reigning still on both shores of the Atlantic, he founded in Pennsylvania a place of refuge for all proscribed opinions; and the germ has been fruitful. In vain I pass from old Europe to young America; I look, I observe, and I do not see that liberty is developed in proportion to the scepticism and the incredulity of nations. I seem, on the contrary, to see that there is perhaps most liberty where there is most real faith.

Some may dispute the validity of these conclusions by remarking that the condition of communities is a complex phenomenon depending upon divers causes. Let us simplify the question. Is it not, it will be said, the literary representatives of the spirit of doubt who have demanded and founded toleration? Is it not . . . But it is not necessary for my supposed questioner to go on.

If he is a Frenchman, he will name Voltaire. No doubt, freedom of opinion has been claimed by sceptics. They have served a good cause; let us know how to rejoice in the fact, and not to be unmindful of what there may have been in their work of noble impulses and generous inspirations. Let us remark however that every proscribed opinion puts forth a natural claim to the liberty of which it is deprived. But it is one thing to claim for one's-self a liberty one would gladly make use of to oppress others, and it is another thing to demand liberty seriously and for all. There was, as I am glad to believe, a certain natural generosity in the motives which led Voltaire to consecrate to noble causes a pen so often sold to evil. Still it is impossible not to suspect that if that apostle of toleration had had a principality under his own sway, the fact of thinking differently from the master would very soon have figured among the number of delinquencies.

The patriarch of Ferney wrote in favor of toleration; some friends of religious indifference have pleaded the cause of liberty of conscience: the fact is certain. But other writers, animated by a living faith, have also demanded liberty for all: the fact is not less certain. Some years ago, at nearly the same epoch, the Père Lacordaire and our own Alexander Vinet consecrated to this noble cause, the former the attractive brilliancy of his eloquence, the latter all the fineness of his delicate analyses. The friends of Lacordaire are gathering up the vibrations of that striking utterance which proclaimed: "Liberty slays not God." * Let us gather up also the good words, which, uttered on the borders of our lake, have gained entrance far and near into many hearts. I should like to take such and such a Parisian journalist, bring him into our midst, and get him to acquaint himself thoroughly with the results of our experience; I should like to conduct him to the cemetery of Clarens, place him by the tomb of Vinet, and tell him what that man was. — If, as he returned to his home, my journalist did not leave behind him at the French frontier, as contraband merchandise, all that he would have seen and learnt in our country, he would perhaps understand that the surest road by which to arrive at respect for the consciences of others is not indifference, but firmness of faith, in humility of heart, and largeness of thought. All the writers who have devoted their pen to the defence of the rights

* *Le Père Lacordaire*, by the Comte de Montalembert, p. 25.

of the human soul have not therefore been sceptics. Without continuing this discussion of proper names, let us settle what is here the true place of writers. Before there are men who demand liberty and digest the theory of it, there must be other men who take it, and who suffer for having taken it. If liberty is consolidated with speech and pen, it is founded with tears and blood; and the sceptical apostles of toleration conveniently usurp the place of the martyrs of conviction. "What we want," rightly observes a revolutionary writer, "is free men, rather than liberators of humanity." *

In fact, liberty comes to us above all from those who have suffered for it. Its living springs are in the spirit of faith, and not, as they teach us, in the spirit of indifference. It is easy to understand, that where no one believes, the liberty to believe would not be claimed by any one.

Let us now endeavor to penetrate below facts, in order to bring back the discussion to sure principles. Let us ask what, in regard to liberty of conscience, are the natural consequences of faith, and the natural consequences of scepticism.

* *De l'autre rive*, by Iscander (in Russian). Iscander is the pseudonyme of M. Herzen.

Faith does appear, at first sight, a source of intolerance. The man who believes, reckons himself in possession of the right in regard to truth, and to God; he has nothing to respect in error. Thus it is that belief naturally engenders persecution. This reasoning is specious, all the more as it is supported by numerous and terrible examples; but let us look at things more closely. Place yourselves face to face with any one of your convictions, no matter which; I hope there is no one of you so unfortunate as not to have any. Suppose that it were desired to impose upon you by force even the conviction which you have. Suppose that an officer of police came to say to you, pronouncing at the same time the words which best expressed your own thoughts: "you are commanded so to believe." What would happen? If you had never had a doubt of your faith, you would be tempted to doubt it, the moment any human power presumed to impose it upon you. The feeling of oppression would produce in your conscience a strong inclination to revolt. Let us analyze this feeling. You feel that it is words, not convictions, which are imposed by force; you feel that declarations extorted by fear from lying lips are an outrage to truth. You feel, in a word, that your belief is the right of God over you, and not the right of your neighbor. Men respect God's right over the souls of their fellow-men, in proportion as they are intelligent in their own faith. The fanaticism which would impose words by force is not an ardent but a blind faith. In order to bring it back into the paths of liberty, it is enough to restore to it its sight.

The establishment of the Christian religion furnishes a great example in support of our thesis. The Christians, when persecuted by the empire, had never allowed themselves to reply to the violence of power by the violence of rebellion. There came, however, and soon enough, a time when they were sufficiently numerous to defend themselves, and had withal the consciousness of their strength; but they had no will to conquer the world, except by the arms of martyrdom, and heroism, and obedience. This was not the case during a few years only, it is the history of three centuries, an ever-memorable page of human annals, in which all ages will be able to learn what are the true weapons of truth. Christendom, too often forgetful of its origin, has in later times allowed the fury of persecution to cloak itself under a pretended regard for sacred interests; but the remedy has proceeded from the very evil. The Christian conscience has protested, in the name of the Gospel, against the crimes of which the Gospel was the pretext, and the passions of men the cause. "We must bewail the misery and error of our time," already St. Hilary was exclaiming, in the fourth century. "Men are thinking that God has need of the protection of men. . . . The Church is uttering threats of banishment and imprisonment, and desiring to compel belief by force, — the Church, which itself acquired strength in exile and in prisons!"

True faith, then, possesses a principle by which it protests against abuses which it is sought to cloak under its name, and this protest comes at last to make itself heard. Faith suppressed, the passions will remain, for in order to be a saint, it is not enough to be a sceptic. The passions will look for other pretexts. Will not the spirit of doubt offer them such pretexts?

It seems at first sight that doubt must promote toleration, since it does not allow any importance to be attached to opinions. This is a specious conclusion, similar to that which placed in belief the source of intolerant passions. Let us once more reflect a little. The first effect of doubt is certainly to dispose the mind to leave a free course to all opinions; but disdain is not the way to respect, and only respect can give solid bases to the spirit of liberty. Believers are in the eyes of the sceptic weak-minded persons, whom he treats at first with a gentle and patronizing compassion. But these weak minds grow obstinate; the sceptic perceives that they do not bend before his superiority, and dare perhaps to consider themselves as his equals. Then irritation arises, and, beneath the velvet paw, one feels the piercing of the claw. The sceptic has in fact a dogma; he has but one, but one he has after all — the negation of truth. The faith of others is a protest against that single dogma on which he has concentrated all the powers of his conviction. He is passionately in earnest for this negation; he feels himself the representative of an idea, of which he must secure the triumph. Now come such surmisings as these: "Here are men who think themselves the depositaries of truth! These pretended believers — may they not be hypocrites?" Place men so disposed in positions of power; let them be the masters of society; what will follow? Beliefs are a cause of disturbances: what seemed at first an innocent weakness, takes then the character of a dangerous madness. For the politician, the temptation to extirpate this madness is not far off. "What if we were to get rid of this troublesome source of agitation! If we declared that the conscience of individuals belongs to the sovereign, what repose we should have in the State! If we proclaimed the true modern dogma, namely, that there is no dogma; if silencing, in short, fanatics who are behind their age, we decreed that every belief is a crime and every manifestation of faith a revolt, what quiet in society!" The incline is slippery, and what shall hold back the sceptic who is descending it?

Faith carries with it the remedy for fanaticism, but where shall be found the remedy for the fanaticism of doubt? In the claims of God? God is but a word, or a worthless hypothesis. In respect for the convictions of others? All conviction is but weakness and folly. All this, be well assured, gives much matter for reflection. When I hear some men who call themselves liberal, tracing the ideal of the society which they desire, the bare imagination of their triumph frightens me, for I can understand that that society would enjoy the liberty of the Roman empire, and the toleration of the Cæsars.

Such are the consequences of scepticism for the leaders of a people. What will those consequences be for the people themselves? The spirit of indifference paralyzes the sources of generous sentiments, and ends in the same results as the spirit of cowardice. And do you not know the part which cowardice has played in history? If I may venture to call up here the most mournful recollections of modern times, do you not know that during the Reign of Terror, two or three hundred scoundrels instituted public massacres in the Capital of France, in the midst of a population shuddering with fright, but who let things go? Now the characteristic of indifference is the letting things go. If fanaticism has something to do with persecution, indifference has a great deal to do with it. The crimes which minds paralyzed by doubt allow to be perpetrated have besides a sadder character than those which are perpetrated by passions, which, wild and erring though they be, have a certain nobleness in their origin. If I must be bound to the stake, I had rather burn with the blind assent of a fanatical crowd, than in the presence of an indifferent populace who came to look on. For just as sceptics find all doctrines equally good, so they find all spectacles equally instructive and curious.*

I have felt it necessary to insist on these considerations. Direct attacks upon religious truth are perhaps less dangerous than the efforts by which modern infidelity endeavors to estrange us from God, by persuading us that doubt is the guarantee of liberty, and that belief rivets the chains of bondage. Many consciences are disturbed by these affirmations. It concerns us therefore to know that God is the great Liberator of souls, and that forgetfulness of God is the road to slavery. The faith which seeks to propagate itself by force inflicts upon itself the harshest of contradictions. The spirit of doubt, in order to become the spirit of violence, has only to transform itself according to the laws of its proper nature.

And now to sum up. One of the noblest spec-

* "The man of thought knows that the world only belongs to him as a subject of study, and, even if he could reform it, perhaps he would find it so curious as it is that he would not have the courage to do so." — Ernest Renan, preface to *Etudes d' histoire religieuse*, 1857. The author has manifested better sentiments in 1859, in the preface to his *Essais de morale et de critique*.

tacles that earth can show, is that of a community animated with a true and profound faith, in which each man, using his best efforts to communicate his convictions to his brethren, respects the while that which belongs to God in the inviolable asylum of the conscience of others. But woe to the society formed by sophists, in which opinion, benumbed by doubt and indifference, arouses itself only to devote to hatred or to contempt every firm and noble conviction!

To unsettle the idea of God, is to dry up at its source the stream of the veritable progress of modern society; it is to attack the foundations of liberty, justice, and love. The material conquests of civilization would serve thenceforward only to hasten the decomposition of the social body. The pure idea of God is the true cause of the great progress of the modern era; religion, in its generality, is, as Plutarch has told us, the necessary condition to the very existence of society. This is what remains for us to prove.

"How sacred is the society of citizens," said Cicero, "when the immortal gods are interposed between them as judges and as witnesses." * Let us raise still higher this lofty thought, and say:

* *De Legibus*, ii. 7.

"How sacred is human society, when, beneath the eye of the common Father, the inequalities of life are accepted with patience and softened by love; when the poor and the rich, as they meet together, remember that the Lord is the Maker of them both; when a hope of immortality alleviates present evils, and when the consciousness of a common dignity reduces to their true value the passing differences of life!" Take away from human society God as mediator, and the hopes founded in God as a source of consolation, and what would you have remaining? The struggle of the poor against the rich, the envy of the ignorant directed against the man who has knowledge, the dullard's low jealousy of superior intelligence, hatred of all superiority, and, by an almost inevitable reaction, the obstinate defence of all abuses, — in one word, war — war admitting neither of remedy nor truce. Such is the most apparent danger which now threatens society.

When I consider these facts with attention, I am astonished every day that society subsists at all, that the burning lava of unruly passions does not oftener make large fissures in the social soil, and overflow in devastating torrents, bearing away at once palace and cottage, field and workshop. This standing danger is drawing anxious attention, and we hear the old adage repeated: "There must be a religion for the people." There are men who wish to give the people a religion which they themselves do not possess, acting like a man who, at once poor and ostentatious, should give alms with counterfeit money. And what result do they attain? We must have a religion for the people, say the politicians, that they may secure the ends they have in view, and conduct at their own pleasure the herds at their disposal. We must have a religion for the people, say the rich, in order to keep peaceably their property and their incomes. We must have a religion for the people, say the *savants*, in order to remain quiet in their studies, or in their academic chairs. What are they doing — these men without God, who wish to preserve a faith for the use of the people? These *savants*, — they say, and print it, that religion is an error necessary for the multitudes who are incapable of rising to philosophy. Where is it that they say it, and print it? Is it in drawing-rooms with closed doors? Is it within the walls of Universities, or in scientific publications which are out of the reach of the masses? No. They say it in political journals, in reviews read by all the world; they print it at full in books which are sold by thousands of copies. Their words are spreading like a deleterious miasma through all classes of society. Thoughtless men! (I am unwilling to suppose a cool calculation on their part of money or of fame which should oblige me to say—heartless men), thoughtless men! they do not see the inevitable consequences of their own proceeding. The people hear and understand. The intellectual barriers between the different classes of society are gradually becoming lower: this is one of the clearest of the ways of Providence in our time. Do you believe that the people will long consent to hear it said that they only live on errors, but that those errors are necessary for them? Do you not see that they are about to rise, and answer, in the sentiment of their own dignity, that they will no longer be deceived, and that they intend to deliver themselves also from superstition? Then, all restraining barriers removed, passions will have free course; and believe me, the rising floods will not respect those quiet haunts of study in which they will have had one of their springs. The proof of this has been seen before. Some men of the last century wished to destroy religion amongst decent folk, but not for the rabble: they are Voltaire's words, who had too much good sense to be an atheist, but whose pale deism is sometimes scarcely distinguishable from the negation of God. "Your Majesty," thus he wrote to his friend the King of Prussia, in January, 1757, "will render an eternal service to the human race, by destroying that infamous superstition, I do not say amongst the rabble, which is not worthy to be enlightened, and to which all yokes are suitable, but amongst honest people." A religion was necessary for the people; but Voltaire and the King of Prussia, the German barons, the French marquises, and the ladies who received their homage, could do without it.

Voltaire died before eating of the fruit of his works; and Alfred de Musset could only address to him his vengeful apostrophe at his tomb:

> Sleep'st thou content, and does thy hideous smile
> Still flit, Voltaire, above thy fleshless bones?*

Voltaire was dead; but many of his friends and disciples were able to meditate, in the prisons of the Terror and as they mounted the steps of the

* Dors-tu content, Voltaire, et ton hideux sourire
Voltige-t-il encor sur tes os décharnés?

scaffold, on the nature of the terrible game which they had played — and lost.

So it fares with men of letters who have no God, but who would have a religion for the people. Other men there are who would have a religion for the people, being themselves the while without restraint, because they are without religious convictions. They abandon themselves to the ardent pursuit of riches, excitements, worldly pleasures. These are they who have made a fortune by disgraceful means, perhaps the public sale of their consciences, and who by their luxurious extravagance overwhelm the honest and economical working-man. These are the courtesans who parade in broad daylight the splendid rewards of their own infamy. Let not such deceive themselves! The people see these things; they form their judgment of them, and if they give way to the bad instincts which are in us all, where God is not in the heart to restrain them, to their hatred is added contempt. If they are forcibly kept back from realizing their cherished hopes, they adjourn them, but without renouncing them.

Put away all belief in God, and you will see the action and reaction of human passions forming, as it were, a mass of opposite electricities, and preparing the thunder-peal and the furies of the tempest. Then appear those disorganized societies which are terrified at their own dissolution, until a strong man comes, and, taking advantage of this very terror, takes and chastises these societies, as one chastises an unruly child. It is a story at once old and new, because, in proportion as God withdraws from human society, in that same proportion the power of the sword replaces the empire of the conscience. There must be a religion for the people! Yes, Sirs, but for that people, wide as humanity, which includes us all.

If the existence of God is denied, man falls into despair, and society into dissolution. What then is my inference? That atheism is false. Such a mode of arguing produces an outcry. "A matter of sentiment!" men exclaim. "You would build up a doctrine according to your own fancy! You do not discuss the question calmly, but appeal to interests and prejudices: you quit the domain of science, which takes cognizance only of facts and reasoning." Such expressions are common enough to make it worth while to study their value. Of course, science must not be an instrument of our caprice. We are bound to search for truth; and we are unfaithful to our obligations if we try to establish doctrines which serve our passions, or favor our interests, or flatter our tastes and our prejudices. But the conscience, the heart, the conditions of the existence of human society, are neither prejudices nor personal interests; they are eternal and living realities. We speak of the conscience, of the heart, of society, and they answer us: "We do not believe that there are true sciences in that domain; we only wish for facts." Occasionally we hear naturalists speak in this way. We only wish for facts! Then our thoughts, our feelings, our conscience are not facts! The man who will give the closest observation to the steps of a fly, or to a caterpillar's method of crawling, has not a moment's attention to give to the impulses of the heart, to the rules of duty, to the struggles of the will; and when addressed on the subject of these realities of the soul, the most certain of all realities, he will reply: "That is no business of mine, I want nothing but facts." Let us pass from this aberration, and listen for a moment to other objectors.

We do not deny, it is often said, the reality of our feelings. Man desires happiness, and seeks it in religious belief; but this is an order of things which science cannot take account of. Science has only truth for its object, and owes its own existence wholly to the reason. If it happens to science to give pain to the heart or to the conscience, no conclusion can thence be drawn against the certainty of its results. "There is no commoner, and at the same time faultier, way of reasoning, than that of objecting to a philosophical hypothesis the injury it may do to morals and to religion. When an opinion leads to absurdity, it is certainly false; but it is not certain that it is false because it entails dangerous consequences." * So wrote the patriarch of modern sceptics, the Scotchman Hume. The lesson has been well learnt; it is repeated to us, without end, in the columns of the leading journals of France, and in the pages of the *Revue des deux Mondes*. The adversaries of spiritual beliefs have changed their tactics. In the last century, they replied to minds alarmed for the consequences of their work: "Truth can never do harm." — "Truth can never do harm," retorted J. J. Rousseau: "I

* Hume, Essay VIII. On liberty and necessity. [Not having access to the original, I re-translate the French translation. — Tr.]

believe it as you do, and this it is that proves to me that your doctrines are not truth." The argument is conclusive. So the adversary has taken up another position; and he says at this day: —" Our doctrines do perhaps pain the heart, and wound the conscience, but this is no reason why they should be false: moral goodness, utility, happiness, are not signs by which we may know what is true."

Philosophy, Gentlemen, has always assumed to be the universal explanation of things, and you will agree that it is on her part a humiliating avowal, that she is enclosed, namely, in a circle of pure reason, and leaves out of view, as being unable to give any account of them, the great realities which are called moral goodness and happiness. One might ask what are the bases of that science which disavows, without emotion, the most active powers of human nature. One might ask whether those who so speak, understand well the meaning of their own words; and inquire also what is the method which they employ, and the result at which they aim. One might ask whether these philosophers are not like astronomers who should say: " Here are our calculations. It matters nothing to us whether the stars in their observed course do or do not agree with them. Science is sovereign; it is amenable only to its own laws, and visible realities cannot be objections in the way of its calculations." Let us leave these preliminary remarks, and let us come to the core of the controversy.

They set the reason on one side, the conscience and heart upon the other, as an anatomist separates the organic portions of a corpse, and they say: Truth belongs only to the reason; the conscience and the heart have no admission into science. Listen to the following express declaration of the weightiest, perhaps, of French contemporary philosophers: "The God of the pure reason is the only true God; the God of the imagination, the God of the feelings, the God of the conscience, are only idols!"* It is impossible to accept this arbitrary division of the divine attributes. There is but one and the same God, the Substance of truth, the inexhaustible Source of beauty, the supreme Law of the wills created to accomplish the designs of His mercy. The conscience, the heart, the reason rise equally towards Him, following the triple ray which descends from His eternity upon our transitory existence.

* Vacherot, *La metaphysique et la science*. Preface, p. xxix.

We cannot therefore seriously admit that God of the pure reason, separated from the God of the conscience and of the heart. Still let us endeavor to make this concession, for argument's sake, to our philosopher. Let us suppose that the reason has a God to itself, a God for the metaphysicians who is not the God of the vulgar. Before we immolate upon His altar the conscience and the heart, it is worth our while to examine whether the statue of the God of the reason rests upon a solid pedestal. Here are the theses which are proposed to us: "It is impossible for our feelings to supply any light for science. Truth may be gloomy, and despair may gain its cause. Virtue may be wrong, and immorality may be the true. Reason alone judges of that which is." I answer: Human nature has always eagerly followed after happiness. Human nature has always acknowledged, even while violating it, a rule of duty. The heart is not an accident, the conscience is not a prejudice: they are, and by the same right as the reason, constituent elements of our spiritual existence. If there exist an irreconcilable antagonism between science and life; if the heart, in its fundamental and universal aspirations, is the victim of an illusion, if the conscience in its clearest admonitions is only a teacher of error, what is our position? In what I am now saying, Gentlemen, I am not appealing to your feelings; the business is to follow, with calm attention, a piece of exact reasoning. If the heart deceives us, if the voice of duty leads us astray, the disorder is at the very core of our being; our nature is ill constructed. If our nature is ill constructed, what warrants to us our reason? Nothing. What assures us that our axioms are good, and that our reasonings have any value? Nothing. The life of the soul cannot be arbitrarily cloven in twain; it must be held for good in all its constituent elements, or enveloped wholly and entirely in the shades of doubt. If the heart and conscience deceive us, then reason may lead us astray, and the very idea of truth disappears. God is the light of the spiritual world. We prove His existence by showing that without Him all returns to darkness. This demonstration is as good as another.

LECTURE III.

THE REVIVAL OF ATHEISM.

(At Geneva, 24th Nov. 1863. — At Lausanne, 18th Jan. 1864.)

GENTLEMEN,

The subject of the present Lecture will be — The revival of Atheism. And I do not employ the word 'atheism' — a term which has been so greatly abused — without mature reflection. When Socrates opposed the idea of the holy God to the impure idols of paganism; when he dethroned Jupiter and his train in order to celebrate "the supreme God, who made and who guides the world, who maintains the works of creation in the flower of youth, and in a vigor always new," * they accused Socrates of being an atheist. Descartes, the great geometrician who proclaimed the existence of God more certain than

* Xenophon, *Memorab. of Socrates*, Bk. iv. 10.

any theorem of geometry, has been denounced as an atheist. When men began to forsake the temples of idols in order to worship the unknown God who had just manifested Himself to the world, the Christians were accused of atheism because they refused to bow down to wood and stone. Such abuses might dispose one to renounce the use of the word. Besides, when a word has been for a long time the signal of persecution and the forerunner of death, one hesitates to employ it. In an age when atheists were burned, generous minds would use their best efforts to prove that men suspected of atheism had not denied God, because they would not have been understood had they attempted to say—"They have denied God perhaps, but that is no reason for killing them." Thence arose the sophistical apologies for certain doctrines, apologies made with a good intention, but which trouble the sincerity of history. These are the brands of servitude, which must disappear where liberty prevails. We are able now to call things by their proper names, for there exist no longer for atheism either stakes or prisons. In affirming that certain writers, some of whom are just now the favorites of fame, are shaking the foundations of all religion, one exposes no one to severities which have disappeared from our manners, one only exposes oneself to the being taxed with intolerance and fanaticism. But candor is here a duty. If this duty were not fulfilled, liberty of thought would no longer be anything else than liberty of negation; and, while truth was oppressed, error alone would be set free.

Let us settle clearly the terms of this discussion. It is often asserted that an atheist does not exist. Does this mean that the lips which deny God, always in some way contradict themselves? Does it mean that every soul bears witness to God, perhaps unconsciously to itself, either by a secret hope, or by a secret dread? This is true, as I think; but we are speaking here of doctrines and not of men. It is true again that the negation of the Creator allows of the existence, in certain philosophies, of generous ideas and elevated conceptions. Such men, while they put God out of existence, desire to keep the true, the beautiful, the good; they hope to preserve the rays, while they extinguish the luminous centre from which they proceed. Such systems always tend to produce the deadly fruits pointed out in my last lecture; but men devoted to the severe labors of the intellect often escape, by a noble inconsistency, the natural results of their theories. Therefore, in the inquiry on which we are about to enter, the term 'atheism' implies, with regard to persons, neither reproach nor contempt. It simply indicates a doctrine, the doctrine which denies God. This denial takes place in two ways: It is affirmed that nature, that is to say matter, force devoid of intelligence and of will, is the sole origin of things; or, the reality is acknowledged of those marks which raise mind above nature, but it is affirmed that humanity is the highest point of the universe, and that above it there is nothing. Such are the two forms of atheism.

Perhaps you expect here the explanation of a doctrine which is often described as holding a sort of middle place between the negation and the affirmation of God, namely, pantheism. Pantheism, in the true sense of that word, is a system according to which God is all, and the universe nothing. This extraordinary thesis is met with in India. A Greek, Parmenides, has vigorously sustained it. We have in it a kind of sublime infatuation. In presence of the one and eternal Being thought collapses in bewilderment; and thenceforward it experiences for all that is manifold and transitory a disdain which passes into negation. In the domain of experience, all is limited, temporary, imperfect; and reason seeks the perfect, the eternal, the infinite. The doctrine of creation alone explains how the universe subsists in presence of its first cause. In ignorance of this doctrine, some bold thinkers have cut the knot which they could not untie. They have declared that reason alone is right, and that experience is wrong: the world does not exist, it is but an illusion of the mind. Whence proceeds this illusion? If perfection alone exists, how comes that imperfect mind to exist which deceives itself in believing in the reality of the world? To this question the system has no answer. Such is true pantheism; but it is not to dangers so noble that most minds run the risk of succumbing. What is commonly understood by pantheism is the deification of the universe. The idea of God is not directly denied, but it undergoes a transformation which destroys it. God is no longer the eternal and Almighty Spirit, the Creator; but the unconscious principle, the substance of things, the whole. The universe alone exists; above it there is nothing; but the universe is infinite, eternal, divine. The higher wants of the reason, mingling with the data derived from experience, form an imposing and confused image, which, while it beguiles the imagination, perverts the understanding, deceives the heart, and places the conscience in peril. In a philosophical point of view, it is a contradiction of thought, which seeks the Infinite Being, and, being unable to discover Him, gives the character of infinity to realities bounded by experience. In a religious point of view, it is an aberration of the heart, which preserves the sentiment of adoration, but perverts it by dispersing it over the universe. "Pantheism," says M. Jules Simon, "is only the learned form of atheism; the universe deified is a universe without God."* From the moment that the reason endeavors to see distinctly, pantheism vanishes like a deceitful glare. Atheism disengages itself from the cloak which was concealing its true nature, and the mind remains in presence of nature only, or of humanity only. We will proceed to take a rapid glance at some few of the countries of Europe, in order to discover and point out in them the traces of this melancholy doctrine. Let us begin with France.

In the year 1844, just twenty years ago, some

* *La Religion naturelle.* Preface.

French writers, representing the philosophy, in some measure official, of the time, united to publish a *Dictionnaire des sciences philosophiques.* M. Franck, the director of this useful and laborious enterprise, said in the preface to the work: "Atheism has well nigh completely disappeared from philosophy; the progress of a sound psychology will render its return for ever impossible." In speaking thus, he expressed the thoughts and hopes of the school of which he remains one of the most estimable representatives. A generous impulse was animating a group of intelligent and learned young men. Their hope was to translate Christianity into a purely rational doctrine, to purify religious notions without destroying them, and, while endowing humanity with a vigorous scientific culture, to leave to it its lofty hopes. The object in view was to establish a philosophy founded upon a serious faith in God; and to this philosophy was promised the progressive and pacific conquest of the human race.* Twenty years have passed, and things bear quite another aspect. To language expressive of security have succeeded the accents of anxiety and words of

* Emile Saisset, in the *Revue des Deux Mondes,* of March, 1845.

alarm. The cause which was proclaimed victorious is defended at this day like a besieged city. You will remark however,—that I may not leave you beyond measure discouraged by the facts of which I have to tell you,—you will remark, I say, that it is the efforts attempted in the cause of good which have helped to set me on the track of evil; it has often been the defence which has fixed my attention upon the attack.

The materialism of the last century seems to have maintained a strong hold upon one part of the Paris school of medicine. We do find in France a good many physicians who, like Boerhave, render homage to religion, and a good many physiologists who, like the great Haller, are ready to defend beliefs of the spiritual order;* but, among men specially devoted to the study of matter, many succumb to the temptation of refusing to recognize anything as real which does not come under the experience of the senses. This however is not one of the points which offer themselves most strikingly for our examination. The atheistic manifestations of the socialist schools have more novelty, and perhaps more importance.

* See the *Lettres sur les vérités, les plus importantes de la révélation*, by Albert de Haller, translated into French by one of his grandsons. Lausanne, Bridel, 1846.

Man is naturally a social being. Good and evil have their primitive seat in the heart of individuals, but good and evil are transferred into institutions of which the influence is morally beneficial or pernicious. If socialism consists in recognizing the importance of social institutions, in cherishing ideas of progress and hopes of reform, I trust that we are all socialists. Do we desire progress by the ever wider diffusion of justice and love? From the moment that, across the conscience whereon divine rays are falling, we have descried the eternal centre of light, we understand that God is the most implacable enemy of abuses. How is it then that atheism sometimes manifests itself in attempts at social reform? We may explain it, without so much as pointing out the influence, but too real, of the faults committed by the representatives of religion. Faith is a principle of action; it is, as history testifies, the grand source of the progress of human society; but faith is also a principle of patience. The brow of every believer is more or less illumined by the rays of His peace who is patient because He is eternal. Eager to effect good to the utmost extent of his ability, he accomplishes his work with that calm activity to which are reserved durable victories. In the impossible (for if the word impossible is not French, it is human) the believer recognizes one of the manifestations of the supreme Will, and immortal hope enables him to support the evils which he does not succeed in destroying. But this is not enough for impatient reformers. Ignorant of the profound sources of evil, they think that institutions can do everything, and that a change of laws would suffice to reform men's hearts; they believe that the organization of society alone hinders the realization of good and of happiness. The resignation of believers appears to them a stupid lethargy, and in their patient expectation of a judgment to come they see only an obstacle to the immediate triumph of justice on the earth. What if the nations were persuaded that there is nothing to be looked for beyond the present life, so that all that is to be done is to make to ourselves a paradise as soon as may be here below! If they were persuaded that all appeal to the Judge in heaven is a chimerical hope, with what ardor would they throw themselves into schemes of revolution! Thus it is that certain political innovators are led to seek in the negation of God one of their means of action.

Two views, therefore, essentially diverse, govern the labors of the renovators of society. The one class desire to realize, in an ever larger measure, justice and love; religious convictions are the strongest support of their work. The other class would uproot from men's minds every principle of faith, in order the more readily to obtain the realization of their theories. These two classes of men seem at times to be fighting all together in the *mêlée* of opinions. They meet, as, in the doubtful glimmer of the dawn, might meet together laborious workmen who are anticipating the daylight, and evil-doers who are fleeing from the sun.

In order to form a just estimate of the labors of the socialist schools, it would be necessary to make a bold and straightforward inquiry into the object of their studies, and to discern, in the midst of mad-brained and guilty dreams, whatever flashes of light might disclose some prophetic vision of the future. This is no task of ours. It is enough for us to remark that in France, as also in the other countries of Europe, the negation of God discovers itself in this order of ideas. It discovers itself at one time by an idolatry of humanity, at another by a materialistic enthusiasm for corporeal indulgences. Disregarding the sensual imaginations which disgrace the works of Fourrier, let us turn our attention elsewhere.

M. Vacherot, a sober philosopher, of high intellectual power and elevated sentiment, has lately published, unhappily, twelve hundred pages destined to maintain the thesis that God does not exist.* Man conceives the idea of perfection, and not finding that perfection realized either in the world or in himself, he rises to the conception of a real and perfect being: such is the usual process of metaphysical reasoning. For M. Vacherot, reality and perfection mutually exclude one another; this is one of his fundamental theses. This thesis does but interpret the result of our experience, by refusing us the right to raise ourselves higher. The world with which we are acquainted is imperfect; therefore — say Plato, Saint Augustine, and Descartes — the perfection of which we have the idea is realized in a Being superior to the world. The world with which we are acquainted is imperfect, therefore there is a contradiction between the ideal and the real, says M. Vacherot, who makes thus of the general result of experience the absolute rule of truth.

* *La Métaphysique et la Science*, 2 tom. Oct. 1858.

To say therefore of God that He is perfect, is to affirm that He does not exist, inasmuch as the ideal is never realized. Thought thus finds itself placed in a situation at once odd and violent. If God is perfect, He does not exist. If God exists, He is not perfect. The respect which we owe to the Being of beings forbids us to believe in Him; to affirm His existence would be to do outrage to His perfection. The author of this theory renders a worship to that ideal which does not exist, and towards which he affirms nevertheless that the world is gravitating by the law of progress. This worship is of too abstract a nature to secure many adherents; it can only become popular by taking another shape, and it does so in this way: We conceive of that perfection which in itself does not exist; it exists therefore in our thought. Since the world, by the law of progress, is tending towards perfection, the world has for its end and law a thought of the human mind. The human mind therefore is the summit of the universe, and it is it that we must adore. We are here out of the region of pure abstraction, and arrive at the doctrines of the Positivist school.

The Positive philosophy, so called because it wishes to have done with chimeras, was founded in France, a few years ago, by Auguste Comte. M. Littré is at present one of its principal representatives. This writer, says M. Sainte-Beuve, is one of those who are endeavoring "to set humanity free from illusions, from vague disputes, from vain solutions, from deceitful idols and powers." * Let us say the same thing in simpler terms: M. Littré professes the doctrines of a school which ignores the Creator in nature, and Providence in history. To ascertain phenomena, and acquaint ourselves with the law which governs them, such, say the positivists, is the limit of all our knowledge. As for the origin of things and their destination, that is an affair of individual fancy. "Each one may be allowed to represent such matters to himself as he likes; there is nothing to hinder the man who finds a pleasure in doing so from dreaming upon that past and that future." †

"In spite of some appearances to the contrary," says M. Littré, "the positive philosophy does not accept atheism." ‡ Why? Because atheism pretends to give an explanation of the universe, and

* *Notice sur M. Littré*, page 57.

† *Paroles de philosophie positive*, page 33.

‡ *Idem*, page 30.

that after a fashion is still theology. Minds "veritably emancipated" profess to know nothing whatever on questions which go beyond actual experience. They do not deny God, they eliminate Him from the thoughts. The attempt is a bold one, but it fails; men do not succeed in emancipating themselves from the laws of reason. The very writer whom I have just quoted is himself a proof of this, for he absolutely proscribes every statement of a metaphysical nature, and then, three pages farther on, in the very treatise in which he makes this proscription, he speaks of the "*eternal* motive powers of a *boundless* universe."* Boundless! eternal! What thoughts are these? Behold the instincts of the reason coming to light! behold all the divine attributes appearing! Adoration is withdrawn from God, and it is given to the universe at large. What is it which, in the universe regarded as a whole, will become the direct object of worship? Another positivist, M. de Lombrail, will tell us, in a work reviewed by Auguste Comte: "Man," he says, "has always adored humanity." Here, we learn, is the true foundation of all religions, and the brief summary of their history. This humanity-

* *Paroles de philosophie positive*, page 34.

god has been long adored under a veil which disguised it from the eyes of its worshippers; but the time is come when the sage ought to recognize the object of his worship and give it its true name.*

The positivist school, then, professes a complete scepticism with regard to whatever is not included in the domain of experience. But its foot slips, and it falls into the negation of God, from which it rises again by means of a humanitarian atheism. All these marks are met with again in the works of the critical school.

The critics group themselves about M. Renan. The praises which they lavished a while ago on a bad book by that author seem at least to allow us to point him out as their chief. They derive their name from studies in history and archæology, with which we here have nothing to do. They are regarded as forming a philosophical and religious school; and it is in that connection that they claim our attention. Their influence is incon-

* *Aperçus généraux sur la doctrine positiviste*, par M. de Lombrail, ancien élève de l' école polytechnique. The author says in his preface: "Auguste Comte examined this work with the conscientious attention which he was accustomed to give to the simplest task. He desired by his useful counsels to render it worthy of publication."

testable, and still, notwithstanding, their doctrinal value is nothing. They form merely a literary branch of the positivist school engrafted upon the electicism of M. Cousin. We find in their writings the pretension to limit science to the experimental study of nature and to humanity. We afterwards find there the pretension to understand and to accept all doctrines alike. Beyond this, nothing. The critics bestow particular attention on the phenomena of religion, of art, and of philosophy; but this interest is purely historical. Nothing is more curious than the successive forms of human beliefs; but the period of beliefs is over. Religious faith no longer subsists except in minds which are behind the age; and philosophy, upheld in a final swoon by Hegel and Hamilton, has just yielded its last breath in the arms of M. Cousin: so M. Renan informs us.* To choose a side between the defenders of the idea of God and its opponents; to choose between Plato and Epicurus, between Origen and Celsus, between Descartes and Hobbes, between Leibnitz and Spinoza, would be to make one's self the Don Quixote of thought. An honest man may find amusement in reading the Amadis of Gaul; the

* *Revue des Deux Mondes*, of 15th Jan. 1860, page 367.

Knight of *la Manche* went mad through putting faith in the adventures of that hero. A like fate befalls those minds which are simple enough to believe still, in the midst of the nineteenth century, in the brave chimeras of former days. Let us study history, let us study nature; beyond that we do not know, and we never shall know, anything. Our fashionable men of letters develop their thesis with so much assurance; they lavish upon believers so many expressions of amiable disdain; they appear so sure of being the interpreters of the mind of the age, that they seem ready to repeat to young people dazzled by their success, the lesson which Gilbert had expressed in these terms:

> Between ourselves — you own a God, I fear!
> Beware lest in your verse the fact appear:
> Dread the wits' laughter, friend, and know your betters:
> Our grandsires might have worn those old-world fetters;
> But in our days! Come, you must learn respect, —
> Content *your age to follow*, not direct.*

---

* Je soupçonne entre nous que vous croyez en Dieu.
N' allez pas dans vos vers en consigner l'aveu;
Craignez le ridicule, et respectez vos maîtres.
Croire en Dieu fut un tort permis à nos ancêtres.
Mais dans notre âge! Allons, il faut vous corriger
Et suivre votre siècle, au lieu de le juger.

To believe in God would be vulgar; to deny the existence of God would be a want of taste; the divine world must remain as a subject for poetry. So our critics speak. Their direct affirmation is scepticism. But they follow the destinies of the positivist school; they do not succeed in maintaining their balance between the affirmation and negation of God. Alfred de Musset has described this position of the soul, and its inevitable issue. Must I hope in God? Must I reject all faith and all hope?

> Between these paths how difficult the choice!
> Ah! might I find some smoother, easier way.
> "None such exists," whispers a secret voice,
> "God *is*, or *is not* — own, or slight, His sway."
> In sooth, I think so: troubled souls in turn
> By each extreme are tossed and harassed sore:
> They are but atheists, who feel no concern;
> If once they doubted they would sleep no more.*

The indifference of the critical philosophers is in fact only a transparent veil to atheistical doc-

* Entre ces deux chemins j'hésite et je m'arrête.
Je voudrais à l'écart suivre un plus doux sentier.
Il n'en existe pas, dit une voix secrète:
En présence du Ciel, il faut croire ou nier.
Je le pense, en effet: les âmes tourmentées
Vers l'un et l'autre excès se portent tour à tour;
Mais les indifférents ne sont que des athées;
Ils ne dormiraient plus, s'ils doutaient un seul jour.

trines. Faith in God the Creator is in their eyes a superstition; this is their only settled dogma. In other respects they indulge in theses the most contradictory. Most generally they deify man, declaring that there is no other God than the idea of humanity, no other infinite than the indefinite character of the aspirations of our own soul. At other times they proclaim an undisguised materialism, and look for the explanation of all things in atoms and in the law which governs them. They make to themselves a two-faced idol, one of these faces being called nature, and the other humanity. What strangely increases the confusion is that all the terms of language change meaning as employed by their pen. They speak of God, of duty, of religion, of immortality; their pages seem sometimes to be extracted from mystical writings; but these sacred words have for them a totally different meaning than for the ordinary run of their readers. Their God is not a Being, their religion is not a worship, their duty is not a law, their immortality is not the hope of a world to come. Amidst these equivocations and contradictions thought is blunted, and the sinews of the intellect are unstrung. The public, bewitched by talent and captivated by success, is deluged with writings which have the same effect as the talk of a frivolous man, or the showy tattle of a woman of the world. They give an agreeable exercise to the mind, without ever allowing it to form either a precise idea or a settled judgment.

Many are the clouds then on the intellectual horizon of France. Glance over the recent productions of French philosophy, and you will have no difficulty in recognizing the gravity of the situation. Works are multiplying with the object of defending the existence of God, Providence, the immortality of the soul: dams are being raised against the rising flood of atheism.* And here is a fact still more significant, namely, that the historians of ideas, whether they are recurring to the most remote antiquity, or are passing in review the worst errors of modern days, cannot meet with the negation of God, without having

* See, for example, *La Religion naturelle*, by Jules Simon; *Essai de philosophie religieuse*, by Emile Saisset; *De la connaissance de Dieu*, by A. Gratry; *La raison et la christianisme, douze lectures sur l'existence de Dieu*, by Charles Secrétan; *Essai sur la Providence*, by Ernest Bersot; *De la Providence*, by M. Damiron; *L'Idee de Dieu*, by M. Caro; *Théodicée, Etudes sur Dieu, la Création et la Providence*, par Amédée de Magerie.

their eyes thus turned to Paris, and their attention directed to contemporary productions.*

I hence infer, that atheism is raising its head in France, and there presenting itself under two forms. Materialism is appearing principally as an heritage from the last century. The new, or rather renewed, doctrine is the adoration of man by man. We are now going to cross the Rhine.

A powerful thinker, Hegel, had supreme sway in the last movement of speculative thought in Germany. Hegel's system of doctrine is enveloped in clouds. It is so ambiguous in regard to the questions which most directly concern the conscience and human interests, that it has been pretended to deduce from it, on the one hand a Christian theology, and on the other a sheer atheism. There is a story, whether a true one or not I cannot say, that this philosopher when near his end uttered the following words: "I have only had one disciple who has understood me — and he has misunderstood me." A man distinguished in metaphysical research by taste, genius, and

* See, for example, the *Etudes orientales* of M. Franck, the *Bouddha* of M. Barthélemy Saint-Hilaire; *L'Histoire de la philosophie au XVIIIe siècle*, of M. Damiron.

science, and who has, in that respect, devoted particular attention to Germany, M. Charles Secrétan, writes with reference to the fundamental principle of the entire Hegelian system: "If you ask me how I understand the matter, I will give you no answer; I do not understand it at all, and I do not believe that any one has ever understood it."* You will excuse me, Gentlemen, from here undertaking the scientific study of so difficult a system. It will be enough for us to render the darkness visible, that is to say, to understand well what it is which the doctrine of the Berlin Professor, in a certain sense, renders incomprehensible.

The foundation of his theory is that the universe is explained by an eternal idea, an idea which exists by itself, without appertaining to any mind. The Hegelians say that the existence of an infinite Mind is an inadmissible conception. They reject this mystery, and prefer to it the palpable absurdity of an idea which exists in itself, without being the act of an intelligence. This idea-God we have already encountered in the writings of M. Vacherot. We shall find it again more than once as we go on. In Germany,

* *Philosophie de la liberté*, vol. i. p. 225.

as in France, the theory only becomes popular by undergoing a transformation. The eternal idea manifests itself in the mind of man, and exists nowhere else. Above this idea there is nothing. Man is therefore the summit of things; it is he who must be adored. And thus it is in fact that Hegel has been understood. In the spring of 1850, Henri Heine wrote as follows in the *Gazette d'Augsbourg:* "I begin to feel that I am not precisely a biped deity, as Professor Hegel declared to me that I was twenty-five years ago." The deification of man: such is the popular translation of the philosophy of the idea. Would you have a further proof of this? The following anecdote was current in my youth, when German idealism was at the height of its popularity. A student going to call on one of his fellow-students, found him stretched on his bed, or his sofa, and exhibiting all the signs of an ecstatic contemplation. "Why, what are you doing there?" inquired the visitor. "I am adoring myself," replied the young adept in philosophy.

I am not examining the doctrines of Hegel with reference to the history of metaphysics, and within the precincts of the school in which it occupies a large place and demands the most serious attention; I am tracing the influence of those doctrines on the public mind at large. This influence is visible in the most disastrous consequences of atheism. "It certainly is not the Hegelian school alone," says M. Saint-Réné Taillandier, "which has produced all the moral miseries of the nineteenth century, all those unbridled desires, all those revolts of matter in a fury;* but it sums them all up in its formulæ, it gives them, by its scientific way of representing them, a pernicious authority, it multiplies them by an execrable propaganda." †

It was through Feuerbach principally that the evolution was to be brought about which has led the Hegelian system, severely idealistic in its commencement, to favor at length *the revolts of matter run mad.* And this evolution is only natural after all. If the universe is the development of an idea, and not the work of an intelligent Will, all is necessary in the world, for the development of an idea is a matter of destiny. Where all is necessary, all is legitimate: the desires of the flesh as well as the laws of thought and of conscience. But, from the moment that the flesh

* *Toutes ces révoltes de la matière en furie.*

† *Revue des Deux Mondes,* April, 1850.

is emancipated, it aims at absolute empire, and ends by obtaining it: this is matter of fact. Feuerbach has put atheism into a definite shape, and disengaged it from all obscurity. There exists no other infinite than the infinite in our thoughts; above us there exists nothing; no law which binds us, no power which governs us: the work of modern science is to set man free from God, for God is an idol. But man thus set free from all bonds and from all duty is not, for Feuerbach, the individual, but humanity. The individual owes himself to his species; "the true sage will make no more silly and fantastic sacrifices, but he will never refuse sacrifices which are really serviceable to humanity." *

Here then is still a bond, a religion, and sacrifices; the emancipation is incomplete. What is this humanity to which man owes himself? An abstraction, an idol still, an idol to be overthrown if he would obtain perfect independence. Listen to the German Stirmer, deducing from the doctrine its extreme consequences: "Perish the people," he exclaims, "perish Germany, perish all the nations of Europe; and let man, rid of all

* *Qu' est-ce la religion?* page 586 of the translation of Ewerbeck.

bonds, delivered from the last phantoms of religion, recover at length his full independence!" * All the mists of abstraction have now disappeared: here we are on ground which is hideously clear. Humanity is no longer in question, but the worship of *self;* it is the complete enfranchisement of selfishness.

While the proud idealism of the Germans was thus, by its own weight, descending into the level flats of thought, a political movement was agitating Germany. Simple-minded poets were celebrating atheism with an enthusiasm which seemed sincere; and, at the same time, men who are not simple-minded, journalists and demagogues, were laying hold of the irreligion as a lever with which to make a breach in the social edifice. In the year 1845, the attention of the Swiss authorities was drawn to certain secret societies, composed of Germans, and having for their object a revolution in Germany, but which had established their basis of operations on the Swiss territory. The inquiries of the police issued in the discovery of twenty-seven clubs bound together by secret correspondence. Working-men were induced on various pretexts to attend meetings, of which the

* *Revue des Deux Mondes* of 15th April, 1850, p. 288.

real object was only gradually disclosed to them. If they were reckoned worthy, they were initiated into the plan of a social reform, the basis of which was atheism.* One of the principal agents in this work of proselytism, Guillaume Marr, exclaimed: "Faith in a personal and living God is the origin and the fundamental cause of our miserable social condition." And he deduced as follows the practical consequence of his theory: "The idea of God is the key-stone of the arch of a tottering civilization; let us destroy it. The true road to liberty, to equality, and to happiness, is atheism. No safety on earth, so long as man holds on by a thread to heaven.—Let nothing henceforward shackle the spontaneity of the human mind. Let us teach man that there is no other God than himself, that he is the Alpha and the Omega of all things, the superior being, and the most real reality." We have still to explain the nature of this spontaneity, free from every shackle. One of the editors of the journal conducted by Marr discloses it by quoting some verses in which

* General Report addressed to the *Conseil d'Etat* of Neuchâtel on the secret German propaganda, and on the clubs of Young Germany in Switzerland, by Lardy, Doctor of law. Neuchâtel, 1845.

Henri Heine expresses the wish to see *great vices, bloody and colossal crimes*, provided he may be delivered from a *worthy-citizen virtue*, and an *honest-merchant morality!** A little later, a journal of German Switzerland asserted, that in order to set free man's natural instincts and propensities, it is indispensable to destroy the idea of God.†

These, I am well aware, are the screams of a savage madness. But after all, and be this as it may, Marr was publishing his journal at Lausanne in 1845, and in 1848 he was named representative of the people, by a considerable majority, in one of the largest cities of Germany. And this was by no means an isolated fact. Atheism showed itself in the ephemeral parliament of Frankfort as a sort of party, of which M. Vogt, says the *Revue des Deux Mondes*, was the great orator.‡

The German revolution was put down by the bayonet, but the doctrines of which it had revealed the existence, left vestiges for a long time in the

* *Pourvu qu' on le délivre d' une vertu bourgeoise et d' une morale d' honnêtes négociants.* Blätter der Gegenwart für sociales Leben.

† See the *Chroniqueur Suisse* of 19 Jan. 1865.

‡ April, 1850, p. 292.

country of the terror which they had inspired. Alarm was felt for the various interests threatened, and noble souls were stirred with compassion by the conviction forced upon them of the spiritual miseries of their brethren. A powerful reaction took place, as well in the religious as the philosophical world. This reaction has produced salutary results; but the object is not fully attained. Open the journals and the reviews, and you will learn that Germany is, in these days, the principal centre of materialism. It is unhappily so rich in this respect, that it can afford to engage in exportation, and to furnish professors of the school to other countries of Europe.

Doctor Büchner has published, under the title of *Force and Matter*, a small volume which has rapidly reached a seventh edition, and has lately been translated into French.* Materialism is there set forth with perfect arrogance, or, to speak more moderately, with perfect audacity. The author pretends to confine himself strictly within the domain of experience, and it is wonderful with what haughtiness he proscribes the re-

* *Force et Matière*, by Louis Büchner, Doctor in medicine: translated into French from the seventh edition of the German work, by Gamper, Leipzig, 1863.

searches of philosophy. It would seem therefore that the question of the nature of things ought to remain outside the circle of his studies. Nevertheless, he declares matter to be eternal and the universe infinite. I ask you how long it would be necessary to have lived in order to pronounce matter eternal in the name of experience; and what journeys it would have been necessary to make, before ascertaining by means of observation that the universe is infinite. We shall have occasion to recur to this subject. Meanwhile we may be very sure that experience supplies no system of metaphysics, and that materialism is a metaphysical system as strongly marked as any. When its adepts cry out, Away with philosophy! they mean by that simply: We will have no good philosophy, that we may be free to make bad philosophy of our own without rivalry. A proceeding which reminds one of certain demagogues who cry with all their might, Down with tyrants! and who thus succeed in making out of the fear of the tyranny of others the solid foundation of their own despotism.

We find then in Germany, first of all the doctrine of the idea set forth with *éclat* by Hegel, then atheism mixed up with political notions and projects, and lastly materialism. The elements are the same as in France, but exhibit themselves in a different order. This diversity suggests some observations worth your attention.

France, setting out with the materialism of the eighteenth century, rose to that adoration of man which characterizes at the present day the greater part of its atheistical manifestations. German atheism, having as its starting-point an abstract idealism of which the adoration of man was the result, has descended to the levels of materialism.* We may inquire into the theory of these facts, and say why materialism rises to the adoration of man by a natural movement; and why, also by a natural movement, the adoration of man descends again to materialism.

* My object is to point out the atheistical systems which are being produced in various parts of Europe, and not to estimate, in a general way, the tendency of contemporary philosophies. The reader, who would understand the position occupied by materialism in relation to German thought in general, may consult with advantage, *Le Matérialisme contemporain*, by Paul Janet, Paris, 1864; and the review of this work by M. Reichlin-Meldegg (*Zeitschrift für Philosophie*, Sechsundvierzigster Band). A Swiss writer, M. Böhner, has lately published a learned work on the subject entitled: *Le Matérialisme au point de vue des sciences naturelles et des progrès de l'esprit humain*, by Nath. Böhner, member of the *Société helvétique des sciences naturelles*, translated from the German, by O. Bourrit, 1 vol. 8vo. (*Genève, imprimerie Fick*), 1861.

Materialism infers from its principles the denial of any future to man, and not only any future, but any true value, any real existence. We are nothing but an agglomeration of molecules, ready to separate without leaving any trace of ever having been together. Is not this a thing to be said sadly, as the saddest thing in the world? Why then are the apostles of matter nearly always assuming the loftiest tone, and uttering shouts of triumph? It is that they feel themselves free, emancipated from that terror which has made the gods,

> . . . that brood of idle fear
> Fine nothings worshipped, — *why*, doth not appear;
> The gods — whom man made, and who made not man.*

Emancipation! Such is the watchword of materialism. Listen, for example, to the conclusion of Baron d'Holbach's *System of Nature:* "Break the chains," says he, "which are binding men. Send back those gods who are afflicting them to those imaginary regions from whence fear first drew them forth. Inspire with courage the intelligent being; give him energy; let him dare at

* . . . Ces enfants de l' effroi,
Ces beaux riens qu' on adore, et sans savoir pourquoi,
Ces dieux que l'homme a faits et qui n' ont pas fait l'homme.
CYRANO DE BERGERAC.

length to love himself, to esteem himself, to feel his own dignity; let him dare to emancipate himself, let him be happy and free." Strange accents these, at the close of a large philosophical treatise intended to prove that there is nothing in the universe but matter. Whence proceeds the dignity of that fragment of matter which calls itself man? Understand well what passes in the mind of these philosophers. In proportion as man lowers his own origin, in the same proportion, — if he does not wish to make himself a brute, in order to live as do the animals, — he exalts himself in an inevitable sentiment of pride. In vain does he give out that the material frame is everything; he feels that thought is more than the material frame; and he accords to himself the first place in the universe. The materialist ignores the Eternal Mind in order to emancipate himself; and whatever he may say, his real deity is not the atom, but himself. The encyclopedists, sons of an age which yielded at once to noble influences and to guilty seductions, united the worship of progress to a degrading philosophy. Consider with what a feeling of pride they lowered man, and you will understand why eternal nature gave place to sacred humanity. When

France had fallen into the delirium of irreligion, it was not a little dust in an earthen vase which was offered for public adoration, but they led in procession through the streets of Paris a woman who was called the goddess Reason.

So it was that materialism ended in the adoration of man. Let us endeavor to understand how the adoration of man turns again to materialism. The mind endowed with intelligence and will is more elevated in the scale of being than inert bodies. This is for us an evident truth. Could one demonstrate it by reasoning? I do not know; but in contesting it, we should contradict the plainest evidence. Reason is superior to matter. If, with the school which extends from Pythagoras to Saint Augustine, and from Saint Augustine to Descartes, we connect reason with God as its principle, the grand science of metaphysics is founded. But if reason does not rise to God, what will happen? This reason, which proclaims itself superior to matter, is not, as we have said already, the individual thought of Francis, Peter, or John. If an individual presented himself as being reason itself, the absolute reason, and said, "I am the truth," it would be necessary to take one of three courses. If we thought that he spoke truly, and if we received his testimony, it would be necessary to worship him, for he would be God. If it were feared that he spoke truly, and those who so feared were unwilling to acknowledge his rule, it would be necessary for them to kill him in order to endeavor to kill the truth. If it were thought that he spoke falsely, it would be necessary to watch him, and the moment he committed an act dangerous for society, to shut him up, for he would be a madman. But the philosophers make no such pretension. The reason of which they speak is the reason common to all, a reason which is not that of an individual, but that of which all rational individuals partake. This common, universal, eternal reason, — where and how does it exist? Reason manifests itself by ideas, and ideas are the acts of minds. To imagine an idea without a mind of which it is the act, is the same thing as to imagine a movement without a body of which it is also the act, in a different sense. Take away bodies, and there is no more movement. Take away intelligences, and there are no more ideas. The philosopher who speaks of an idea which is not the idea of an intelligence, utters words which have no meaning. The reason which is not that of any created individual remains therefore absolutely inconceivable without the eternal Spirit, or God. Idealism is based upon this impossible conception. Thus it is that thought, trying in vain to maintain itself in this abstract domain, ends by holding as chimerical the world of ideas in which it has met with nothing to which to cling. It is seized with giddiness and falls. Whither does it fall? To the ground. It is always thither one falls. Wearied with its efforts to find footing on shifting clouds, the human mind comes back to the *positive* by a violent reaction. Here is the secret of that haughty and derisive materialism of certain modern Germans, who jeer and scoff at the lofty pretensions of philosophy. So it was that Hegel brought upon the scene Doctor Büchner and his fellows.

The great conflict of the spiritual world is not, as it is often said to be, the combat of idealism against materialism. Idealism begins well, and we must not refuse to acknowledge the services which it has rendered to the cause of truth. But philosophy must follow the road traced out in an ancient adage: *Ab exterioribus ad interiora, ab interioribus ad superiora.** If the mind does not

* From outer to inner things, and from inner to higher.

go to the end of this royal road; if idealism, having surmounted the fascinations of the senses, remains in ideas, without ascending to the supreme Mind, the worship of matter and the worship of the idea call mutually one to another, and revolve in a fatal circle. The struggle between these two forms of atheism reminds one of those duels, in which, after having satisfied honor, the adversaries breakfast together, and gather strength to combat, in case of need, a common enemy. The great combat which forms the main subject of the history of ideas is the combat between belief in God and an atheistical philosophy. Whether atheism admits for its first principle an atom without a Creator, or a reason without an Eternal Mind, is a fact very important for the history of philosophy, but the importance of which is small enough in regard to the interests of humanity.

We passed the Rhine in order to penetrate into Germany, let us now cross the British Channel, and observe what is going on in England.

England, at the close of the seventeenth and the beginning of the eighteenth century, was the principal centre of irreligion. France gave the patent of European circulation to ideas which proceeded in part from this foreign source. An active propaganda for the diffusion of impious and immoral writings had been established in Great Britain. A strong reaction set in, and, dating from the year 1698, we see formed various societies having for their object the diffusion of good books and respectable journals.* These efforts were crowned with success. England, by its zeal in the work of Missions, by its sacrifices for the diffusion of the Holy Scriptures, and by its respect for the Lord's-day,† assumed ‡ the characteristic marks of a Christian nation. Grand measures adopted in the interests of liberty and humanity, placed it at the same time at the head of a seriously philanthropic civilization; but as Père Gratry has remarked, "more than in any other people, there are in the English people the old man and the new." § The strange contrasts which are presented by the political action of this

* See the Report of Mr. H. Roberts, in the *Comptes rendus du Congrès international de bienfaisance de Londres*, vol. ii. page 95, and the 23rd *Bulletin de la Société genevoise d' utilité publique*, 1863.

† Par son respect pour le jour du Dimanche.

‡ revêtit.

§ *La Paix méditations historiques et religieuses*, par A. Gratry, prêtre de l' Oratoire. — Septième méditation : l' Angleterre.

double-people are found also in the productions of its thought, in which, while the spirit of piety is displayed full of life, the spirit of irreligion is also manifested with terrible energy. A book is instanced, of materialistic tendency,* published in 1828, of which a popular edition was printed with a view to extend the opinions which it advocated. There was sold of this edition, in a short time, more than eighty thousand copies. A thoughtful writer, Mr. Pearson, mentions a statistical statement, according to which English publications, openly atheistical, reached, in the year 1851, a total of six hundred and forty thousand copies.†

If we pass from the current literature to scientific publications, we shall meet with facts of the same order. The Hegelianism and the scepticism of the critical school are creeping into the works of some theologians. The theories of positivism, reduced to shape in France, have passed the channel, and have obtained in England more attention perhaps than in the country of their

* *The Constitution of Man*, by G. Combe. The popular edition was printed at the expense of Mr. Henderson.

† *Infidelity: its aspects, causes, and agencies*, by Thomas Pearson. People's edition, 1854, page 263.

origin. They have been adopted by a distinguished author, Mr. Stuart Mill; and a female writer, Miss Martineau, has set them forth, in her mother-tongue, for the use of her fellow-countrymen.* Positivism is even in vogue, and has become "*fashionable*" amongst certain literary and intellectual circles in Great Britain.†

In less elevated regions of the intellectual world of England, an organized sect commends itself to our attention. This sect has given to its system of doctrine the name of *Secularism*. It has a social object — the destruction of the Established Church and the existing political order. It has a philosophy, the purport and bearing of which we will inquire of Mr. Holyoake. The following is the answer of the chief of the secularists: — "All that concerns the origin and end of things, God and the immortal soul, is absolutely impenetrable for the human mind. The existence of God, in

* *Auguste Comte et la Philosophie positive*, par E. Littré, page 276.

† "Positivism, within the last quarter of a century, has become an active, and even fashionable mode of thought, and nowhere more so than amongst certain literary and intellectual circles in England." *The Christ of the Gospels and the Christ of modern Criticism, Lectures on M. Renan's 'Vie de Jésus,'* — by John Tulloch, D.D., Principal of the College of St. Mary in the University of St. Andrew. Macmillan and Co., 1864.

particular, must be referred to the number of abstract questions, with the ticket *not determined.* It is probable, however, that the nature which we know, must be the God whom we inquire after. What is called atheism is found *in suspension* in our theory." * The practical consequence of these views is, that all day-dreams relating to another world must be put aside, and we must manage so as to live to the best advantage possible in the present life.† Hence the name of the system. *Secularism* teaches its disciples to have nothing to do with religion in any shape, that they may confine themselves strictly to the present life. It is an attempt of which the express object is to realize life without God.

These doctrines formed the subject of public discussions, in London in 1853, and at Glasgow in 1854. The meeting at Glasgow numbered, it is said, more than three thousand persons.‡ The sect employs as its means of action open-air speeches, the publication of books and journals,§

* See Pearson: *Infidelity*, particularly page 316, and *Christianity and Secularism, the public discussion*—, particularly page 8. † —*dans le siècle.*

‡ Vapereau's *Dictionnaire des contemporains*—Art. HOLYOAKE.

§ I have had in view here the first numbers of *The Secular* and assemblies for giving information and holding debates in lecture-rooms. There are five of these lecture-rooms in London. I have seen the programme, for 1864, of the meetings held at No. 12, Cleveland Street, under the direction of Messrs. Holyoake and J. Clark. There are, every Sunday, — a discourse at eleven o'clock, a discussion at three o'clock, a lecture at seven o'clock. The programme invites all free-thinkers to attend these meetings. Some of the assemblies are public; for others a small entrance fee is demanded. London is the principal centre of the association; but it has branches all over the country, and it numbers in Great Britain twenty-one lecture-rooms, particularly at Liverpool, Manchester, Birmingham, Glasgow, and Edinburgh.* Secularism naturally seeks to magnify, as much as may be, its own importance; and it is not to the declarations of its apostles that we must refer in order to estimate the extent and influence of its action. At the same time the existence of a society, the avowed object of which is the diffusion of practical atheism, cannot be regarded with indif-

World, and of *The National Reformer*, *Secular Advocate*, for 1864.

* *The National Reformer* of 2nd Jan. 1864.

ference. At the present moment the affairs of the sect would not appear to be flourishing. A year ago a secularist orator had delivered a vehement speech in favor of virtue. Just as he had resumed his seat, a policeman entered the room and took him into custody. A few days afterwards the *Times* informed its readers that the orator of virtue had just been condemned for theft to twelve months' hard labor.* In the *Secular World* of the 1st January, 1864, Mr. Holyoake complains that a great many *mauvais sujets* seem to seek in secularism a kind of cheap religion. He declares that he is going to use energetic efforts to purify the sect, and seems to intimate that he shall retire if his efforts fail. Let us leave him to wrestle against the invasion of the orators of virtue, and let us pass from England into Italy.

While Italy is seeking to deliver itself from the bayonets of Austria, it is threatened with subjection to the influence of the most pernicious German doctrines. After having bent, like nearly all Europe, in the eighteenth century, beneath the blast of sensualism, Italy made a noble effort to renew more generous traditions. Two eminent men, Rosmini and Gioberti, the second espe-

* MS. information.

cially, succeeded in exciting in the youth of Italy a passionate interest in doctrines in which liberty and vigor of thought were united with the confidence of faith. This intellectual movement preceded and prepared a national movement, the course of which has been precipitated by the intrigues of politics and the intervention of the arms of the foreigner. At the present time the influence of Rosmini and of Gioberti is on the decline. Hegelianism is being installed with a certain *éclat* in the university of Naples. Nothing warrants us in hoping that this system will not produce upon the shores of the Mediterranean the same depravation of philosophic thought which it has produced in Germany. In the ancient university of Pisa, M. Auguste Conti, a brave defender of Christian philosophy, steadfastly maintains the union of religion and of speculative inquiry,* and the centre of Italy is less affected perhaps than the extremities of the Peninsula by the spirit of infidelity. But as we go further north, we encounter in the writings of Ferrari the utterance

* Readers unacquainted with the Italian language will find a compendious exposition of M. Conti's philosophy, in a small volume published, in 1863, under the title of *Le Camposanto de Pise ou le Scepticisme.* (Paris, librairies Joël Cherbuliez et Auguste Durand; 1 vol. in - 18.)

of a gloomy scepticism, and in those of Ausonio Franchi, formerly a journalist at Turin, and now a Professor at Milan, the manifestations of an almost undisguised atheism. Ausonio Franchi, or rather the man who assumes that pseudonyme, is an ex-priest, who, "while maintaining severely the rule of good morals and the dignity of life," * has turned with violent animosity against his former faith. He exerts some influence over the youth of Italy, and has met with warm admirers in England and Germany. Franchi's profession of faith reduces itself to these very simple terms:—"The world is what it is, and it is *because it is;* any other reason whatever of its essence and of its existence can be nothing but a sophism or an illusion." † All inquiry into the origin of things is a pure chimera, and we must therefore limit ourselves to the experience of the present life, and look for nothing beyond it. The author treats with sufficient disdain arguments which satisfied Descartes, Newton, and Leibnitz. It has seemed to me that his understanding, a little

* Such is the testimony rendered to him by M. Aug. Conti in his work, *La Philosophie italienne.* (Paris, Joël Cherbuliez et Auguste Durand; one small vol. 18mo.)

† *Le Rationalisme* (in French), published with an introduction, by M. D. Bancel, Brussels, 1858, page 27.

obscured by passion, misconceives the true purport of the reasonings which it rejects, and by thus impairing their force, assumes to itself the right to despise them.

The religious negations of Ausonio Franchi do not stop at Christian dogma. He denies all value to those higher aspirations of the human soul which constitute *reason*, in the philosophical meaning of the term. Now, this radical negation of the reason is what those Italians who do not scruple to practise it denominate *Rationalism*. And this very unwarrantable use of a word is in fact only a particular case of a general phenomenon. To criticise, means to examine the thoughts which present themselves to the mind in order to distinguish error from truth. The Frenchmen, who call themselves the *critics*, are men who require that the intellect shall make itself the impartial mirror of ideas, but shall renounce the while all discrimination between truth and error. The term scepticism, in its primary signification, contains the idea of inquiring, of examining; and they give the name of *sceptics* to the philosophers who declare that there is nothing to discover, and consequently nothing to examine, or to search for! One is a *free-thinker* only on the express condition of renouncing all such free exercise of thought as might lead to the acceptance of beliefs generally received. This is verily the carnival of language, and the *bal masqué* of words. These corruptions of the meaning of terms are highly instructive. Doctrines contrary to the laws of human nature bear witness in this way to a secret shame in producing themselves under their true colors. Just as hypocrisy is an homage which vice pays to virtue, so these barbarisms are an homage which error pays to truth.

To return to Italy: that beautiful and noble country has not escaped the revival of atheism. The intoxication of a new liberty, and the political struggles in which the Papacy is at present engaged, will favor for a time, it may be feared, the development of evil doctrines.* But the lively genius of the Italians will not be long in attaching

* The learned author appears to intimate that the distractions of the Papacy, consequent on its political struggles for temporal power, hinder the salutary influence which it might otherwise exercise in the suppression of evil doctrines. The Translator feels it due to himself to state here, once for all, that he has no sympathy whatever with such a view of the influence of the Papacy. On the contrary, he is disposed to attribute to the Church of Rome most of the evils which afflict, not Italy only, but all the countries over which she has any power. Perhaps, having "felt the weight of too much liberty" in

itself again to the grand traditions of its past history; and the inhabitants of the land, whose soil was trodden by Pythagoras and Saint Augustine, will not link themselves with doctrines which always run those who hold them aground sooner or later upon the sad and gloomy shores of a vulgar empiricism.

We have not leisure, Gentlemen, to extend our study to all parts of the globe, and besides, there are countries with regard to which information would fail me. Therefore I say nothing of Holland, where we should have, as I know, distressing facts to record. The silence imposed on Spain upon the subjects which we are discussing would render the study of that country a difficult one. I am wanting in data regarding America. Let us conclude our survey by a few words about Russia.

his own Church, the excellent author, fundamentally sound in his own views of Christian doctrine, as is proved abundantly by his writings, has been led by a natural reaction to give too much weight to the opposite principle of authority. The concluding pages of his former work, *La Vie Eternelle*, indicate a mind too painfully and sensitively averse to all controversy with a corrupt Church, in consideration of the acknowledged excellences of many of her individual members, — her Pascals, Fénélons, Martin Boos, Girards, Gratrys, and Lacordaires. — *Translator.*

If we are warranted in making general assertions in speaking of that immense empire, we may say that the Russian people, taken as a whole, is good and pious, badly instructed, and often the victim of ignorance or of superstition, but disposed to open its heart to elevated and pure influences. The clergy is ignorant, though with honorable and even brilliant exceptions. It is too much cut off from general society, and consigned to a sort of caste, of which it would be most desirable to break down the barriers, in order to allow the influence of the representatives of religion to extend itself more freely. The young nobles, and the university students in general, are, in too large a proportion, imbued with irreligious principles. Various atheistical writings, those of Feuerbach amongst others, have been translated into Russian, printed abroad, and furtively introduced into the empire. M. Herzen, a well-known writer, has published, under the pseudonyme of Iscander, a work full of talent, but in which come plainly into view the worst tendencies of our time.* In his eyes, life is itself its own end and cause. Faith in God is the portion of the ignorant crowd, and atheism, like all the high truths of science,

* *De l' autre rive* (in Russian).

like the differential calculus and the laws of physics, is the exclusive possession of the philosophical few. When Robespierre declared atheism aristocratic, he was right in this sense, for atheism is above the reach of the vulgar; but when he concluded that atheism was false, he made a great mistake. This error, which led him to establish the worship of the Supreme Being, was one of the causes of his fall. When he began to follow in the wake of the *conservatives*, as a necessary consequence he would lose his power.* The writings of Iscander hàve exerted a veritable influence in Russia. M. Herzen appears to have lost much of his repute, by the exaggerated and outrageous course he has taken in politics; but it is to be feared that the traces of his action are not altogether effaced.

The Russian Empire has been for a long time, in the eyes of the West, only an immense garrison; but now for some years past it has been taking rank among the number of intellectual

* *De l' autre rive.* v. Consolatio. — This chapter is a dialogue between a lady and a doctor. I have considered the doctor as expressing the thoughts of the writer. The form of dialogue, however, always allows an author to express his thoughts, while declining, if need be, the responsibility of them.

powers, and nowhere in Europe is the ascending march of civilization displaying itself by signs so striking. The summons to liberty of so many millions of men, which has just been accomplished by the generous initiative of the ruling power, and with the consent of the nation, testifies that that vast social body is animated by the spirit of life and of progress. But in the solemn phase through which she is passing, Russia is exposed to a great danger. She is running the risk of substituting for a national development, drawn from the grand springs of human nature, a factitious civilization, in which would figure together the fashions of Paris, the morals of the *coulisses* of the Opera, and the most irreligious doctrines of the West. May God preserve her!

We have passed in review some of the symptoms of the revival of atheism, and it is impossible not to acknowledge the gravity of the facts which we have established. What must especially awaken solicitude is, that the irreligious manifestations of thought have assumed such a character of generality, that the sorrowful astonishment which they ought to produce in us is blunted by habit. Fashionable reviews, (I allude especially to the French-speaking public), widely-circulated journals which take good care not to violate propriety, and which could not with impunity offend the interests or prejudices of the social class from which their subscribers are recruited, are able to entertain without danger, and without exciting energetic protestations, the productions of an open, or scarcely disguised, atheism. Here are ample reasons for thoughtfulness; but this thoughtfulness must not be mingled with fear. We have to do with a challenge the very audacity of which inspires me with confidence, rather than with dread. In fact all the productions of irreligious philosophy rest on one and the same thought, the common watchword, of the secularism of the English, of the rationalism of the Italians, of the positivism of the French, and which may even be recognized, with a little attention, under the haughty formulas which bear the name of Hegel. And the thought is this: The earth is enough for us, away with heaven; man suffices for himself, away with God; reality suffices for us, away with chimeras! Wisdom consists in contenting ourselves with the world as it is. It is attempted ridiculously enough to place this wisdom under the patronage of the luminaries of our age. We are bidden, forsooth, to see in the negation of the real and living God, a conflict of progress with routine, of science with a blind tradition, of the modern mind with superannuated ideas.* We know of old this defiance hurled against the aspirations of the heart, the conscience, and the reason. We know the destined issue of this ancient revolt of the intellect against the laws of its own nature. There were atheists in Palestine in the days when the Psalmist exclaimed, "The fool hath said in his heart, There is no God." † There were atheists at Rome when Cicero wrote, ‡ that the opinion which recognizes gods appeared to him to come nearest to the resemblance of truth. A poet of the thirteenth century has expressed in a Latin verse the thoughts which are in vogue among a great many of our contemporaries: "He dares nothing great, who believes that there are gods." § There were atheists in the seventeenth century, when Descartes exerted himself to confound them, and they reckoned themselves the fine spirits of their time. || And who, again, does

* *Le Rationalisme*, par Ausonio Franchi, page 19. — *Force et matière*, par le docteur Büchner, page 262. — *Paroles de philosophie positive*, par Littré, page 36. — *La Métaphysique et la Science*, par Vacherot, page xiv. (Première edition.)

† Ps. xiv. 1.

‡ De Naturâ Deorum.

§ Nil audet magnum qui putat esse Deos.

|| See Bossuet: *Sermon sur la dignité de la religion.*

not know that in the eighteenth century atheism marched with head aloft, and filled the world with its clamors. The attempt to do without God has nothing modern about it, it is met with at all epochs. The means employed now-a-days to attain this end have nothing new about them. Atheism exhibits itself in history with the characters of a chronic malady, the outbreaks of which are transient crises. The moment the negation is blazoned openly, humanity protests. Why? Because man will never be persuaded to content himself with the earth, and with what the earth can give him: his nature absolutely forbids it. When we compare the reality with the desires of our souls, we can all say with the aged patriarch Jacob: "Few and evil have been the days of my pilgrimage;" * we can all say with Lamartine:

> Though all the good desired of man
> In one sole heart should overflow,
> Death, bounding still his mortal span,
> Would turn the cup of joy to woe.†

---

* Gen. xlvii. 9.

† Quand tous les biens que l'homme envie
Déborderaient dans un seul cœur,
La mort seule au bout de la vie
Fait un supplice du bonheur.

And it is not the heart only which is concerned here; without God man remains inexplicable to his own reason. The spiritual creature of the Almighty, free by the act of creation, and capable of falling into slavery by rebellion, — he understands his nature and his destiny; but it is in vain that the apostles of matter and the worshippers of humanity harangue him in turn to explain to him his own existence. Man is too great to be the child of the dust; man is too miserable to be the divine summit of the universe. "If he exalts himself, I abase him; if he abases himself, I exalt him; and I contradict him continually, until he understands at last that he is an incomprehensible monster."*

"The proper study of mankind is man;" and man remains an enigma for man, if he do not rise to God. So it is that our very nature is a living protest against atheism, and never allows its triumphs to be either general, or of long duration. A solid limit is thus set to our wanderings; and, to the errors of the understanding, as to the tides of the ocean, the Master of things has said, "Ye shall go no further." Therefore atheists may become famous, but, destitute of the ray which

* Pascal.

renders truly illustrious, humanity refuses them the aureole with which it encircles the brows of its benefactors. This aureole it reserves for the sages which lead it to God, for the artists which reveal to it some of the rays of the immortal light, for all those who remind it of the titles of its dignity, the pledges of its future, the sacred laws of the realm of spirits. Humanity desires to live; and to live it must believe; for it must believe in order to love and to act. Atheism is a crisis in a disease, a passing swoon over which the vital forces of nature triumph. Now the vital forces of humanity are neither extinct nor stupefied in our time. The world of literature is sick, and grievously sick in some of its departments; but even there again are manifesting themselves noble and powerful reactions. Then look in other directions. Contemplate the religious movement of society at large, the wide efforts making in the domain of active beneficence, the progressive conquests of civilization, the awakening of conscience on many subjects: — I could easily instance numerous facts in proof of what I advance, and say to you:

Know, by these speaking signs, a God to-day
As yesterday the same — the same for aye:
Veiling, revealing, at His sovereign will,
His glory, — and His people guarding still.*

Wrestle then against the invasion of deadly doctrines, wrestle and do not fear. If men rise against God in the name of the modern mind, of the science of the age, of the progress of civilization, do not suffer yourselves to be stunned by these clamors. Let the past be to you the pledge of the future! To make of atheism a novelty, is an error. To make of it, in a general way, the characteristic of our epoch, is a calumny.

* Reconnaissez, *Messieurs*, à ces traits éclatants,
Un Dieu tel aujourd'hui qu'il fut dans tous les temps.
Il sait, quand il lui plaît, faire éclater sa gloire,
Et son peuple est toujours présent à sa mémoire.

LECTURE IV.

NATURE.

(At Geneva, 27th Nov. 1863.—At Lausanne, 25th Jan. 1864.)

GENTLEMEN,

The thoughts of man are numberless; and still, in their indefinite variety, they never relate but to one or another of these three objects: nature, or the world of material substances, which are revealed to our senses; created spirits, similar or superior to that spirit which is ourselves; and finally God, the Infinite Being, the universal Creator. Therefore there are two sorts of atheism, and there are only two. The mind stops at nature, and endeavors to find in material substances the universal principle of existence; or, rising above nature, the mind stops at humanity, without ascending to the Infinite Mind, to the Creator. We have seen how clearly these two doctrines appear in contemporary literature. We have now to enter upon the examination of them, and this will afford us matter for two lectures.

The word nature has various meanings; we employ it here to designate matter, and the forces which set it in motion, those forces being conceived as blind and fatal, in opposition to the conscious and free force which constitutes mind. Matter and the laws of motion are the object of mechanics, of chemistry, and of physics. Do these sciences suffice for resolving the universal enigma? Such is precisely the question which offers itself to our examination.

Let us first of all determine what, in presence of the spectacle of the universe, is the natural movement of human thought, when human thought possesses the idea of God. I open a book trivial enough in its form, but occasionally profound in its contents: the *Journey round my room*, of Xavier de Maistre. The author is relating how he had undertaken to make an artificial dove which was to sustain itself in the air by means of an ingenious mechanism. I read:

"I had wrought unceasingly at its construction for more than three months. The day was come for the trial. I placed it on the edge of a table, after having carefully closed the door, in order to keep the discovery secret, and to give my friends a pleasing surprise. A thread held the mechanism motionless. Who can conceive the palpitations of my heart, and the agonies of my self-love, when I brought the scissors near to cut the fatal bond? — Zest! — the spring of the dove starts, and begins to unroll itself with a noise. I lift my eyes to see the bird pass; but, after making a few turns over and over, it falls, and goes off to hide itself under the table. Rosine (my dog), who was sleeping there, moves ruefully away. Rosine, who never sees a chicken, or a pigeon, or the smallest bird, without attacking and pursuing it, did not deign even to look at my dove which was floundering on the floor. This gave the finishing stroke to my self-esteem. I went to take an airing on the ramparts.

"I was walking up and down, sad and out of spirits as one always is after a great hope disappointed, when, raising my eyes, I perceived a flight of cranes passing over my head. I stopped to have a good look at them. They were advancing in triangular order, like the English column at the battle of Fontenoy. I saw them traverse the sky from cloud to cloud. — Ah! how well they fly, said I to myself. With what assurance they seem to glide along the viewless path which they follow. — Shall I confess it? alas! may I be forgiven! the horrible feeling of envy for once, once only, entered my heart, and it was for the cranes. I pursued them, with jealous gaze, to the boundaries of the horizon. For a long while afterwards, motionless in the midst of the crowd which was moving about me, I kept observing the rapid movement of the swallows, and I was astonished to see them suspended in the air, just as if I had never before seen that phenomenon. A feeling of profound admiration, unknown to me till then, lighted up my soul. I seemed to myself to be looking upon nature for the first time. I heard with surprise the buzzing of the flies, the song of the birds, and that mysterious and confused noise of the living creation which involuntarily celebrates its Author. Ineffable concert, to which man alone has the sublime privilege of adding the accents of gratitude! Who is the author of this brilliant mechanism? I exclaimed in the transport which animated me. Who is He that, opening his creative hand, let fly the first swallow into the air? It is He who gave commandment to these trees to come forth from the ground, and to lift their branches toward the sky!"

Here is a charming page, and containing, though apparently trivial in style, a good and sound philosophy. Let us translate this delightful description into the heavier language of science.

The intellect is one of the things with which we are best acquainted; logic is the science of thought, and logic is perhaps, among all the sciences, the one best settled on its bases. The intellect discovers itself to us in the exercise of our activity. We pursue an object, we combine the means for attaining it, and it is the intellect which operates this combination. What happens if we compare the results of our activity with the results of the power manifested in the world? When we consider in their vast *ensemble* the means of which nature disposes, when we remark the infinite number of the relations of things, the marvellous harmony of which universal life is the produce, we are dazzled by the splendor of a wisdom which surpasses our own as much as boundless space surpasses the imperceptible spot which we occupy upon the earth. Think of this: the science of nature is so vast that the least of its departments suffices to absorb one human life-time. All our sciences are only in their very beginning; they are spelling out the first lines of an immense book. The elements of the universe are numberless; and yet, notwithstanding, all hangs together; all things are linked one to another in the closest connection. The *savants* therefore find themselves in a strange embarrassment. They are obliged to circumscribe more and more the field of their researches, on pain of losing themselves in an endless study; and, on the other hand, in proportion as science advances, the mutual relation of all its branches becomes so manifest that it is ever more and more clearly seen that, in order to know any one thing thoroughly, it would be necessary to know all. It needs not that we seek very high or very far away for occasions of astonishment: the least of the objects which nature presents to our view contains abysses of wisdom.

The acquired results of science appear simple through the effect of habit. The sun rises every day; who is still surprised at its rising? The solar system has been known a long while; it is taught in the humblest schools, and no longer surprises any one. But those who found out, after long efforts, what we learn without trouble, the discoverers, reckoned their discoveries very surprising. Kepler, one of the founders of modern astronomy, in the book to which he consigned his immortal discoveries, exclaims: * "The wisdom of the Lord is infinite, as are also His glory and His power. Ye heavens! sing His praises. Sun, moon, and planets, glorify Him in your ineffable language! Praise Him, celestial harmonies, and all ye who can comprehend them! And thou, my soul, praise thy Creator! It is by Him, and in Him, that all exists. What we know not is contained in Him as well as our vain science. To Him be praise, honor, and glory for ever and ever!" These words, Gentlemen, have not been copied from a book of the Church; they are read in a work which, as all allow, is one of the foundations of modern science.

I pass on to another example, and I continue to keep you in good and high company. Newton set forth his discoveries in a large volume all bristling with figures and calculations.† The work of the mathematician ended, the author

* *Harmonices mundi, libri quinque.*

† *Philosophiæ naturalis principia mathematica.*

rises, by the consideration of the mutual interchange of the light of all the stars, to the idea of the unity of the creation; then he adds, and it is the conclusion of his entire work: "The Master of the heavens governs all things, not as being the soul of the world, but as being the Sovereign of the universe. It is on account of His sovereignty that we call Him the Sovereign God. He governs all things, those which are, and those which may be. He is the one God, and the same God, everywhere and always. We admire Him because of His perfections, we reverence and adore Him because of His sovereignty. A God without sovereignty, without providence, and without object in His works, would be only destiny or nature. Now, from a blind metaphysical necessity, everywhere and always the same, could arise no variety; all that diversity of created things according to places and times (which constitutes the order and life of the universe) could only have been produced by the thought and will of a Being who is *the Being*, existing by Himself, and necessarily."

Here, Sirs, are noble thoughts, expressed in noble style. I recommend you to read throughout the pages from which I have quoted a few fragments. Let us now analyze the ideas of this great astronomer as thus expounded. We may note these three affirmations:

1. The universe displays an admirable order which reveals the wisdom of the Power which governs it.

2. The universe lives; it is not fixed, and its variations suppose an intelligent Power which directs it.

3. The variable existence of the universe shows that it is not necessary; it must have its cause in a Being who is *the* Being, necessarily, by His proper nature.

Such are the views of Newton. Examine this course of thought, and see if it is not natural. Observation reveals to us facts. Facts in themselves, isolated facts, are nothing for the mind; but in the facts of nature, human reason discovers an order, and in that order it recognizes its own proper laws. To keep within the domain of astronomy — there is harmony between our mind and the course of the stars. If you have any doubt about this, I appeal to the almanac. We there find it stated that in such a month, on such a day, at such an hour, there will be an eclipse of the sun or of the moon. How comes the editor of the almanac to know that? He has learnt it from the savants who have succeeded in explaining the phenomena of the skies. The savant therefore can in his study meet with the intelligence which directs the universe. If he makes no mistake in his calculations, the eclipse begins at the precise hour which he has indicated. If the eclipse did not take place at the instant foreseen, no one would suspect Nature of not following the course prescribed by the directing intelligence; the inference would be that there had been a fault in observation, or an error of figures on the part of the astronomer.

When science, then, does its part well, the mind of man encounters another mind which is governing the world and maintaining it in order. The special science of nature stops there, as we shall explain further on; but this is not all that man requires, when he makes use of all his faculties. All is passing and changing in the domain of experience; and reason seeks instinctively the cause of changeable facts in an unchangeable Being, the cause of transient phenomena in an eternal Being. Nature, therefore, does not suffice to account to us for itself. It demands a power to direct it, an intelligence to regulate it; an absolute eternal Being as its cause. This is what reason imperatively requires; and when we possess the idea of God, nature reveals to us His power and His wisdom.

This is an old argument, and they call it commonplace. It is commonplace, in fact; it has appeared over and over again in the discourses of Socrates, in the writings of Galen, of Kepler, of Newton, of Linnæus. Yes, this argument has fallen so low as to be public property, if we can say that truth falls when it shines with a splendor vivid enough to enlighten the masses. If I desired to bring together here the testimony of all the savants who have seen God in nature, the song of all the poets who have celebrated the glory of the Eternal as manifested by the creation, the enumeration would be long, and I should soon tire out your patience. You can understand therefore that if there are, as the misanthrope Rousseau says there are, philosophers who hold in such contempt vulgar opinions that they prefer error of their own discovery to truth found out by other people, then the ancient argument, which infers the wisdom of the Creator from the order of the creation, must be the object of but small esteem with them. Still I for my part take this old argument for a good one, and I mean to defend it.

Nature is verily and indeed a marvel placed before the observation of our minds. The growth of a blade of grass, the habits of an ant, contain for an attentive observer prodigies of wisdom. A drop of dew reflecting the beams of morning, the play of light among the leaves of a tree, reveal to the poet and the artist treasures of poetry. But too often, blinded by habit, we are unable to see; and when our mind is asleep, it seems to us that the universe slumbers. A sudden flash of light can sometimes arouse us from this lethargy. If science all at once delivers up to us some one of those grand laws which reveal in thousands of phenomena the traces of one and the same mind, the astonishment of our intellect excites in our soul an emotion of adoration. When the first rays of morning light up with a pure brightness the lofty summits of our Alps; when the sun at his setting stretches a path of fire along the waters of our lake, who does not feel impelled to render glory to the supreme Artist? When dark cold fogs rest upon our valleys at the decline of autumn, it only needs sometimes to climb the mountain-side, in order to issue all at once from the gloomy region, and see the chain of high peaks, resplendent with light, mark themselves out upon a sky of incomparable blue. Often have I given myself the delight of this grand spectacle, and always at such a time my heart has uttered spontaneously from its depths that hymn of adoration :

> Tout l' univers est plein de sa magnificence.
> Qu' on l' adore, ce Dieu, qu' on l' invoque à jamais ! *

Such is, in the presence of nature, the spontaneous movement of the heart and of the reason. But a false wisdom obscures these clear verities by clouds of sophisms. When your heart feels impelled to render glory to God, there is danger lest importunate thoughts rise in your mind and counteract the impulse of your adoration. Perhaps you have heard it said, perhaps you have read, that the accents of spiritual song, those echoes, growing ever weaker, of by-gone ages, are no longer heard by a mind enlightened by modern science. I should wish to deliver you from this painful doubt. I should wish to protect you from the fascinations of a false science. I should wish that in the view of nature, even those

* The whole universe is full of His magnificence.
May this God be adored and invoked for ever !

who have as yet no wish to adore, with St. Paul, Him whose invisible perfections are clearly seen when we contemplate His works, may at least feel themselves free to admire, with Socrates, "the supreme God who maintains the works of creation in the flower of youth and in a vigor ever new." Let us examine a few of the prejudices which it is sought to disseminate, in order to deprive of their force the reasonings of Newton, and to turn us from the opinions of Kepler.

It is said that science leads away from God, and that faith continues to be the lot only of the ignorant. Listen on this head first of all to the Italian Franchi. "The class of society in which infidels and sceptics especially abound is that of savants and men of letters, — men, in short, who have gone through studies, in the course of which they have certainly become acquainted with the famous demonstrations of the existence of God. But no sooner have they examined them with their own eyes, and submitted them to the criterion of their own judgment, than these demonstrations no longer demonstrate anything; these reasonings turn out to be only paralogisms." * Here we have the thesis in its general form: to

* *Le Rationalisme*, page 19.

become an infidel or a sceptic, it is enough to be a well educated man. The German Büchner will now show us the application of this notion to the special study of nature. "At this day, our hardest laborers in the sciences, our most indefatigable students of nature, profess materialistic sentiments." * The same tendencies are often manifested among French writers. The author of a recent astronomical treatise, for example, draws a veil of deceitful words over the profound faith of Kepler, and takes evident pleasure in throwing into relief the tokens of sympathy bestowed unfortunately by the learned Laplace upon atheism.† Here then we have open attempts to found a prejudice against religion on the authority of science; and these attempts disturb the minds of not a few. I ask two questions on this head. Is it true, in fact, that modern naturalists are generally irreligious? Is it possible that the science of nature, rightly considered, should lead to atheism? ‡

* *Force et Matière*, page 262.

† *Les Mondes Causeries astronomiques* by Guillemin; see p. 122 (3rd edition), where Kepler is described as an intelligence "penetrated by a profound faith in nature and exalted by a noble pride." See also pages 327 and 336.

‡ The question discussed in these pages must not be confounded with that of the relations between the science of

Let us begin with the question of fact; and first of all let us settle clearly the bearing and object of this discussion. I wish to destroy a prejudice, and not to create one. I am not proposing to you to take the votes of savants, in order to know whether God exists. No. Though all the universities in Europe should unite to vote it dark at mid-day, I should not cease on that account to believe in the sun, and that, Gentlemen, in common with you all, and with the mass of my fellow-men. I have instituted a sort of inquiry in order to ascertain whether modern naturalists have in general been led to atheistical sentiments, as some would have us believe. In appealing to the recollections of my own earlier studies and subsequent reading, I have marked the names of the men best known in the various sciences, and I have inquired what religious opinions they may

nature and the documents of revelation. Whether nature can be explained without God is one question. Whether geology is in accordance with the language of the book of Genesis is another question, as regards both its nature and its importance. This latter subject does not come within the scope of these lectures. I will merely call attention to the fact, that if nature and the sacred text are fixed elements, this is not the case with the interpretations of theologians, and the results of geology. It is difficult to pronounce upon the exact relation of two quantities more or less indeterminate.

have publicly manifested. I will now give you briefly the result of my labor.

I have left astronomy out of the question, considering that, notwithstanding the great notoriety of Laplace, we have in Kepler and Newton a weight of authority sufficient to counterbalance that which it is desired to connect with his name. Descending to the earth, we encounter first of all the general science of our globe, or geography. In this order of studies a German, Ritter, enjoys an incontestable preeminence. He is called, even in France, the "creator of scientific geography." Scientific geography rests for support on nearly all the sciences: it proceeds from the general results of chemistry, physics, and geology. Had then the vast knowledge of Ritter turned him away from God? I had read somewhere* that he was one of those savants who have best realized the union of science and faith. One of my friends who was personally acquainted with him has described him to me, not only as a man who adored the Creator in the view of the creation, but as an amiable and zealous Christian, who exerted himself to communicate to others his own convictions.

* In the writings of M. de Rougemont, if I am not mistaken.

From the general study of the globe, let us pass to that of the organized beings which people its surface. Does botany teach the human mind to dispense with God? Let us listen to Linnæus. I open the *System of Nature*,* and on the reverse of the title-page I read: "O Lord, how manifold are Thy works! in wisdom hast Thou made them all: the earth is full of Thy riches." † I turn over a few leaves, and I meet with a table which comprises, under the title, *Empire of Nature*, the general classification of beings. The commencement is as follows: "Eternal God, all-wise and almighty! I have seen Him as it were pass before me, and I remained confounded. I have discovered some traces of His footsteps in the works of the creation; and in those works, even in the least, even in those which seem most insignificant, what might! what wisdom! what inexplicable perfection!—If thou call Him *Destiny*, thou art not mistaken, it is He upon whom all depends. If thou call Him *Nature*, thou art not mistaken, it is He from whom all takes its origin. If thou call Him *Providence*, thou speakest truly; it is by His counsel that the universe subsists." Another great naturalist, George

* *Systema naturæ*. † Ps. civ. 24.

Cuvier, takes care to point out that "Linnæus used to seize with marked pleasure the numerous occasions which natural history offered him of making known the wisdom of Providence." * Thus modern botany was founded in a spirit of piety. Has it, at a later period, made any discoveries calculated to efface from the life of vegetables the marks of Divine intelligence? Allow me to introduce here a personal *souvenir*. I received lessons in my youth from an old man, who, having once been the teacher of De Candolle, remained his friend.† By a rather strange academical arrangement, M. Vaucher found himself set to teach us — not botany, for which he possessed both taste and genius, ‡ but a science of which he knew but little, and which he liked still less. So it came to pass that a good part of the hour of lecture was often filled up with familiar conversations. These conversations took us far away from church history, which we were supposed to be learning. The misplaced botanist reverted, by a natural impulse, to his much-loved

* *Biographie universelle.*

† *A. P. de Candolle*, by A. de la Rive, pp. 12 and 13.

‡ M. Vaucher's principal title to scientific distinction is his *Histoire des conferves d' eau douce*, Genève, an XI (1803), 4°.

science; and I have seen him shed tears of tender emotion, in his Professor's chair, as he spoke to us of the God who made the primrose of the spring, and concealed the violet under the hedge by the wayside. Therefore is the recollection of that old man not only living in my memory, but also dear to my heart. Still he was a savant, an enthusiastic naturalist; and, in the broad light of the nineteenth century, he felt and spoke like Linnæus.

Let us pass to the study of animals. I had the wish, some years ago, to procure the best of modern treatises upon physiology. I was directed to the work of Professor Müller, of Berlin. This book has not lost its value,—for, this very morning, a student of our faculty of sciences came to me to borrow it, by the advice of his masters. Müller was a great physiologist, and he made an open profession of the Christian religion. Have we not the right to conclude that he believed in God? In France, I could cite more than one name in support of my thesis; I confine myself to a single fact. The attention of the scientific world has very recently been occupied with the discoveries of M. Pasteur. M. Pasteur has ascertained that the decomposition of organized bodies, after death, is effected by the action of small animals almost imperceptible, the germs of which the larger animals carry in themselves, as living preparatives for their interment. The design of Providence reveals itself to his understanding, and he writes: "The immediate elements of living bodies would be in a manner indestructible, if from the beings which God has created were taken away the smallest, and, in appearance, the most useless. Life would thus become impossible, because the return to the atmosphere and to the mineral kingdom of all that has ceased to live would be all at once suspended." * In other words: I have studied facts hitherto incompletely observed, and my study has revealed to me a new manifestation of that Divine wisdom of which the universe bears the impression.

England possesses a naturalist of the first order, whom his fellow-countrymen take a pleasure in comparing to George Cuvier — Professor Owen. This savant lectured, a few months ago, before a numerous auditory, on the relations of religion and natural science.† He is fully possessed of

* *Comptes rendus de l'Académie des Sciences* of 20 April, 1863, page 738.

† Exeter Hall Lectures — *The Power of God in His Animal*

all the information which the times afford,—is not ignorant of modern discoveries,—is, in fact, one of the princes of contemporary science. Well, Gentlemen, Mr. Owen repeats, with reference to animals, what Newton was led to say by his contemplation of the heavens, and Linnæus by his study of the plants. He is not afraid to admire with Galen the marvellous wisdom which presided over the organization of living bodies. His discourse is entitled, *The Power of God in His Animal Creation*. The more we understand, he says, the more we admire, the more we adore. He pauses in view of the marvellous productions of nature, beside which the most delicate works of human industry appear, beneath the microscope, but coarse, rough hewings; he compares our most highly finished machines to the living machines made by the hand of God, and infers that, not to discern intelligence in the relation of means to ends, necessarily implies in the mind a defect similar to that of eyes which are unable to

Creation, pamphlet in 12mo. This remarkable lecture contains a twofold protest—against the blindness of those savants who fail to recognize the presence of God in nature; and against the pretensions of those theologians who attack the certain results of the study of nature, relying upon texts more or less accurately interpreted.

distinguish colors. Mr. Owen declares that such a state of mind and feeling in a naturalist may provoke blame from some and pity from others, and remains for him, so far as he is concerned, absolutely incomprehensible.

Again, do the most learned chemists find in the study of the elements of matter a revelation of atheism? M. Liebig, I have been told, is one of the first chemists of our epoch. He believed he had discovered an application of chemistry to agriculture, the effect of which would be to furnish a remedy to the exhaustion of the soil. His discovery turned out false, and a more attentive study of his subject led him to ascertain that the object which he was pursuing was actually realized by Divine Providence in a way of which he had had no suspicion. The following is his own account of this, published in 1862: "After having submitted all the facts to a new and very searching examination, I discovered the cause of my error. I had sinned against the wisdom of the Creator, and I had received my just punishment. I was wishing to perfect His work, and, in my blindness, I thought that in the admirable chain of laws which preside over life at the surface of the earth, and maintain it ever in freshness, there was wanting a link which I, feeble and impotent worm, was to supply. Provision had been made for this beforehand, but in a way so wonderful, that the possibility of such a law had not so much as dawned upon the human understanding."* Here is a confession very noble in its humility; and to this chemist, who thus renders glory to God, no one of his colleagues could say: "If you had as much science as we, you would say no more about the wisdom of the Creator."

Let us pass on to natural philosophers. I have taken a special interest in this part of my inquiry, because I had read in the productions of a literary man of Paris, that modern physics have placed those at fault who defend the doctrine of the living and true God. I inquired accordingly of a man, very well able to give me the information, whether there exists in Europe a natural philosopher holding a position of quite exceptional distinction. I received for reply: "You may say boldly that, by the unanimous consent of men of science, Mr. Faraday, in regard both to the greatness and range of his discoveries, is the first natural philosopher living." After having thus made myself

* *Chemistry applied to Agriculture and to Physiology* (in German). Seventh edition. Introd. page 69.

sure, therefore, on this point, I took the liberty of writing to Mr. Faraday the following letter:

"GENEVA, 30th October, 1863.

"SIR,

"I have the intention of commencing shortly, at Geneva, and for an auditory of men, a course of lectures designed to combat the manifestations of contemporary atheism. To this deplorable error I desire to oppose faith in God, as it has been given to the world by the Gospel, faith in the Heavenly Father.

"One of my lectures will be specially devoted to the removal of prejudices against religion which have their origin in natural science. It is said very often, and very boldly, that modern physics and modern chemistry demonstrate the unfounded character of religious beliefs. These theses are maintained at Geneva as elsewhere. I should wish to reply that natural science does not of itself turn men from God, and that without being able to give faith, it confirms the faith of those who believe: this I should wish to establish by citing names invested, in science, with an incontestable and solid renown. Will you, Sir, authorize me to make use of your name?"

Mr. Faraday, in reply, sent me the following letter, dated 6th Nov. 1863.

"SIR,

. . . . . "You have a full right to make use of my name: for although I generally avoid mixing up things sacred and things profane, I have, on one occasion, written and published a passage which accords to you this right, and which I maintain. I send you a copy of it. I hope you will find nothing in any other part of my researches, to contradict or weaken in any way whatever the sense of this passage.

"I beg you to transmit my best remembrances to my friend M. de la Rive. . . . . ."

The passage thus indicated establishes a line of demarcation, very strongly (perhaps too strongly) drawn between researches of the reason and the domain of religious truth, and contains a profession of positive faith in Revelation. The author affirms that he has never recognized any incompatibility between science and faith, and makes the following declaration: "Even in earthly matters I reckon that 'the invisible things of God from the creation of the world are clearly seen, being understood by the things that are made, even his eternal power and Godhead.'"

A literary man of Paris declares to us that natural science leads away from God: one of the first savants of our time informs us that the scientific contemplation of nature renders the wisdom of God manifest. The question is one of fact. To whom shall we give our confidence? For my part, since it is natural philosophy which is in question, I rank myself on the side of the Natural Philosopher.

We will here terminate this review. It is time, however, which fails us, not subject-matter, for continuing it. You may have noticed that the name of no one of the savants of Switzerland figures in this inquiry. Nevertheless our country would have furnished a rich mine for my purpose. It contains (and it is one of its best privileges) a goodly number of savants, whom the observation of the facts of matter have not caused to forget the claims of mind, and who know how to raise their souls to the Author of the marvels which they study. You will understand therefore that it has not been from anxiety for my cause, but from a motive of discretion, that I have forborne to bring into this discussion the names of men in whom we have a near interest, and many of whom perhaps are present in this assembly. I will take advantage of Mr. Faraday's letter to make a single exception, by naming M. de la Rive. More than once, and in public, we have heard him distinctly point out the place occupied by the sciences of mind in relation to the natural sciences, and render glory to the Creator. And I do not think that any one, in Switzerland or elsewhere, can claim to speak with disdain, in the name of the physical sciences, of the religious convictions boldly professed by our learned fellow-countryman.*

Recollect, Gentlemen, that I have not undertaken to prove the existence of God, by making appeal to the authority of men of science. All I have sought to do has been to destroy a prejudice. They tell us, and scream it at us, that the best naturalists become atheists. This is not true, as I think I have shown. There do exist atheists who cultivate the natural sciences, — no doubt of the fact. But even though half the whole number of naturalists were atheists, inasmuch as other naturalists, and those some of the greatest, find in their studies new motives to adoration, we are forced to the conclusion, that the true cause why

* Since these words were spoken, M. de la Rive has been named an associated member of the Institute of France (Academy of Sciences), and thus elevated to the first of scientific dignities. It might be shown, I believe, that the greater number of the eight associates of the Academy of Sciences to be found in the world, make profession of their faith in God the Creator, the Almighty and Holy One. The silence which others may have preserved on the subject would, moreover, be no authority for concluding that they do not share in beliefs and sentiments which they have not had the occasion perhaps of publicly expressing.

these savants repudiate religion has nothing to do with their science. We shall come to be more strongly confirmed in this opinion, if we pass now from the question of fact to considerations of sound reason.

The weakness of the human mind leads it to forget the facts with which it is not occupied. All special culture of the intellect risks consequently the paralyzing a part of our faculties. Hegel, lost in abstractions, persuades himself that he will be able to construct by pure reasoning the history of nature and that of the human race. A geometrician, who no longer saw in the world anything but theorems and demonstrations, asked, after the representation of a dramatic masterpiece, "And what does that prove?" A physiologist absorbed in the study of sensible phenomena says: "Where is that soul they talk of? I have never seen it." These are phenomena of the same order. This infirmity of the mind, which leads certain savants to think that the ordinary subject of their studies is everything, must not be imputed to science. A man accustomed to the exclusive observation of material phenomena, may become a materialist by the effect of his mental habits, and this really happens, in fact, in too many instances; but the study in itself is not responsible for this result. Let us endeavor to prove this, by clearly defining the object of the natural sciences.

When the matter of a phenomenon is given to us, the understanding proposes to itself three questions:

1. How does the fact manifest itself? what is the mode of its existence? The answer gives us the law of the phenomenon. Bodies fall to the ground at a determined rate of speed: the determination of this rate is the law of their fall.

2. What is the real effective power which produces the phenomenon? This is the inquiry after the cause.

3. What is the intention which presided at the production of the phenomenon? This is the search after the object, which philosophers call the final cause.

What we call understanding or explaining a fact, is answering these three questions; it is finding the law, the cause, the end. This analysis was made by Aristotle, and seems to have been well made. The science of nature, as it is conceived by the moderns, does not undertake to satisfy entirely the desires of the human mind.

It confines itself to the first question; it classes phenomena; it then seeks their law; arrived at this, it stops. The cause and design of things remain out of the sphere of its investigations; the question of God therefore continues foreign to it.

A story is told that when Buonaparte expressed his astonishment that the Marquis de la Place could have written a large book on the system of the universe, without making any mention of the Creator, the learned astronomer replied to his sovereign: "Sire, I had no need of that hypothesis." The answer is admissible if we regard only the science of nature. An astronomer has no need of God in order to follow out the series of his calculations, and compare their results with the course of the stars; a chemist has no need of God in order to ascertain the simple elements combined in composite bodies; a natural philosopher has no need of God in order to determine the laws of waves of sound or of electric currents. The science of nature does not demonstrate the existence of God; still less can it deny His existence. To deny God, it would be necessary for science to demonstrate that there is no order, and consequently no cause of the order to discover; for when we point out the harmony of the universe, we manifestly prepare a basis for the argument which, from the intelligence recognized in the phenomena, will infer the intelligence of the Power which governs them. To prove that there is no order would be to prove that there is no science. For any one who well understands the value of terms, the words *atheistical science* contain a contradiction; they signify science which proves that there is no science.

Such, Gentlemen, is the real state of the question. Our savants, when they remain faithful to their method, seek to determine the laws of phenomena, and do not occupy themselves either with the First Cause of nature, or with its general object; they leave the question of God on one side. Whence come then the negations of naturalists? They arise in this way: those savants who succeed in strictly confining themselves within the limits of their science are rare exceptions. Almost always the *man* introduces his thoughts into the work of the savant, and the results of his study appear to him religious or irreligious, according to his views of religion. Newton ends his book with a hymn to the Creator; but it is not the *mathematical principles* of nature which have revealed to him the Sovereign God. He perceives the rays of His glory because he believes in Him. In the same way, the atheist thinks that his researches disprove the existence of God, because God is veiled from his soul. In both cases it is a doctrine foreign to pure natural science which gives a color to its results. Self-deception is very common in this matter, and in both directions. The religious mind does not understand how it is possible to contemplate the universe, and not see inscribed upon it distinctly the name of its Author; and the intrusion of atheism into the sciences of observation is veiled beneath confusions of ideas which it is of importance for us to dissipate.

Modern science, as we have said, stops at laws, without troubling itself with causes. The laws which determine the series of facts as they offer themselves to observation express the mode of the action of the causes. There are here two ideas absolutely distinct: the power which acts, and the manner in which it acts. If the naturalist thinks that his science is everything, he must conclude that we can know nothing beyond the laws, and that an insuperable ignorance hides from our view the power of which they express the action. But he rarely succeeds in keeping this position, and deceives his reason by confounding the laws which he discovers with the causes with which his mind is not able to dispense. He says first of all with Franchi, "the universe is what it is"; this is the general formula of all the truths of experience; then he adds with the same author, "it is because it is." This *because* means nothing, or means that laws are their own causes. If it is asked, What is the cause of the motion of the stars? they will give for answer the astronomical formulæ which express this motion, and will think that they have explained the phenomena by stating in what way they present themselves to observation. This is a curious example of that confusion of ideas which opens the door to atheism.

An English naturalist, Mr. Darwin, has shown that in the successive life of animal generations, the favorable variations which are produced in the organization of a being are transmitted to its descendants and insure the perpetuity of its race, while the unpropitious variations disappear because they entail the destruction of the races in which they are produced. He tells us: "This preservation of favorable variations and the rejection of injurious variations, I call Natural Selection." * What does the author understand by law? He answers: "the series of facts as it is known to us." † Here we have the true definition of law: it is the simple expression of the series of the facts; the cause remains to be sought for. I open the book in another part. The author is speaking of the eye; and his doctrine is that the eye of the eagle was formed by the slow transformations of an extremely simple visual apparatus. There will have been then, in the development of animal existence, first of all a rudimentary eye, then an eye moderately well formed, and then the eye of the eagle, because the favorable modifications of the organ of sight will have been preserved and increased in the course of ages. Such is the series of facts, such is the law; suppose we grant it. What is the cause? The optician makes our spectacles; who made the eye of the eagle, by directing the slow transformations which at length produced it? Let us listen to the author: "There exists an intelligent power, and that intelligent power is nat-

* *On the Origin of Species*, page 81. Fifth edition.

† *On the Origin of Species.* The text is — "the *necessary* series of facts;" but it would be to do the writer wrong to impute to him the idea that observation reveals to us what is *necessary*, in the philosophical import of the word.

ural selection, constantly on the watch for every alteration accidentally produced in the transparent layers, in order carefully to choose such of those alterations as may tend to produce a more distinct image. . . . Natural selection will choose with infallible skill each new improvement effected."* Natural selection is a law; a law is the series of facts; it seems that we must seek for the power which directs this series of facts; but, lo, the series of facts itself is transformed into a power—into an intelligent power—into a power which chooses with infallible skill! The confusion of ideas is complete. The mind is on a wrong scent; it concludes that the law explains everything, and has itself no need of explanation. The idea of the cause disappears, and, as Auguste Comte expresses it, "science conducts God with honor to its frontiers, thanking Him for His provisional services. † This is not perhaps the idea of Mr. Darwin, but it is at any rate the idea of some of his disciples, as we shall see by-and-by.

Thus the idea of the cause is kept out of sight. Let us now see the fate to which are consigned

* *On the Origin of Species.*

† Caro, *L' Idée de Dieu,* page 47.

those other requirements of the reason — the eternal and the infinite. I take up Dr. Büchner's book, and I read: "We are incapable of forming an idea, even approximately, of the *eternal* and the *infinite*, because our mind, shut up within the limits of the senses, in what regards space and time, is quite unable to pass these bounds so as to rise to the height of these ideas." I follow the text, and thirteen lines further on, in the same page, I read, "Therefore matter and space must be eternal." * Observe well the use which this writer makes of the great ideas of the reason. Is it desired to employ them to prove the existence of God? He will have nothing to do with them. Is the object in question to deny God's existence? He makes use of them; and all in the same page. This is coarse work, no doubt, and Dr. Büchner damages his cause; but, under forms, often more subtle and more intelligent, the same sophism turns up in all systems of materialism.† It is affirmed that we have no real idea

* *Force et Matière*, page 181.

† The Büchner proceeding is found again pretty exactly in *Les Mondes* of M. Amédée Guillemin. This writer affirms (page 60 of the third edition) that science does not approach metaphysical questions; and asserts in the same page, ten lines further on, that astronomical experience leads our reason to the idea of *the eternity of the universe*. After that, he may laugh, if he will, at *lovers of the absolute*.

of the infinite, and it is sought at the same time to beguile the need which reason feels of this idea by applying it to matter.

Pray do not suppose that I am here attacking the natural sciences, in the interest of metaphysics. I am not attacking but defending them. I am endeavoring, as far as in me lies, to avenge them from the outrages which are offered to them by materialism, while it seeks to cover with their noble mantle its own shameful nakedness. Naturalists on the one hand, and theologians and philosophers on the other, are too often at war. They are men, and as nothing human is foreign to them, they are not unacquainted either with proud prepossessions, or with jealous rivalries, or with the miserable struggles of envy: with these things the passions are chargeable. But never render the sciences responsible for the errors of their representatives. Take away human frailties, and you shall see harmony established; the study of matter will thus agree with the study of mind, and the idea of nature with the idea of God. You will see all the sciences rise together in a majestic harmony. I say rise, and I say it advisedly; for the sciences also form a part of that golden chain which should unite the earth to heaven.

The assertion that the science of nature leads away from God, expresses nothing but a prejudice. It is not true in fact, and on principles of right reason it is impossible: the demonstration is complete. Atheism is a philosophy for which the natural sciences are in no degree responsible. We shall not undertake here the general discussion of this philosophy. Let us confine ourselves to the examination of the pretence which it puts forward to find a new support in the results of modern science.

The nineteenth century bestows particular attention upon history, and it is not only to the annals of the human race that it directs its investigations. Geology and palæontology dive into the bowels of the earth in order to ask of the ground which carries us testimony as to what it carried of old. Astronomy goes yet further. It endeavors to conjecture what was the condition of our planet before the appearance of the first living being. It remarks that the sun is not fixed in the heavens, and that our earth does not twice travel over the same line in its annual revolutions. It appears that stars are seen in course of formation; it is suspected that some have wholly disappeared. Nature is not fixed, but is undergoing modifications — lives, in fact. The actual state of the universe is but a momentary phase in a development which supposes thousands of ages in the past, and seems to presage thousands more in the future. These conceptions are the result of solid and incontestable discoveries. They have disturbed men's minds, but what is their legitimate import? Why, Newton's argument receives new force from them. From a blind metaphysical necessity, everywhere and always the same, said this great man, no variation could spring. The more it is demonstrated that the universe is in course of development and modification, the more clearly comes into view the necessity of the supreme Power which is the cause of its modifications, and of the Infinite intelligence which is directing them to their end. This appears to be solid reasoning, and nevertheless atheism has endeavored to strike its roots in the ground of modern discoveries. It does this in the following way.

If the universe as it is, with the infinite variety of beings which people it and the marvellous relations which connect these beings mutually together, could be shown to have sprung all at once from nothing, or to have emerged from chaos at a given instant, in its full harmony, the boldest mind would not venture to regard this miracle of intelligence as the product of chance. But modern science, it is said, no longer admits of this simple explanation of things: "God created the heavens and the earth." This phrase is henceforward admissible only in the catechism. We know that all has been produced by slow degrees, starting from weak and shapeless rudiments. This grand marvel of the universe was not made all of one piece. Man is of recent date; quadrupeds at a certain epoch did not exist; animals had a beginning, and plants also. The earth was once bare. Formerly, it was perhaps only a gaseous mass revolving in space. In course of time, matter was condensed; in time it was organized in living cellules; in time these cellules became shapeless animals; in time these animals were perfected. Time appears therefore to be the "universal factor"; and for the ancient formula, "the universe is the creation of God," we are able to substitute this other formula, the result, most assuredly, of modern science, "the universe is the work of time."

In all this, Gentlemen, I have invented nothing. All I have done has been to put into form the theory, the elements of which I have met with in various contemporary productions.* They bewilder us by heaping ages upon ages, and in order to explain nature they substitute the idea of time for the ideas of power and intelligence. They seem to suppose that what is produced little by little is sufficiently explained by the slowness of its formation.

These aberrations of thought have recently been manifested in a striking manner on the occasion of the publication of Mr. Darwin's book. This naturalist has given his attention to the transformation of organized types. He has discovered that types vary more than is generally supposed; and that we probably take simple varieties for distinct species. His discoveries will, I suppose, leave traces strongly marked enough in the history of science. But Mr. Darwin is not merely an observer; he is a theorist, dominated evidently by a disposition to systematize. Now minds of this character, which render, no doubt, signal services to the sciences of observation, are all like Pyrrhus, who, gazing on Andromache as he walked by her side,

Still quaffed bewildering pleasure from the view.†

* See in particular the *Revue des Deux Mondes*, passim.

† S'enivrait en marchant du plaisir de la voir.

Their theory is their lady-love; they love it passionately, and passionate love always strongly excites the imagination. Mr. Darwin then has put forth the hypothesis, that not only all animals, but all vegetables too, might have come from one and the same primitive type, from one and the same living cellule. This supposes that there was at the beginning but one single species, an elementary and very slightly defined organization, from which all that lives descended in the way of regular generation. The oak and the wild boar which eats its acorn, the cat and the flea which lodges in its fur, have common ancestors. The family, originally one, has been divided under the influence of soil, climate, food, moisture, mode of life, and by virtue of the natural selection which has preserved and accumulated the favorable modifications which have occured in the organism. Mr. Darwin, I repeat, appears to me a man strongly disposed to systematize, but I do not on this account conclude that he is mistaken. The question is, what opinion we must form of his doctrine on principles of experimental science? Professor Owen * does not appear to allow it any value; M. Agassiz does not admit it

* See the lecture above mentioned.

at all;* and, without crossing the ocean, we might consult M. Pictet,† who would reply, that judging by the experimental data which we have at present, this doctrine is an hypothesis not confirmed by the observation of facts. We will leave this controversy to naturalists. What will remain eventually in their science of the system under discussion? The answer belongs to the future enlightened by experience and by the employment of a sage induction. What is the relation existing between these systematic views and the question of the Creator? This is the sole object of our study.

The opinions of the English naturalist are very dubious as to the vital questions of religious philosophy. I have pointed out to you the confusion of his ideas in the use which he makes of natural selection. In the text of his book, he admits, in the special case of life, the intervention of the Creator for the production of the first living being, and he does not speak of man, except in an incidental sentence, which only attentive readers will take any notice of. If we do not take the liberty

* *Lettres sur les Etats-Unis d' Amérique*, by Lieutenant-Colonel Ferri Pisani, page 400. — Letter of 25 Sept. 1861.

† On the origin of species, in the *Archives des sciences de la Bibliothèque universelle*, March, 1860.

to look a little below the surface, we must say that Mr. Darwin remains on the ground of natural history. Therefore I spoke to you of the aberrations of philosophic thought which have been produced *on the occasion* of his book. These aberrations are the following:

First of all, natural selection has been taken for a cause, or rather as dispensing with the necessity for a cause, by means of a confusion of ideas for which the author is responsible. The system has therefore been understood as implying, that organized beings were formed without plan, without design, by the mere action of material causes, and as the result of modifications casual at first, and slowly accumulated. Divine intelligence and creative power thus seemed to be disappearing from the organization of the universe, and to disappear especially before the lapse of time and the infinitely slow action of physical causes. But while the system was taking wing, and soaring aloft, lo! the Creator at the commencement of things, and man conceived as a distinct being at the highest point of nature, have risen up as two idols and paralyzed its flight. To Mr. Darwin, however, have speedily succeeded disciples compromising their master's authority, and addressing him in some such language as this: "You, our master, do not fully follow out your own opinions; you strain off gnats,* and swallow camels. It is not more difficult to see in the living cellule a transformation of matter, and in man a transformation of the monkey, than to point out in a sponge the ancestor of the horse. Cast down your idols, and confess that matter developed in course of time, under favorable circumstances, is the origin of all that is." Matter, time, circumstances — these things have taken the place of God.

This, Gentlemen, is a philosophy, properly so called, which vainly pretends to find a support in the observation of facts. Geoffroy Saint-Hilaire, the rival of Cuvier, set forth views analogous to those which Mr. Darwin has lately reproduced. But in his replies to the attacks which were made upon his system, he affirmed that his theory offered "one of the most glorious manifestations of creative power, and an additional motive for admiration, gratitude, and love." † Two differ-

* Vous coulez des moucherons.

† In his *Principes de philosophie zoologique*, a collection of answers made by Geoffroy, in the discussions of the *Académie des Sciences*, in 1830.

ent interpretations may therefore be given to the system. I wish to show you that these interpretations proceed in all cases from considerations external to the system. The system in itself, as a theory of natural history, could not in any way affect injuriously the great interests of spiritual truth.

In order solidly to establish this assertion, I will suppose the hypotheses of the most advanced disciples of Mr. Darwin to have been verified by experimental science. I take for granted that it has been proved that all plants and all animals have descended, by way of regular generation, from living cellules originally similar; and that the material particles of the globe, at a given moment, drew together to form these cellules. And now where do we stand? Will God henceforward be a superfluous hypothesis? Do the atheistical consequences which it is desired to draw from this doctrine proceed logically from it? Most certainly not!

I observe first of all that there exists a great question relative to the beginning of things. Matter is perfected and organized in process of time — but whence comes matter itself? Is it also formed little by little in process of time? Does non-existence become existence little by little? So it is said in the preface to the French translation of Mr. Darwin's book. But this appertains to high metaphysics; and I pass on.

If time is the factor of all progress by a necessary law, this necessity must be everywhere the same. Have the elements of matter all the same age? If so, why have some followed the law of progress, and others not? Why has this mud and this coal remained mud and coal, age after age, while these other molecules have risen, in the hierarchy of the universe, to the dignity of life? Why have these mollusks remained mollusks throughout the succession of their generations, while others, happily transformed, have gradually mounted the steps of the ladder up to man? Whence comes this aristocracy of nature? Are the beings which we call inferior only the cadets of the universe, and are they too in their turn to mount all the steps of the ladder? Must we admit that there is going on the continual production, not only of living cellules which are beginning new series of generations, but also of new matter, which, setting out from the most rudimentary condition, is beginning the evolution which is to raise it into life? They do not venture to put forth theses of this nature, and, in order to account for the diversity of things, recourse is had to circumstances. The diversity of circumstances explains the diversity of developments. But whence can come the variety of circumstances in a world where all is produced in the way of fatal necessity, and without the intervention of a will and an intelligence? This is the remark of Newton. Study carefully the systems of materialism: their authors declare that to have recourse to God in order to account for the universe is a puerile conception unworthy of science, because all explanation must be referred to fixed and immutable laws; and then you will be for ever surprising them in the very act of the adoration of *circumstances*. Convenient deities these, which they summon to their aid in cases which they find embarrassing.

But we will not insist on these preliminary considerations. We have allowed, for argument's sake, that all organized beings have proceeded by means of generation from cellules presenting to sensible observation similar appearances. Natural history cannot prove, nor even attempt to prove, more. Let us transport ourselves, in thought, to the moment at which the highest points of the continents were for the first time emerging from the primitive ocean. We see, on the parts of the soil which are half-dried, and in certain conditions of heat and electricity, particles of matter draw together and form those rudiments of organism which are called living cellules. These cellules have the marvellous faculty of self-propagation, and the faculty, not less marvellous, of transmitting to their posterity the favorable modifications which they have undergone. Generations succeed one another; gradually they form separate branches. New characteristics show themselves; the organisms become complicated, and becoming complicated they separate. The vegetable is distinguished from the animal; the plant which will become the palm-tree is distinguished from the oak which is in course of formation, and the ancestor of the future bird is already different from that of the fish. We follow up this great spectacle. The ages pass, they pass by thousands and by millions, they pass by tens of millions. We need not be stinting in our allowance of time; our imagination will be tired of conceiving of it sooner than thought of supplying it. And at what shall we have arrived at last? At the universe as it has been for some few thousands of years past; at the world with its vegetables of a thousand forms, grouped by classes and series, with the families of animals, with the relations of animals to plants, with the unnumbered harmonies of nature. Let us choose out one particular, on which to fix our attention. Shall it be a she-goat —

> Upstretched on fragrant cytisus to browse?

This will suit our purpose, although the cytisus, unless I am mistaken, has no perfume except in M. de Lamartine's verses. Let us fix our attention on a cytisus with its yellow clusters hanging down, and the goat bending its pliant branches as it browses on the foliage. Here is a very small detail in the ample lap of nature. Let us come closer, and to help our ignorance, let us provide ourselves with a naturalist who will answer for us the questions suggested by this simple spectacle. And what have we now before us? The various relations of the animal's organization to the vegetables on which it feeds. In the organization and functions of these two living beings, in the equilibrium and movements of their frames, in the circulation of sap and of blood, we have the application of the most secret laws of mechanism, of physics, and of chemistry. Then again, in the relations which the animal and the plant sustain with the ground which bears them, with the air they breathe, with the sun which enlightens them, with heat and light, with the moisture of the air and its electricity — in all this we see the universal relations which connect all the various parts of the wide universe with each one of its minutest details. In this simple spectacle we have, in fact, reciprocal relations, the balance of things, the harmony which maintains the universal life — intelligence, in short, in the organization of beings, in the characteristics which divide them, in the classes which unite them, in the relations of these classes amongst themselves; — wonders of intelligent design, of which the sciences we are so proud of are spelling out, letter by letter, line after line, the inexhaustible abysses: this is what we find everywhere. Let us now come back to our primitive cellules.

All the living beings which people the surface of the globe are composed materially of some of the elements of the earth's substance. The birth therefore of the first living beings could only offer to the view the bringing together of some of the elements of the soil; this is not the matter in question. The primitive cellules were to all appearance alike. Weighed in scales, opened by the scalpel, placed beneath the microscope, they would have offered no appreciable difference; I grant it: it is the supposition we have agreed to make. Therefore they were identical, say you. I deny it, and here is my proof: If the cellules had been identical, they would not have given, in the successive development of their generations, the diverse beings which people the world, and the relations which unite them. Alike to your eyes, the cellules differed therefore by a concealed property which their development brought to light. You have told me as a matter of history how the organization of the world was manifested by slow degrees; you have given me no account of the cause of that organization.

It is said in reply: "We do know the origin of those developments which you refer to a supposed intelligence. The living beings are transformed by the action of food, climate, soil, mode of life. They experience slight variations in the first instance; but these variations are established, and increase; and where you see a plan, types, and species, there is really only the result of modifications slowly accumulated. Nature disposes of periods which have no limit, and everything has come at its proper time, in the course of ages." They are always proposing to us to accept of time as the substitute for intelligence. I am tempted to say with Alcestis:

Time in this matter, Sirs, has nought to do.*

You know what intelligence is; you know it by knowing yourself. Is there, or is there not, intelligence in the universe? Allow me to reproduce some old questions: If a machine implies intelligence, does the universe imply none? If a telescope implies intelligence in the optician, does the eye imply none in its author? The production of a variety of the camelia, or of a new breed of swine, demands of the gardener and the breeder the patient and prolonged employment of the understanding; and are our entire flora and fauna to be explained without any intervention of mind? And if there is intelligence in the universe, is this intelligence a chemical result of the combination of molecules? is it a physical result of caloric or of electricity? It is in vain that you give to material agents an unlimited time; what has time to do here? Whether the world as it now exists arose out of nothing, or whether it was

* Voyons, Messieurs, le temps ne fait rien à l'affaire.

slowly formed during thousands of ages, the question remains the same. With matter and time, you will not succeed in creating intelligence; this were an operation of transcendent alchemy utterly beyond our power. In the theory of *slow causes*, the adjective ends by devouring the substantive; it seems that by dint of becoming slow the causes become superfluous. A breath of reason upsets, like a house of cards, the structures of this erring and misnamed science. Time has a relative meaning and value. We reckon duration as long or short, by taking human life as our measure. But they tell of insects which are born in the morning, arrive at mature age at mid-day, and only reach the evening if they are patriarchs of their race. Is it not easy to conceive of beings organized for an existence such that our centuries would be moments with them, and centuries heaped together one of our hours? Suppose one of these beings to be contemplating our geological periods, and slow causes will to him appear rapid causes, and the question of intelligence will be the same for him as for us.

It is manifest that the attempt is being made to restore the worship of the old *Chronos*, to whom the ancients had erected temples. Let us look the idol in the face. Time appears at first to our imagination as the great destroyer. He is armed with a scythe, and passes gaunt and bald over the ruins of all that has lived. When he lifts up his great voice and cries —

> Mighty nations famed in story
> Into darkness I have hurled, —
> Gone their myriads and their glory
> (Lo! ye follow) from the world:
> My dark shade for ever covers
> Stars I quenched as on they rolled: —

the beautiful and frightened girl in the song is not singular as she exclaims in her terror:

> Ah! we're young, and we are lovers,
> Spare us, Reaper gaunt and old! *

Such is the first impression which time makes upon us. But birth succeeds to death. From an inexhaustible spring, nature sends gushing forth new products and new developments. Youth full of hope trips lightly over the ground, without a

* Sur cent premiers peuples célèbres,
J' ai plongé cent peuples fameux,
Dans un abîme de ténèbres
Où vous disparaîtrez comme eux.
J' ai couvert d' une ombre éternelle
Des astres éteints dans leur cours.
— Ah! par pitié, lui dit ma belle,
Vieillard, épargnez nos amours!

thought that the ground it treads on is the vast cemetery of all past generations. If we fix our thoughts on the permanence of life and the manifestations of progress, time appears to us as the great producer. Destroyer of all that is, producer of all that is to be, time has thus a double form. It is a mysterious tide, ever rising and ever receding; it is the power of death, and it is the power of life. All this, Gentlemen, is for the imagination. In the view of a calm reason, time is the simply negative condition of all development, as space is the negative condition of all motion. Just as without bodies and forces infinite space could not produce any motion; so, without the action of causes, ages heaped on ages could neither produce nor destroy a single atom of matter, or a single element of intelligence. Time is the scene of life and of death; it neither causes to be born, nor to die.

The struggle which we are now maintaining against the philosophers of matter is as ancient as science, and was going on, nearly in the same terms, more than two thousand three hundred years ago. About five hundred years before the Christian era was born at Clazomenæ, a city of Ionia, the son of Eubulus, who was to become famous by the name of Anaxagoras. He fixed his abode at Athens, and the Athenian people gave him a glorious surname, — they called him *Intelligence*. On what account? There were taught at that time doctrines which explained the world by the transformations of matter rising progressively to life and thought, without the intervention of a mind. The philosopher Anaximander gave out that the first animals had their origin in the watery element, and became modified by living in drier regions, so that man was only a fish slowly transformed. "I am quite willing to grant it," replied Anaxagoras; "but for your transformations there must be a transforming principle. Matter is the material of the world, no doubt; but it could not produce universal order except as ruled by intelligence." The Athenians admired this discovery. For us, Gentlemen, the discovery has been made a long while. Let us not then be talking in this discussion about modern science and the lights of the age. Our natural history is much advanced as compared with that of the Greeks; but the vital question has not varied. Does nature manifest the intervention of a directing mind, or do we see in it only a fortuitous aggregation of atoms?

Intelligence radiates from the face of nature, and it is in vain that men endeavor to veil its splendor. Nevertheless I consent to forget all that has just been said, in order to intrench myself in an argument, which of itself is sufficient for the object we have in view to-day. Our object is to prove that material science does not contain the explanation of all the realities of the universe. Even though they had succeeded in persuading us that there is no intelligence in nature, it would still be necessary to explain the origin of that intelligence which is in us, and the existence of which cannot be disputed. Whence proceeds the mind which is in ourselves?

Let us first of all give our attention to a strange contradiction. Those savants who make of the human soul a simple manifestation of matter, are the same who wish to explain nature without the intervention of the Divine intelligence. In order to keep out of view the design which is displayed in the organization of the world, they take a pleasure in finding nature at fault, and in pointing out its imperfections. Still, they do not pretend to be able to do better than nature; they would not undertake the responsibility of correcting the laws of life, and regulating the course of the seasons. They do not say, "We could make a better world," but "We can imagine a world more perfect than our own." Now what is our answer? Simply this: "You are right." Nature is not the supreme perfection, and therefore we will not worship it. How admirable soever be the visible universe, we have the faculty of conceiving more and better. We understand that the atmosphere might be purified, so that the tempest should not engulf the ships, nor the thunderbolt produce the conflagration. We dream of mountain-heights more majestic than the loftiest summits of our Alps, of waters more transparent than the pure crystal of our lakes, of valleys fresher and more peaceful than the loveliest which hide among our hills. The spectacle of nature awakens in us the powers of thought, and the sentiment of beauty draws us on to the pursuit of an ideal which surpasses all realities. Nature is not perfect: let us be forward to acknowledge it, and let us draw from the fact its legitimate consequence. The stream cannot rise higher than its source. If man conceives an ideal superior to nature, he is not himself the mere product of nature. By what strange contradiction is it affirmed at once that our spirit overpasses the bounds of all the realities which encompass it, and that it has not a source more elevated than those realities? Listen to a thought of that weighty writer Montesquieu: * "Those who have said that a blind fatality has produced all the effects which we see in the world, have said a great absurdity; for what greater absurdity than a blind fatality which should have produced intelligent beings?" Without restricting ourselves to this simple and solid argument, let us see how they will explain man by nature. For this end, we must examine the theory of the perfected monkey, which, introduced to us by the lectures of Professor Vogt and the spirited rejoinders of M. de Rougemont, made a great noise as it descended a short time ago from the mountains of Neuchâtel.† A celebrated orator said one day to an assembly of Frenchmen: "I am long, Gentlemen; but it is your own fault: it is your glory that I am recounting." Have not I the right to say to you: "I am long, Gentlemen, but it is worth while to be so; it is our own dignity which is in question."

* *Esprit des Lois*, Bk. I. chap. 1.

† *Leçons sur l'homme*, by Carl Vogt (lectures delivered during the winter of 1862–1863, at Neuchâtel and at Chaux-de-Fonds), 1 vol. 8vo. Paris, 1865. — *L' Homme et le Singe*, by Frédéric de Rougemont, pamphlet, 12mo. Neuchâtel, 1863.

Man is a perfected monkey! I have three preliminary observations to make before I proceed to the direct examination of this theory.

In the first place, this definition transgresses the first and most essential rules of logic. We must always define what is unknown by what is known. This is an elementary principle. What a man is, I know. To think, to will, to enjoy, to hope, to fear, are functions of the mental life. These words answer to clear ideas, because those ideas result directly from our personal consciousness. But what is the soul of a monkey? The nature of animals is a mystery, one which is perhaps incapable of solution, and which, in all cases is wrapped in profound darkness, because the animal appears to us an intermediate link between the mechanism of nature and the functions of the spiritual life, which are the only two conceptions we have that are really clear and distinct. In taking the monkey therefore as our point of departure for the definition of man, we are defining what is clear by what is obscure.

My second remark is this: If it is affirmed that there is but one species, including all the animals and man, so that man is only a monkey modified, and the monkey, in its turn, an inferior animal modified; when once we have established the reality of man we arrive at this result: all animals whatsoever are only inferior developments of humanity, living fœtuses which, without having come to their full term, have nevertheless the faculty of living and reproducing themselves. The animal then is an incomplete man; a theory which raises great difficulties, but which is more serious and more easy to understand than the doctrine which would have man to be a consummation of the monkey.

In fact, — and this is my third observation, — when the theory which I am examining is adopted, it must be carried out to its consequences, and the bearing of it clearly seen. Man, it is said, is the consummation of the monkey. The monkey is an improvement upon some quadruped or other, and this quadruped is an improvement upon another, and so on. We must descend, in an inevitable logical series, to the most elementary manifestations of life, and thence, finally, to matter. If it is not admitted that pure matter is a man in a state of torpor, it must be admitted that man is a *mélange* of carbon, oxygen, hydrogen, azote, phosphorus — a *mélange* which has been brought little by little to perfection. Such is the final inference from the doctrine which we are examining; and there are theorists who deduce it clearly. Now what is it that goes on in the minds of these savants? When the object is to banish God from nature, the creative Intelligence is resolved into thousands of ages. When it is desired to get rid in man of the reality of mind, they seek to resolve the human intelligence into a long series of modifications which have caused life to spring from matter, superior animals from simpler organisms, and man from the animal. Do not allow yourselves to be caught in this trap. Maintain firmly, that, whatever the degree of intelligence, of will, of spiritual essence, which may exist in animals, if that element is really found in them, it demands a cause, and cannot, without an enormous confusion of ideas, be regarded as a mere perfecting of matter. In fact, a thing in perfecting itself, realizes continually more fully its own proper idea, and does not become another thing. A perfect monkey would be of all monkeys the one which is most a monkey, and would not be a man. But let us leave the animals in the darkness in which they abide for our minds, and let us speak of what for us is less obscure.

Our spiritual existence is a fact; it is of all facts

the one which is best known to us; it is the fact without which no other fact would exist for us. And whence proceeds our spirit? To this question, natural history has no answer. It is easy to see this, though we grant once again to natural history, when made the most of by our adversaries, all that it can pretend to claim. Suppose it proved, that in the historical development of nature, man has a monkey for his mother. I will grant it, and grant it quite seriously in order to ascertain what will be the influence of this hypothesis upon the problem on which we are engaged.

If all monkeys were fossils, and if we had a natural history, also fossil, setting forth to us the customs and habits of these animals; if the savages that are said to be the nearest neighbors to monkeys were all fossils; we should find ourselves in presence of a progressive and continued development of beings, and, for an inattentive mind, all would be easily explained by the slow and continued action of time. But this is not the case. All the elements of nature are before our eyes, from inorganic matter up to man. We do not see that time suffices for savages to become civilized, and still less for monkeys to become men. I was, in the spring of this year, in the *Jardin des plantes* at Paris, musing on the question which we are discussing, and I took a good look at the monkeys. Come now, I said to myself, canst thou recognize them as thine ancestors? The question was badly put. The monkeys are not our ancestors, inasmuch as they are living at the same time with us; they can only be our cousins, and it would seem that they are the eldest branch, as they have best preserved the primitive type. But let us speak more seriously. The races of monkeys have lived as long or longer than we: it is neither time nor climate which has made men of them. Recollect, I pray you, that the words 'time' and 'progress' explain nothing. There must have occurred favorable circumstances to transform the earth's substance into living cellules, and the living cellules into plants clearly marked, and into animals properly so called; and in the same way there must have been a propitious circumstance to transform the monkey into man. I think so, in fact; and this propitious circumstance well deserves to be studied with attention.

Man presents characteristics which distinguish him profoundly from the animal races: no one disputes it. He possesses speech; he is capable of religion; he exhibits the varied phenomena of civilization, while the animals succeed one another generations after generations in the unrecorded obscurity of a life for ever the same. Suppose we admit that human phenomena presented themselves at first in a very elementary form; in rudiments of language and rudiments of religion, — although the historical sciences do not quite give this result: — still suppose the case that at a given moment a branch of the monkey species presented the germ, as little developed as you please, but real, of new phenomena. One variety of the monkey species has been endowed with speech, has become religious, capable of civilization, and the other varieties of the species have not offered the same characteristics, although they have had the same number of ages in which to develop themselves. Observe well now my process of reasoning. Remark attentively whether I oppose theories to facts, whether I substitute oratorical declamations for arguments. I grant the hypotheses best calculated, as commonly thought, to contradict my theses. I assume that natural history demonstrates by solid proofs that the first man was carried in the bosom of a monkey; and I ask: What is the circumstance which set apart in the animal species a branch which presented new phenomena? What is the cause? That monkey-author of our race which one day began to speak in the midst of his brother-monkeys, amongst whom thenceforward he had no fellow; that monkey, that stood erect in the sense of his dignity; that, looking up to heaven, said, My God! and that, retiring into himself, said: I!—that monkey which, while the female monkeys continued to give birth to their young, had sons by the partner of his life and pressed them to his heart; that monkey—what shall we say of it? What climate, what soil, what regimen, what food, what heat, what moisture, what drought, what light, what combination of phosphorus, what disengagement of electricity, separated from the animal races, not only man, but human society? humanity with its combats, its falls, its risings again, its sorrows and its joys, its tears and its smiles; humanity with its arts, its sciences, its religion, its history in short, its history and its hopes of immortality? That monkey, what shall we say of it? Do you not see that the breath of the Spirit passed over it, and that God said unto it: Behold, thou art made in mine image: remember now thy Father who is in heaven? Do you not see that though we grant everything to the extreme pretensions of naturalists, the question comes up again whole and entire? When by dint of confusions and sophisms such theorists imagine that they have extinguished the intelligence which radiates from nature, that intelligence again confronts them in man, and there, as in an impregnable fortress, sets all attacks at defiance. Mark then where lies the real problem. Whether the eternal God formed the body of the first man directly from the dust of the earth; or whether, in the slow series of ages, He formed the body of the first man of the dust of the earth, by making it pass through the long series of animality — the question is a grave one, but it is of secondary importance. The first question is to know whether we are merely the ephemeral product of the encounter of atoms, or whether there is in us an essence, a nature, a soul, a reality in short, with which may connect itself another future than the dissolution of the sepulchre; whether there remains another hope than annihilation as the term of our latest sorrows, or, for the aspirants after fame, only that evanescent memory which time bears away with everything beside.

This is the question. Do not allow it to be put out of sight beneath details of physiology and researches of natural history, which can neither settle, nor so much as touch the problem. If therefore you fall in with any one of these philosophers of matter, bid him take this for all your answer: "There is one fact which stands out against your theory and suffices to overthrow it: that fact is — myself!" And since, to have the better of materialism, it is sufficient to understand well what is one thought of the mind, one throb of the spiritual heart, one utterance of the conscience, — add boldly with Corneille's Medea:

I, — I say, — and it is enough.

In fact, nature does not explain man, and to this conclusion has tended all that I have said to you to-day.

LECTURE V.

HUMANITY.

(At Geneva, 1st. Dec., 1863.)

GENTLEMEN,

Man has need of God. If he be not fallen into the most abject degradation, he does not succeed in extinguishing the instinct which leads him to inquire after his Creator. A false wisdom labors to still the cravings which the truth alone can satisfy; but false wisdom remains powerless, and betrays itself continually by some outrageous contradiction. Here is a curious example of this:

In a book which was famous in the last century, and which was called the gospel of atheism,* the Baron d' Holbach explains as follows the existence of the universe: "The universe,

* *Système de la Nature*, published under the pseudonyme of Mirabaud.

that vast assemblage of all that exists, everywhere presents to our view only matter and motion.—Nature is the grand whole which results from the assemblage of different material substances, from their different combinations, and from the different motions which we see in the universe." * Here is a clear doctrine: all that exists, the soul included, is nothing but matter in motion. I pass from the beginning to the end of the work, and I arrive at this conclusion: "O nature! sovereign of all beings! and ye, her adorable daughters, virtue, reason, truth! be ye for ever our sole divinities; to you it is that the incense and the homage of the earth are due." † If we try to translate this sort of hymn in accordance with the express definitions of the author, we shall obtain the following result: "O matter in motion! sovereign of all material substances in motion! and ye, virtue, reason, truth, who are various names of matter which moves, be ye the only divinities of that moving matter which is ourselves." Yet this author was no blockhead. What then passed in his mind? He laid down the thesis of materialism: bodies in motion are the

* *Système de la Nature*, Part I. chap. I.
† *Ibid.* Part II. chap. 14.

only reality. But he is all the while a man. The need for adoration is not destroyed in his soul, and he deceives himself. He defines nature as consisting wholly of matter, and when he sets himself to worship it, he entirely forgets his definition. This is not on his part a piece of philosophical jugglery, but the manifestation of the real condition of our nature, which is always giving the lie, in one direction or another, to erroneous systems. The power of wholly maintaining himself in error has not been granted to man. He who denies God is always deifying something; and all worship which is not that of the Eternal and Infinite Mind is stultified by glaring contradictions. Here is a recent example of this: We were not a little surprised a short time since to see M. Ernest Renan deny clearly enough the immortality of our persons, and, in the opening of the very book in which this negation appears, to find him invoking the soul of his sister at rest with God.* Elsewhere, the same writer says that the Infinite Being does not exist, that absolute reason and absolute justice exist only in humanity, and he concludes his exposition of these views by an invocation of the Heavenly Father.† The Baron

* *Vie de Jésus.* Dedication.

† *Revue des Deux Mondes* of 15 January, 1860.

d'Holbach had put eight hundred and thirty-nine pages between his materialistic definition of the universe and his invocation of nature. Now-a-days everything goes faster; and M. Renan places but a few pages of the *Revue des Deux Mondes* between his denial of God and his prayer to the Heavenly Father. With this difference, which is to the advantage of the writer of the eighteenth century, the process is absolutely the same. The philosopher declares God to be an imaginary being, and the future life an illusion; but the man protests, and, by a touching illusion of the heart, the man who in his system of doctrine has neither God nor hope, finds that he has a sister in the realms eternal, and a Father in the heavens. It is impossible not to see, especially in literary works destined to a success of fashion, the seductive influence of art, the precautions of prudence, the concessions made to public opinion; but we cannot wholly explain the incredible contradictions of the Holbachs and Renans, without allowing full weight to that need for God which shows itself even in the farthest wanderings of human thought by sudden and abrupt returns.

The illusion which deifies matter in motion is gross enough. It belongs only to minds which

Cicero called, in the aristocratic pride of a Roman gentleman, the plebeians of philosophy.* It requires, in fact, no great reflection to understand that truth, beauty, and goodness are neither atoms nor a certain movement of atoms. The attempt, which is to form the subject of our study to-day, that of deifying man, is a far more subtle one. Let us first of all inquire into the origin of the strange worship which humanity accords to itself.

Nature, considered separately from the beings which receive sensible impressions from it, has neither heat nor light. In a world peopled by the blind, light would have no name. If all men were entirely paralyzed as to their sensations, the idea of heat would not exist. Light and heat, regarded as existing in matter itself, without reference to sensitive organizations, are, in the opinion of our natural philosophers, only determinate movements. In the same way, if nature were without any spectator whatever, beauty would not exist; if there were nowhere any intelligence, truth would no longer be. In the same way again, if there were no wills, goodness, which is nothing else than the law of the will, would be a word

* Plebeii philosophi qui a Platone et Socrate et ab eâ familiâ dissident.

deprived of all meaning. Beauty expresses the object of the perceptions of the soul. Truth denotes the quality of the judgments of intelligences. Goodness (I speak of moral goodness) expresses a certain direction of the free will. There exists no means of causing to proceed from nature, or from matter, the attributes of the spiritual being. This is only done by imaginary transformations, by a course of arrant juggling. The flame does not feel its own heat, light does not see itself, the planets know nothing of the laws of Kepler. Materialism is the result of a modesty wholly misplaced which leads man to forget himself, in order to attribute gratuitously to nature realities which exist only in spiritual beings connected with nature by a marvellous harmony. In order therefore to account for the universe, we must raise ourselves above the atom in motion, and penetrate into a higher world where truth, beauty, goodness become the objects of thought. Truth, beauty, goodness conduct the mind to God, their eternal source. But there is a philosophy which endeavors to stop midway in the ascent of the Divine ladder, and thinks to satisfy itself in the contemplation of the true, the beautiful, the good, without connecting them with their cause.

This philosophy considers the true, the beautiful, the good, as ideas which exist by themselves, without a supreme Spirit of which they are the manifestation. It has received, in consequence, the name of idealism.

To conceive of ideas without a mind, ideas having an existence by themselves, is a thing impossible; such a conception is expressed by words which give back a hollow sound, because they contain nothing. We have already stated this thesis; let us now confirm it by an example. A literary Frenchman, M. Taine, would make us understand in what manner the universe may be explained without reference to God, and by means of a pure idea. Listen well, not to understand, but to make sure that you do not understand: "The universe forms a unique being, indivisible, of which all the beings are members. At the supreme summit of things, at the highest point of the luminous and inaccessible ether, pronounces itself the eternal axiom; and the prolonged resounding of this creative formula composes, by its inexhaustible undulations, the immensity of the universe. Every form, every change, every movement, every idea is one of its acts." *

* *Les philosophes français du XIXe siècle*, chap. XIV.

M. Taine is a man of humor, and the burlesque has a place in his philosophical writings; but in the words which I have just read to you he seems to have intended seriously to expound the system which replaces God by an idea. Try now to form a definite conception of this universe composed of the undulations of an axiom. Do you understand how an axiom undulates, and how the heavens and the earth are only the undulations of an axiom? Making all allowance for rhetoric and figures, do you understand what can be the acts of an axiom, and how an axiom *pronounces itself* without being pronounced? You do not understand it, as neither do I. Such doctrines, then, as we have said, can only be the portion of a small number of thinkers who have lost, by dint of abstraction, the sentiment of reality. The ideas — truth, beauty, good — will only exist for the common order of men, under such a system, in the human mind, where we have cognizance of them; and thenceforward, the ideal, or God, is nothing else than the image of humanity which contemplates itself in a sort of mirage. Thus it is that the adoration of man by man is disengaged from the high theories of idealism. Let us proceed to the examination of this worship, which is cried up now-a-days in divers parts of the intellectual globe.

I open the *Revue des Deux Mondes*, of the 15th February, 1861. As the author of the article I refer to * appears to admit "that one assertion is not more true than another opposed to it," † we will not be so simple as to ask whether he adopts the opinions which he propounds. He presents to us, in a rapid sketch, the principal tendencies of the modern mind. The modern mind is here characterized by one of its declared partisans; you will not take therefore for a wicked caricature the picture which he puts before us. Here then are the thoughts of the modern mind: "There is only one infinite, that of our desires and our aspirations, that of our needs and our efforts.‡ The true, the beautiful, the just are perpetually occurring; they are for ever in course of self-formation, because they are nothing else than the human mind, which, in unfolding itself, finds and knows itself again." § This is only the French translation of a saying celebrated in Germany: "God is not: He becomes." What we call God is the human mind. What was there at the beginning

* *Hégel et l' Hégélianisme* par M. Ed. Schérer.
† Page 854. ‡ Page 852. § Page 856.

of things? The human mind, which did not know itself. What will there be in the end? The human mind, which, in unfolding itself, will have come to know itself, and will adore itself as the supreme God. If this be indeed the final object of the universe, it appears that, in the opinion of these philosophers, the consummation of all things must be near. Once that humanity, faithful to their doctrine, shall have pronounced the lofty utterance, "I am God, and there is none else," the world will no longer have any reason for existing.

Such is the system of which we have to follow out the consequences. Let us take as our point of comparison the old ideas which we are urged to abandon.

We usually explain human destinies by the concurrence of two causes, infinitely distinct, since the one is creative and the other created, but both of which we hold for real: man, and God. Humanity has received from its Author the free power which we call will, and the law of that will which we name conscience. The law proceeds from God, the liberty proceeds from God; but the acts of the created will, when it violates its law and revolts against its Author, are the creation of the creature. God is the eternal source of good, and liberty is a good; but God is not the source of evil, which is distinctly a revolt against Him, the abuse of the first of His gifts. Together with will, man has received understanding, and gives himself to the search after truth. Truth is the object of the understanding, its Divine law. Error is a deviation from the law of the understanding, as evil is a deviation from the law of the will. Lastly, with will and understanding, man has received the faculty of feeling. This faculty applies itself to the world of bodies, from which we receive pain or pleasure. But our faculty of feeling does not stop there. Above the animal life, the mind has enjoyments which are proper to it, and the object of which is beauty. Beauty is not only in nature and in works of art, it is everywhere, in whatever attracts our love. The sciences are beautiful, and the harmony of the truths which are discovered in their order and mutual dependence causes us to experience a feeling similar to that produced by the most delightful music. Virtue is beautiful; it shines in the view of the conscience with the purest brightness, and, as was said by one of the ancients, if it could reveal itself to our eyes in a sensible form, it would excite in our souls feelings of inexpressible love. Vice is ugly when once stripped of the delusive fascination of the passions; the vicious excesses of the lower nature are ugly and repulsive as soon as the intoxication is over. Error is ugly too; there are no beautiful errors but those which contain a larger portion of truth than the prosaic verities, which are nothing else than falsehoods put in a specious way. Beauty therefore is the law of our feelings, as truth is the law of our thought, and good the law of our will. We will not inquire now what secret relations shall one day bring together in an indissoluble unity of light, the good, the true, and the beautiful, and in a unity of darkness, evil, deformity, and falsehood. Let it suffice to have pointed out how a threefold aspiration leads man to God, under the guidance of the conscience, the understanding, and the feelings; and that a threefold rebellion estranges him from God, by sinking him into the dark regions of deformity, error, and evil. Humanity has therefore a law; it has been endowed with liberty, but that a liberty of which the legitimate end is determined. It advances towards this end, or it swerves from it. There is a rule above its acts. The thing as it is may not be the thing as it ought to be; rebellion is not obedience, and good is not evil.

All these consequences are included in the idea of creation. The struggle between two opposite principles, a struggle which sums up human destiny, is a fact of which each one of us can easily assure himself in his own person. What will happen when man, sensible of the law of his nature, and conscious of this struggle, proceeds to encounter humanity? Each one of us carries humanity in his own bosom. But humanity, the character of man which is common to us, and which makes the spiritual unity of our species, is found to be altered by the influence of places, times, and circumstances. Our reason is encumbered by prejudices of birth and education, and by such as we have ourselves created in our minds in the exercise of our will. Our sense of beauty is vitiated and narrowed by local influences and habits. Our conscience is likewise subjected to influences which impair its free manifestation. Every one needs to enlarge his horizon. By seeking occasions of intercourse with our fellows, we shall learn to discriminate true and eternal beauty in the diversity of its manifestations; we shall distinguish the truth from the individual prepossessions of our own minds; good and evil, disengaged from the narrownesses of habit, will appear to us in their real and enduring nature. Our taste will be formed, our conscience purified, our mind enlarged; we shall more and more become men, in the high and full acceptation of the term. In order that the meeting together of the individual and of humanity may produce such fruits, God must dwell continually in the sanctuary of the conscience. The inner light is kindled in the intercourse of the soul with its Creator; it is afterwards brightened and nurtured by the soul's intercourse with the traces of God which humanity reveals. But this light makes manifest within us, and without us, great darkness. We have no right to abandon ourselves to every spectacle which strikes our view. If, in presence of what is passing in the world, we are tempted to regard the prosperity of the wicked with cowardly envy; if we would fill up, for the satisfaction of our evil desires, the abyss which separates the holy from the impure, the inner voice lifts itself up and cries to us: "Woe! woe to them who call evil good, and good evil." * God is our Master, even as He is our good and

* Isa. xx. 20.

our hope. The fact of the revolts of humanity can have no effect against His sovereign will. Soldiers in the service of the Almighty, life is for us a conflict, and duty imposes on us a combat.

Such, Sirs, is the explanation of our destinies, an old, and, if you like, a vulgar one. Let us now give our attention to the doctrine which deifies humanity, and follow out its consequences. Humanity carries within its bosom the idea of truth, the love of beauty, the sense of good. What does it need more? These noble aspirations mark for it the end of its efforts. What will be wanting to a life regulated by duty, enlightened by truth, ennobled by art? What will be wanting to such a life? Nothing, or everything. Nothing, if the search after good, truth, and beauty leads to God. Everything, if it be sought to carry it on without any reference to God, because from the moment that man desires to be the source of light to himself, the light will be changed into darkness, as we said at the beginning of this lecture. Put God out of view, and good, beauty, and truth will disappear; while you will see produced the decline of art, the dissolution of thought in scepticism, the absolute negation of morality.

Let us consider with the attention it deserves, and in contemporary examples, this sad and curious spectacle.

I open a treatise by M. Taine. The English historian Macaulay speaks of literary men who "have taken pains to strip vice of its odiousness, to render virtue ridiculous, to rank adultery among the elegant fashions and obligatory achievements of a man of taste." The honest Englishman takes the liberty to judge and to condemn men who have made so pernicious a use of their talents. This pretension to make the conscience speak is in the eyes of the French man of letters a gothic prejudice. Listen how he expresses himself on the subject: "Criticism in France has freer methods.—When we try to give an account of the life, or to describe the character, of a man, we are quite willing to consider him simply as an object of painting or of science. . . . We do not judge him, we only wish to represent him to the eyes and to set him intelligibly before the reason. We are curious inquirers and nothing more. That Peter or Paul was a knave matters little to us, that was the business of his contemporaries, who suffered from his vices— At this day we are out of his reach, and hatred has disappeared with the danger — I experience neither aversion nor disgust; I have left these feelings at the gate of history, and I taste the very deep and very pure pleasure of seeing a soul act according to a definite law —." * You understand, Gentlemen: the distinction between good and evil, as that between error and truth; these are old sandals which must be put off before entering into the temple of history; and the man of the nineteenth century, if he has taste and information, is merely an historian, and nothing more. The sacred emotion which generous actions produce in us, the indignation stirred in us by baseness and cruelty, are childish emotions which are to disappear in order that we may be free to contemplate vice and virtue with a pleasure always equal, very deep, and very pure. We have not here the aberration of a young and ill-regulated mind, but the doctrine of a school. I open again the *Revue des Deux Mondes*, and there I encounter the theory of which M. Taine has made the application: "We no longer know anything of morals, but of manners; of principles, but of facts. We explain everything, and, as has been said, the mind ends *by approving of all that it explains*.

* *Essais de critique et d' histoire*, pp. 8 and 9.

Modern virtue is summed up in toleration.* — Immense novelty! That which is, has for us the right to be.† — In the eyes of the modern savant, all is true, all is right in its own place. The place of each thing constitutes its truth." ‡

I cut short the enumeration of these enormities. All rule has disappeared, all morality is destroyed; there is no longer any difference between right and fact, between what is and what ought to be. And what is the real account to give of all this? It is as follows: Humanity is the highest point of the universe; above it there is nothing; humanity is God, if we consent to take that sacred name in a new sense. How then is it to be judged? In the name of what rule? since there is no rule: in the name of what law? since there is no law. All judgment is a personal prejudice, the act of a narrow mind. We do not judge God, we simply recount His dealings; we accept all His acts, and record them with equal veneration. All science is only a history, and the first requisite in a historian is to reduce to silence his conscience and his reason, as sorry and deceitful exhibitions of his petty personality,

* *Revue des Deux Mondes*, 15 Feb. 1861, page 855.

† Page 853. ‡ Page 854.

in order to accept all the acts of the humanity-deity, and establish their mutual connection. The deification of the human mind is the justification of all its acts, and, by a direct consequence, the annihilation of all morality. Let us look more in detail at the origin and development of these notions.

The individual placing himself before humanity is to accept everything: this is the disposition recommended to us, in the name of the modern mind. Good and evil are narrow measures which minds behind the age persist, ridiculously enough, in wishing to apply to things. "We no longer transform the world to our image by bringing it to our standard; *on the contrary, we allow ourselves to be modified and fashioned by it.*" * The individual goes therefore to meet humanity without any inner rule: he gives himself up, he abandons himself to the spectacle of facts. But the world is large, and history is long. Even those who spend their whole life in nothing else than in satisfying their curiosity, cannot see and know everything. To what then shall be directed that vague look, equally attracted to all points for want of any fixed rule? At what shall it stop?

* *Revue des Deux Mondes* of the 15th Feb. 1861, page 854.

It will rest on that which shines most brilliantly, like a moth attracted by light. Now, nothing shines more brightly than success; nothing more solicits the attention. The glorification of success is the first and most infallible consequence of moral indifference. In leaving ourselves to be fashioned by the world instead of bringing it to our standard, we shall begin by according our esteem to victory. This philosophy is come to us from Germany. It was set forth on one occasion, in France, with great *éclat*, by the brilliant eloquence of a man who has rendered signal services to philosophy, and whose entire works must not be judged of by the single particular which I am about to mention. In the year 1829, M. Cousin was developing at the Sorbonne the meaning of these verses of La Fontaine, which introduce the fable of the Wolf and the Lamb:

> La raison du plus fort est toujours la meilleure:
> Je vais le montrer tout à l' heure.

He had written as the programme of one of his lectures: *Morality of Victory*. Now see how he justified this surprising title: "I have absolved victory as necessary and useful; I now undertake to absolve it as just in the strictest sense of the word. Men do not usually see in success anything else than the triumph of strength, and an honorable sympathy draws us to the side of the vanquished; I hope I have shown that since there must always be a vanquished side, and since the vanquished side is always that which ought to be so, to accuse the conqueror is to take part against humanity, and to complain of the progress of civilization. We must go farther; we must prove that the vanquished deserved to be so, that the conqueror not only serves the interests of civilization, but that he is better, more moral than the vanquished, and that it is on that account he is the conqueror. . . . It is time that the philosophy of history should place at its feet the declamations of philanthropy." *

These words are worth considering. When Brennus the Gaul was having the gold weighed which he exacted from the vanquished Romans, he threw his heavy sword into the balance, exclaiming, *Væ victis!* Woe to the conquered! He simply meant to say that he was the stronger, and did not foresee that a Gaul of the nineteenth century, availing himself of the labors of learned Germany, would demonstrate that being the

* *Introduction à l' histoire de la philosophie.* Neuvième leçon.

stronger he was on that very account the more just. But we must not wander too far from our subject.

When the spectacle of the world is freely indulged in without any application to it of the measure of the conscience, what first strikes the view is success. It is necessary therefore to begin with rendering glory to success by declaring victory good. Now, mark well here the conflict of the old notions with the so-called modern mind. From the old point of view, victory in the issue belongs to good, because while man is tossed in strife and tumult, God is leading him on; but the success of good is realized by conflict, and the victory is often reached only after a long series of defeats. There are bad triumphs and impious successes. What is proposed to us is, to put aside the rule of our own judgments, and to declare that victory is good in itself. The old point of view, that of the conscience, does not surrender without an energetic resistance; and that resistance shows itself in the very words of M. Cousin. His thesis is, that all victory is just. His intention is therefore to *approve* victory. Why does he say *absolve?* it is the term which he employs. Since the matter in question is to absolve victory, it is placed on trial. It is accused of being, like fortune and fame, at one time on the side of good and justice, at another on the side of injustice and evil. Which then is the party accused? Victory. Who is the advocate? An eloquent professor. Who finally is the accuser? Do you not see? It is the human conscience; the conscience which protests in the soul of the orator against the theory of which he is enamoured, and which forces him to say *absolve* when he should say *glorify*. And in fact the choice must be made: either to glorify victory, by treading under foot that narrow conscience which sometimes ranks itself with Cato on the side of the vanquished; or to glorify conscience by impeaching the victories which outrage it.

It is not sufficient, however, to sacrifice the conscience in order to rescue from embarrassment the philosophy of success. It strikes on other rocks also. The same causes are by turns victorious and vanquished, and it is hard to make men understand that, in conflicts in which their dearest affections are engaged, they must beforehand, and in all cases, take part with the strongest. It will be in vain for the philosopher to say that the Swiss of Morgarten were right, for that they beat the Austrians; but that the heroes of Rotenthurm were greatly in the wrong, because, crushed without being vanquished, they were obliged to yield to numbers, and leave at last their country's soil to be trodden by the stranger; — the children of old Switzerland will find it hard to admit this doctrine. Even in France, in that nation so accustomed to encircle its soldiers' brows with laurel, this difficulty has risen up in the way of M. Cousin. Béranger, when asked for a souvenir of Waterloo,

> Replied, with drooping eyelid, tear-bedewed:
> Never that name shall sadden verse of mine.*

But philosophy would be worth little if it had not at its disposal more extensive resources than those of a song-writer. M. Cousin therefore looked the difficulty in the face. Victory is always good. But how shall young Frenchmen be made to hear this with regard to that signal defeat of the armies of France? Listen: "It is not populations which appear on battle-fields, but ideas and causes. So at Leipzig and at Waterloo two causes came to the encounter, the cause of paternal monarchy and that of military democracy.

* Il répondit, baissant un œil humide:
Jamais ce nom n' attristera mes vers.

Which of them carried the day, Gentlemen? Neither the one nor the other. Who was the conqueror and who the conquered at Waterloo? Gentlemen, there were none conquered. (*Applause.*) No, I protest that there were none: the only conquerors were European civilization and the map. (*Unanimous and prolonged applause.*)" *

To make the youth of Paris applaud at the remembrance of Waterloo is perhaps one of the most brilliant triumphs of eloquence which the annals of history record. But this rhetorical success is not a triumph of truth. There were those who were conquered at Waterloo; and, to judge by what has been going on for some time past in Europe, it would seem that those who were conquered are bent on taking their revenge. We may infer from these facts that all triumphs are not good, since truth may be for a moment overcome by a false philosophy tricked out in the deceitful adornments of eloquence.

But let us admit, whatever our opinion on the subject, that the Waterloo rock has been passed successfully; we have not yet pointed out the main difficulty which rises up in the way of this

* *Introduction à l'histoire de la philosophie.* Treizième leçon.

system. If victory is good, it seems at first sight that defeat is bad. But defeat is the necessary condition of victory; and being the condition of good, it seems therefore that it also is good; and the mind comes logically to this conclusion: "Victory is good;—defeat is good, since it is the condition of victory;—all is good." We set out with the glorification of victory, and, lo! we are arrived at the glorification of fact. All that is, has the right to be; in the eyes of the modern savant whatever is, is right. M. Cousin laid down the principle; he laid it down in a general manner in his philosophical eclecticism, of which it was easy to make use, as has in fact been done, in a sense contrary to his real intentions. Our young critics, wasting an inheritance of which they do not appear always to recognize the origin, are doing nothing else, very often, than catching as they die away the last vibrations of that surpassing eloquence.

In the eyes of the modern savant, everything is right and good: such is the axiom for which the labors of more than one modern historian had prepared us. We are to seek for the relation of facts one to another, that is to explain; and all that we explain, we must approve. Let us follow out this thought in a few examples.

It was necessary that Louis XVI should be beheaded and the guillotine permanently set up, in order to manifest the result of the disorders of Louis XIV, of the shameful excesses of Louis XV, and of the licentious immorality of French society. It was necessary for Louis XIV to be an adulterer, Louis XV a debauchee, the clergy corrupt, and the nobility depraved, to bring about the shocks of the revolution. The facts mutually correspond; I explain, and I approve. In the eyes of the modern savant everything is right.

It was necessary that Buonaparte should throw the *Corps législatif* out of the window, that he should let loose his armies upon Europe, and leave thousands of dead bodies in the snows of Russia, in order to end the revolution, and extinguish the restless ardor of the French. It needed the massacres of September, the gloomy days of the Terror, the anarchy of the period of the Directory, to throw dismayed France into the arms of the crowned soldier who was to carry to so high a pitch her glory and her influence. The facts correspond; I explain, and I approve. In the eyes of the modern savant, everything is right.

I consider the character of Nero. I take him at the commencement of his reign, when, being forced to sign the death-warrant of a criminal, he exclaimed — "Would I were unable to write!" And then again I regard him after he has perpetrated acts such that to apply his name in future ages to the cruellest of tyrants shall appear to them a cruel injury. What has taken place in the interval? The development of his natural character, Agrippina, Narcissus . . . I understand the play of all the springs which have made a monster. As I am out of his clutches, my detestation vanishes with the danger. "I taste the very deep and very pure pleasure of seeing a mind act according to a definite law." I understand, I explain, I approve. In the eyes of the modern savant, everything is right.

It would be impossible, Gentlemen, to pursue this reasoning to its extreme limits without offending against the commonest decency. We should have to descend into blood and mire, continuing to declare the while that everything is right. I pause therefore, and leave the rest to your imaginations. Open the most dismal pages of history. Choose out the acts which inspire the most vivid horror and disgust, the blackest examples of ingratitude, the meanest instances of cowardice, the cases of most refined cruelty, and the most hideous debaucheries: thence let your thoughts pass to facts which bedew the eyelid with the tear of tenderest emotion, to the cases of most heroic self-devotion, to sacrifices the most humble in their greatness; and then try to apply the rule of the modern savant, and to say that all this is equally right and good, and that whatever is has the right to be. Open the book of your own heart. Think of one of those base temptations which assault the best of us, one of those thoughts which raise a blush in solitude; then think of the best, the purest, the most disinterested of the feelings which have ever been given to your soul; and try again to apply the rule of the modern savant, and to affirm that all this is equally good, and that all that is has the right to be. I know very well that in general these doctrines are applied to things looked at in the mass, and to the far-off past of history; but this is a poor subterfuge for the defenders of these monstrous theses. Things viewed in the mass are only the assemblage of things viewed in detail. If the distinction of good and evil do not exist for general facts, how should it exist for particular facts? And how can we apply to the past a rule which we refuse to apply to the present, seeing that the present is nothing else than the past of the future, and that the facts of our own time are matter for history to our posterity? These, I repeat, are but vain subterfuges. If humanity is always adorable, it is so in the faults of the meanest of men as in the splendid sins of the magnates of the earth; it is so to-day as it was thirty centuries ago; the god in growing old does not cease to be the same.

When the mind is engaged in these pernicious ways, the spring of the moral life is broken, and the practical consequence is not long in appearing. The philosophers of success, having become the philosophers of the *fait accompli*, accept all and endure all; but in another sense than that in which charity accepts all, that it may transform all by the power of love. It is the morality of Philinte:

> I take men quietly, and as they are:
> And what they do I train my soul to bear.*

These instructions are not very necessary. There will always be people enough found ready to applaud victory, and to fall in with the *fait*

* Je prends tout doucement les hommes comme ils sont,
J' accoutume mon âme à souffrir ce qu' ils font.

accompli. But is it not sad to see men of mind, men of heart too, perhaps, making themselves the theorists of baseness, and the philosophers of cowardice?

There is still more to be said. From the glorification of success the mind passes necessarily, as we have just seen, to the glorification alike of all that is. It would appear at first sight that the adept in the doctrine must find himself in a condition of indifference with regard to what prejudiced men continue to call good and evil. This indifference however is only apparent. When it is granted that nothing is evil, the part of good disappears in the end. There had been formed in ancient Rome, under pretence of religion, a secret society, which had as its fundamental dogma the aphorism that *nothing is evil*.* The members of the society did not practise good and evil, it appears, with equal indifference, for the magistrates of the republic took alarm, and smothered, by a free employment of death and imprisonment, a focus of murders, violations, false witness, and forged signatures. This fact reveals, with ominous clearness, a movement of thought on the nature of which it is easy to speculate.

* *Nihil nefas ducere, hanc summam inter eos religionem esse.* (Tit. Liv. lib. xxxix. c. 13.)

When man casts a vague glance over the world, extinguishing the while the inner light of conscience; when he resigns himself to the things he contemplates without applying to them any standard, what first strikes his attention, as we have said before, is success. And what next? Scandal. Nothing comes more into view than scandal. In a vast city, thousands of young men gain their livelihood laboriously, and devote themselves to the good of their families: no one speaks of them. A libertine loses other men's money at play, and blows out his brains: all the city knows it. Honest women live in retirement; the king's mistresses form the subject of general conversation. Crime and baseness hide themselves; but up to the limits of what the world calls infamy, evil delights in putting itself forward, because *éclat* and noise supply the means of deadening the conscience; while, as regards the grand instincts of charity, it has been well said that — "the obscure acts of devotedness are the most magnificent." The poor and wretched shed tears in obscurity over benefits done secretly, while folly loves to display its glittering spangles, and shakes its bells in the public squares. There is in each one of us more evil than we think; but there is in the world more good than is commonly known. There are concealed virtues which only show themselves to the eye of the faith which looks for them, and of the attention which discovers them. Bethink you, especially, how the laws of morality set at defiance appear again triumphant in the sorrows of repentance; those laws have their hour, and that hour is usually a silent one. Let a poet of genius defile his works by the impure traces of a life spent in dissipation, and his brow shall shine in the sight of all with the twofold splendor of success and of scandal. But if, stretched on a bed of pain, he renders a tardy but sincere homage to the law which he has violated, to the truth which he has ignored, his voice will often be confined to the sick chamber; his companions in debauchery and infidelity will mount guard perhaps around his dwelling, in order to prevent the public from learning that their friend is a *defaulter*. The ball and the theatre make a noise and attract observation; but men turn their eyes from hospitals, those abodes in which, in the silence of sickness, or amidst the dull cries of pain, there germinate so many seeds of immortality. Yes, Sirs, evil is more apparent than good. The violations of the divine law have more *éclat* than penitence. And what is the consequence? The man who abandons himself to the spectacle of the world, and who takes that spectacle for the rule of his thoughts, will see the world under a false aspect, and, in his estimation, evil will have more advantage over good than it has in reality. It will appear to him altogether dominant, and will thenceforward become his rule. From the glorification of success, we passed to the glorification of fact; from the glorification of fact, we arrive at last at the glorification of evil. We have seen how is illustrated the morality of victory. In the same current of ideas, a book famous now-a-days, and quite full of outrages to the conscience, supplies us with illustrations of the morality of falsehood. M. Ernest Renan, in his explanation of Christianity, has applied, point after point, the theory which I have just set forth to you. In order to estimate the grand movements of the human mind, he frees himself from the vulgar prejudices which make up the ordinary morals, and abandons himself to the impression of the spectacle which he contemplates. Jesus had a success without parallel. This success was based on charlatanism; and it is habitually so. To lead the nations by deceiving them is the lesson of history, and the good rule to follow. We find falsehood fortunate as matter of fact, we explain it, we approve it.

Whither then are we bound, under the guidance of modern science? An irresistible current is drawing us on, and causing us to leave the morals of Philinthe in our rear. We are coming to those which Racine has engraven in immortal traits in the person of Mathan. When once conscience is put aside, all means are good in order to succeed; and the experience of the world teaches us that, to succeed, the worst means are often the best.

It is not only at the theatre that such lessons are received; they come out but too commonly from the ordinary dealings of life. Set a young man face to face with the world as it exhibits itself, and tell him to give himself up to what he sees, to let himself be fashioned by life. He will soon come to know that strict probity is a virtue of the olden times, chastity a fantastic excellence, and conscientious scruples an honorable simplicity. Evil will become in his eyes the ordinary rule of life. When the socialist Proudhon wrote that celebrated sentence, "Property is robbery," there arose an immense outcry. Ought there not to arise a louder outcry around a theory which arrives by a fatal necessity at this consequence: "Evil is good"?

But do these doctrines exercise any influence for the perversion of public morals? Much; their influence is disastrous. And do the men who profess them believe them, taking the word 'believe' in its real and deep meaning? No; they often do mischief which they do not mean to do, and do not see that they do. They are intoxicated with a bad philosophy, and intoxication renders blind. It is easy to prove that these optimists, who in theory find that everything is right, are perpetually contradicting themselves in practice. Address yourselves to one of them, and say to him: "Your doctrine is big with immorality. You do not yourself believe it; and when you pretend to believe it, you lie." This man who tolerates everything will not tolerate your freedom of speech. He will get angry, and, according to the old doctrines, he will have the right to be so, for insult is an evil. Then say to him: "Here you are, it seems to me, in contradiction with your system. Everything is right; the vivacity of my speech therefore is good. All that is has the right to be; my indignation is therefore a legitimate fact, and it appears to me that yours cannot be so unless you allow (an admission which would be contrary to your system) that mine is not so." If you have to do with a sensible man, he will begin to laugh. If you have met with a blockhead, he will be more angry than ever. This contradiction comes out in every page, and in a more serious manner, in the writings of our optimists. One cannot read them with attention, without meeting incessantly with the protest of their moral nature against the despotism of a false mode of reasonig. The man is at every moment making himself heard, the man who has a heart, a conscience, a reason, and who contradicts the philosopher without being aware of it. Contradictions these, honorable to the writer, but dangerous for the reader, because they serve to invest with brilliant colors doctrines which in themselves are hideous.

No, Gentlemen, it is impossible to succeed in adoring humanity, preserving the while the least consistency of reasoning. In vain men wish to accept everything, to tolerate everything; in vain they wish to impose silence on the inner voice: that voice rebels against the outrage, and its revolt declares itself in the most manifest contradictions. The Humanity-God is divided, and the affirmation — "Everything is right" — will continue false as long as there shall be upon the earth a single conscience unsilenced, as long as there shall be in a single heart

> . . . . . . that mighty hate
> Which in pure souls vice ever must create; *

that hatred which is nothing else than the indirect manifestation of the sacred love of goodness.

The doctrine that all is equally good, equally divine, in the development of humanity, explains nothing, because humanity, torn by a profound struggle, condemns its own acts, and protests against its degradations. It cries aloud to itself that there are principles above facts, a moral law superior to the acts of the will; and all the petty clamors of a deceitful and deceived philosophy cannot stifle that clear voice. Not only do these doctrines explain nothing, they do not even succeed in expressing themselves; language fails them. "Everything is right and good." What will these words mean, from the time there is no longer any rule of right? How is it possible to

* . . . . . . Ces haines vigoureuses
Que doit donner le vice aux âmes vertueuses.

approve, when we have no power to blame? The idea of good implies the idea of evil; the opposition of good and evil supposes a standard applied to things, a law superior to fact. He who approves of everything may just as well despise everything. But contempt itself has no longer any meaning, if esteem is a word void of signification. We must say simply that all is as it is, and abandon those terms of speech which conscience has stamped with its own superscription. We must purify the dictionary, and consign to the history of obsolete expressions such terms as good, evil, esteem, contempt, vice, virtue, honor, infamy, and the like. The doctrine which, to be consistent with itself, ought to reduce us to a kind of stupid indifference, does such violence to human nature that its advocates are incapable of enunciating it without contradicting themselves by the very words they make use of.

All these extravagances are the inevitable consequence of the adoration of humanity. The Humanity-God has no rule superior to itself. Whatever it does must be put on record merely, and not judged: it is the immolation of the conscience. But on what altar shall we stretch this great victim? Shall we sacrifice it to pure reason, to reason disengaged from all prejudice? Allow me to claim your attention yet a few minutes longer.

The Humanity-God in all its acts escapes the judgment of the conscience. What measure shall we be able to apply to its thoughts? None. The God which cannot do evil, cannot be mistaken either. For the modern savant all is true, for exactly the same reason that all is right. The human mind unfolds itself in all directions; all these unfoldings are legitimate; all are to be accepted equally by a mind truly emancipated. Furnished with this rule, I make progress in the history of philosophy. The Greek Democritus affirms that the universe is only an infinite number of atoms moving as chance directs in the immensity of space: I record with veneration this unfolding of the human mind. The Greek Plato affirms that truth, beauty, good, like three eternal rays, penetrate the universe and constitute the only veritable realities: I record with equal veneration this other unfolding of the human mind. I pass to modern times. Descartes tells me that thought is the essence of man, and that reason alone is the organ of truth. Helvetius tells me that man is a mass of organized matter which receives its ideas only from the senses. These two theses are equally legitimate, and I admit them both. I quit now philosophers by profession to address myself to those literary journalists who deal out philosophy in crumbs for the use of *feuilletons* and reviews. There I find all possible notions in the most astounding of jumbles. "The villain has his apologist; the good man his calumniator. . . . Marriage is honorable, so is adultery. Order is preached up, so is riot, so is assassination, provided it be politic." * I contemplate with a calm satisfaction, with a very deep and very pure pleasure, these various unfoldings of the human mind; I place them all, with the same feelings of devotion, in the pantheon of the intelligence. I cannot do otherwise, inasmuch as there is no rule of truth superior to the thoughts of men, and because the human mind is the supreme, universal, and infallible intelligence.

But will our mind be able to entertain together two directly opposite assertions? Will contradiction no longer be the sign of error? We must come to this; we must acknowledge that the modern mind, breaking with superannuated tra-

* *Mélanges de Töpffer.* De la mauvaise presse considerée comme excellente.

ditions, has proclaimed the principle "that one assertion is not more true than an opposite assertion." We must proclaim that the thinker has not to disquiet himself "about the *real* contradictions into which he may fall; and that a true philosopher has absolutely nothing to do with consistency." * The fear of self-contradiction may be excused in Aristotle and Plato, in St. Anselm and St. Thomas, in Descartes and Leibnitz. These writers were still wrapped in the swaddling clothes of old errors; the light of the nineteenth century had not shone upon their cradles; but the epoch of enfranchisement is come. These things, Gentlemen, are printed now-a-days; they are printed at Paris, one of the metropolises of thought!

Mark well whereabouts we are. We must admit — what? that all is true. But, if all is true, there is nothing true, just as if all is good, there is nothing good. There are thoughts in men's heads; to make history of them is an agreeable pastime; but there is no truth. We must not say that two contradictory propositions are equally

* *Revue des Deux Mondes* of 15 Feb. 1861, page 854. — *Etudes critiques sur la littérature contemporaine*, par Edmond Scherer, page x. et xi.

true; that would be to make use of the old notion of truth; we must say that they are, and that is all about it. The night is approaching, the sun of intelligence is sinking towards the horizon, and thick vapors are obscuring its setting. But wait!

If the Humanity-God is always right, it must be that two contradictory propositions can be true at the same time, since contradictions abound in the history of human thoughts. If two contradictory propositions can be true, there is no more truth. What then is our reason, of which truth is the object? We are seized with giddiness. Might not everything in the world be illusion? and myself— ? Listen to a voice which reaches us, across the ages, from the countries crowned by the Himalayas. "Nothing exists. . . . By the study of first principles, one acquires this knowledge, absolute, incontestable, comprehensible to the intelligence alone: I neither am, nor does anything which is mine, nor do I myself, exist."* What is there beneath these strange

* Sa'nkya—ka'rika', 61 and 64. The text 61 in which occur the words "Nothing exists" is hard to understand, but there appears to be no doubt of the meaning of No. 64. *Non sum, non est meum, nec sum ego.*

lines? The feeling of giddiness, which seeks to steady itself by language. Here is now the modern echo of these ancient words. One of those writers who accept all, in the hope of understanding all, describes himself as having come at last to be aware that he is "only one of the most fugitive illusions in the bosom of the infinite illusion." One of his colleagues expresses himself on this subject as follows: "Is this the last word of all? — And why not? — The illusion which knows itself — is it in fact an illusion? Does it not in some sort triumph over itself? Does it not attain to *the sovereign reality*, that of the thought which thinks itself, that of the dream which knows itself a dream, that *of nothingness which ceases to be so*, in order to recognize itself and to assert itself?" * We are gone back to ancient India. You will remark here three stages of thought. The fugitive illusion is man. The infinite illusion is the universe. The universal principle of the appearances which compose the universe is nothingness. Here is the explanation of the universe! Nothingness takes life; nothingness takes life only to know itself to be nothingness; and the nothing-

* *Etudes critiques sur la littérature contemporaine*, par Edmond Scherer. — M. Sainte-Beuve, p. 354.

ness which says to itself, "I am nothingness," is the reason of existence of all that is. I said just now that the sun was declining to the horizon. Now the last glimmer of twilight has disappeared; night has closed in — a dark and starless night. Yes, Sirs, but there is never on the earth a night so dark as to warrant us in despairing of the return of the dawn. If the modern mind is such as it is described to us, it has lost all the rays of light; but the sun is not dead.

The doctrine of non-existence and of illusion is entirely incomprehensible, in the sense in which to comprehend signifies to have a clear idea, and one capable of being directly apprehended. But, if one follows the chain of ideas as logically unrolled, in the way that a mathematician follows the transformations of an algebraical formula, without considering its real contents, it is easy to account for the origin of this theory. If the human mind has no rule superior to itself, if it is the absolute mind, God, all its thoughts are equally true, since we cannot point out error without having recourse to a rule of truth. If all doctrines are equally true, propositions directly and absolutely contradictory are equally true. If all is true, there is no truth; for truth is not conceived except in opposition to at least possible error. If there is no truth, the human reason, which seeks truth by a natural impulse belonging to its very essence, as the magnetized needle seeks the pole, — reason, I say, is a chimera. The truth which reason seeks is an exact relation of human thought to the reality of the world. If the search for this relation is chimerical, the two terms, mind, and the world, may be illusions. A fugitive illusion in presence of an infinite illusion: there is all. You see that these thoughts hang together with rigorous precision. The darkness is becoming visible to us, or, in other words, we are acquiring a perfect understanding of the origin and developments of the absurdity. Put God aside, the law of our will, the warrant of our thought; deify human nature; and a fatal current will run you aground twice over — on the shores of moral absurdity, and on those of intellectual absurdity. These sad shipwrecks are set before our eyes in striking examples; it has been easy to indicate their cause.

The consideration of the beautiful would give occasion to analogous observations. The human mind becoming the object of our adoration, we must give up judging it in every particular, and suppress the rules of the ideal in art, as those of morals in the conduct, and truth in the intellect. We must form a system of æsthetics which accepts all, and finds equally legitimate whatever affords recreation to the Humanity-God, in the great variety of its tastes. Then high aspirations are extinguished, the beautiful gives place to the ageeable; and since the ugly and misshapen please a vicious taste, room must be made for the ugly in the Pantheon of beauty. Art despoiled of its crown becomes the sad, and often the ignoble slave of the tastes and caprices of the public. I do not insist further. The pretension of the worshippers of humanity is to make their conscience wide enough to accept all, and to have their intellect broad enough to understand all. They explain all, except these three small particulars — the conscience, the heart, and the reason. Goodness and truth avenge themselves in the end for the long contempt cast upon them; and the first punishment those suffer who accept all, in the hope of understanding all, is no longer to understand what constitutes the life of humanity.

Let us not, Sirs, be setting up altars to the human mind; for an adulterous incense stupefies it, and ends by destroying it. Man is great, he is sublime, with immortal hope in his heart, and the divine aureole around his brow; but that he may preserve his greatness, let us leave him in his proper place. Let us leave to him the struggles which make his glory, that condemnation of his own miseries which does him honor, the tears shed over his faults which are the most unexceptionable testimony to his dignity. Let us leave him tears, repentance, conflict, and hope; but let us not deify him; for, no sooner shall he have said, "I am God," than, deprived that instant of all his blessings, he shall find himself naked and spoiled.

Before they deified man, the pagans at least transfigured him by placing him in Olympus. At this day, it is humanity as it is upon earth that is proposed to our adoration, humanity with its profound miseries and its fearful defilements. They seek to throw a veil over the mad audacity of this attempt, by telling us of the progress which is to bring about, by little and little, the realization of our divinity. But, alas! our history is long already, and no reasonable induction justifies the vague hopes of heated imaginations. Great progress is being effected, but none which gives any promise that the profound needs of our nature can ever be satisfied in this life. Charity has appeared on the earth; but there are still poor amongst us, and it seems that there always will be. A breath of justice and humanity has penetrated social institutions; still politics have not become the domain of perfect truth and of absolute justice, and there seems small likelihood that they ever will. Industry has given birth to marvels; we devour space in these days, but we shall never go so fast that suffering and death will not succeed in overtaking us. The great sources of grief are not dried up; the song of our poets causes still the chords of sorrow to vibrate as in the days of yore. Progress is being accomplished, sure witness of a beneficent Hand which is guiding humanity in its destinies; but everything tells us that the soil of our planet will be always steeped in tears, that the atmosphere which envelops us will always resound with the vibrations of sorrow. Far as our view can stretch itself, we foresee a suffering humanity, which will not be able to find peace, joy, and hope, except in the expectation of new heavens and a new earth, wherein dwelleth righteousness.

If there be no God above humanity, no eternity

above time, no divine world higher than our present place of sojourn; if our profoundest desires are to be for ever deceived; if the cries we raise to heaven are never to be heard; if all our hope is a future in which we shall be no more; if humanity as we know it is the perfection of the universe; if all this is so, then indeed the answer to the universal enigma is illusion and falsehood. Then, before the monster of destiny which brings us into being only to destroy us, which creates in our breast the desire of happiness only to deride our miseries; in view of that starry vault which speaks to us of the infinite, while yet there is no infinite; in presence of that lying nature which adorns itself with a thousand symbols of immortality, while yet there is no immortality; in presence of all these deceptions, man may be allowed to curse the day of his birth, or to abandon himself to the intoxication of thoughtless pleasure. But, a secret instinct tells us that wretchedness is a disorder, and thoughtless pleasure a degradation. Let us have confidence in this deep utterance of our nature. Good, truth, beauty descend as rays of streaming light into the shadows of our existence; let us follow them with the eye of faith to the divine focus from whence they proceed.

All is fleeting, all is disappearing incessantly beneath our steps; but our soul is not staggered at this swift lapse of all things, only because she carries in herself the pledges of a changeless eternity. "The ephemeral spectator of an eternal spectacle, man raises for a moment his eyes to heaven, and closes them again for ever; but during the fleeting instant which is granted to him, from all points of the sky and from the bounds of the universe, sets forth from every world a consoling ray and strikes his upward gaze, announcing to him that between that measureless space and himself there exists a close relation, and that he is allied to eternity." *

And are these sublime *pressentiments* only dreams after all? Dreams! Know you not that our dreams create nothing, and that they are never anything else than confused reminiscences and fantastic combinations of the realities of our waking consciousness? What then is that mysterious waking during which we have seen the eternal, the infinite, the perfection of goodness, the fulness of joy, all those sublime images which come to haunt our spirit during the dream of life? Recollections of our origin! foreshadowings of

* Xavier de Maistre.

our destinies! While then all below is transitory, and is escaping from us in a ceaseless flight, let us abandon ourselves without fear to these instincts of the soul —

> As a bird, if it light on a sprig too slight
> The feathery freight to bear,
> Yet, conscious of wings, tosses fearless, and sings,
> Then drops — on the buoyant air.*

---

* Soyons comme l' oiseau posé pour un instant
Sur des rameaux trop frêles,
Qui sent ployer la branche et qui chante pourtant,
Sachant qu' il a des ailes. — VICTOR HUGO.

LECTURE VI.

THE CREATOR.

(At Geneva, 4th Dec. 1863. — At Lausanne, 27th Jan. 1864.)

GENTLEMEN,

Man is not a simple product of nature; in vain does he labor to degrade himself by desiring to find the explanation of his spiritual being in matter brought gradually to perfection. Man is not the summit and principle of the universe; in vain does he labor to deify himself. He is great only by reason of the divine rays which inform his heart, his conscience, and his reason. From the moment that he believes himself to be the source of light, he passes into night. When thought has risen from nature up to man, it must needs fall again, if its impetus be not strong enough to carry it on to God. These assertions do but translate the great facts of man's intellectual history. "There is no nation so barbarous," said Cicero,* "there are no men so savage as not to have some tincture of religion. Many there are who form false notions of the gods; . . . but all admit the existence of a divine power and nature. . . . Now, in any matter whatever, the consent of all nations is to be reckoned a law of nature." No discovery has diminished the value of these words of the Roman orator. In the most degraded portions of human society, there remains always some vestige of the religious sentiment. The knowledge of the Creator comes to us from the Christian tradition; but the idea, more or less vague, of a divine world is found wherever there are men.

Cicero brings forward this universal consent as a very strong proof of the existence of the gods. The supporters of atheism dispute the value of this argument. They say: "General opinion proves nothing. How many fabulous legends have been set up by the common belief into his-

* Firmissimum hoc afferri videtur, cur deos esse credamus, quod nulla gens tam fera, nemo omnium tam sit immanis, cujus mentem non imbuerit deorum opinio. Multi de diis prava sentiunt, id enim vitioso more effici solet; omnes tamen esse vim et naturam divinam arbitrantur. . . . Omni autem in re consentio omnium gentium, lex naturæ putanda est. — *Tuscul.* i. 13.

toric verities! All mankind believed for a long time that the sun revolved about the earth. Truth makes way in the world only by contradicting opinions generally received. The faith of the greater number is rather a mark of error than a sign of truth." This objection rests upon a confusion of ideas. Humanity has no testimony to render upon scientific questions, the solution of which is reserved for patient study; but humanity bears witness to its own nature. The universality of religion proves that the search after the divine is, as said the Roman orator, a law of nature. When therefore we rise from matter to man, and from man to God, we are not going in an arbitrary road, but are advancing according to the law of nature ascertained by the testimony of humanity. It needs a mind at once very daring and very frivolous not to feel the importance of this consideration.

In our days atheism is being revived. In going over in your memory the symptoms of this revival, as we have pointed them out to you, you will perceive that the direct and primitive negation of God is comparatively rare; but that what is frequently attempted is, if I may venture so to speak, to effect the subtraction of God. Any religious theory whatever is put aside as inadmissible, and with some such remarks as these : " How is it that real sciences are formed? By observation on the one hand, and by reasoning on the other. By observation, and reasoning applied to observation, we obtain the science of nature and the science of humanity. But do we wish to rise above nature and humanity? We fail of all basis of observation ; and reason works in a vacuum. There is therefore no possible way of reaching to God. Is God an object of experience? No. Can God be demonstrated *à priori* by syllogisms? No. The idea of God therefore cannot be established, as answering to a reality, either by the way of experience or by the way of reasoning ; it is a mere hypothesis. We do not, however, it is added, in our view of the matter, pretend (Heaven forbid!) to exclude the sentiment of the Divine from the soul, nor the word *God* from fine poetry. We accept religious thoughts as dreams full of charm. But is it a question of reality? then God is an hypothesis, and hypothesis has no admission into the science of realities."

These ideas place those who accept them in a position which is not without its advantages. When a man of practical mind says with a smile,

"Do you happen to believe in God?" one may reply to him, smiling in turn, "Have I said that God is a real Being?" And if a religious man asks, "Are you falling then into atheism?" one may assume an indignant tone, and say: "We have never denied God: whoever says we have is a slanderer!" So God remains, for the necessities of poetry and art. But as we cannot know either what He is, or whether He is, real life goes on in complete and entire independence of Him. The taking up of this position with regard to religion may, in certain cases, be a literary artifice. In other cases it is seriously done. There are certain natures of extreme delicacy, which, touched by the breath of modern scepticism, have lost all positive faith; but their better aspirations, and an instinctive love of purity, guard and direct them, in the absence of all belief, and they do not deny that which they believe no longer. Such a mind is in an exceptional position. Is it yours? and would you preserve it? Keep a solitary path, and do not seek to communicate your ideas to others. Contact with the public, and such an unfolding even of your own thoughts as would be required in carrying on a work of proselytism, would place you under the empire of those laws which govern the human mind in these matters. Now what are these laws? A poet has already answered for us this question:

En présence du Ciel, il faut croire ou nier.*

A famous writer expands the same thought as follows: "Doubt about things which it highly concerns us to know," says Jean-Jacques Rousseau, "is a condition which does too great violence to the human mind; nor does it long bear up against it, but in spite of itself comes to a decision one way or another, and likes better to be mistaken than to believe nothing." † Such is the law. We have met with the pretension to maintain the mind independent of God, without either denying or asserting His existence, and we have seen how completely this pretension fails in the presence of facts. The sceptic makes vain efforts to continue in a state of doubt, but the ground fails him, and he slips into negation: he affirms that humanity has been mistaken, and that God is not. But neither does this negation succeed any the more in keeping its ground; it strikes too

* *In presence of Heaven, we must believe or deny.* See Lecture III.

† *Profession de foi du vicaire Savoyard.*

violently against all the instincts of our nature. The human mind is under an imperious necessity to worship something; if God fails it, it sets itself to adore nature or humanity; atheism is transformed into idolatry. Recollect the destinies of the critical school and of the positive philosophy! Let us now examine, with serious attention, that attempt to *eliminate* God which is the starting-point in this course along which the mind is hurried so fatally.

God is not, I grant, an object of experience. I grant it at least in this sense, that God is not an object of sensible experience. The experience of God (if I may be allowed the expression), the feeling of His action upon the soul, is not a phenomenon open to the observation of all, and apart from determined spiritual conditions. In order to be sensible of the action of God, we must draw near to Him. In order to draw near to Him, we must, if not believe with firm faith in His existence, at least not deny Him. The captives of Plato's cavern can have no experience of light, so long as they heap their raillery on those who speak to them of the sun. I grant again that God cannot possibly be the object of a demonstration such as the science of geometry requires; I grant it fully, I have already said so. Every man who reasons, affirms God in one sense; and the foundation of all reasoning cannot be the conclusion of a demonstration. God therefore, in the view of science formed according to our ordinary methods, is, I grant, an hypothesis. And here, Gentlemen, allow me a passing word of explanation.

When I say that God is an hypothesis, I run the risk of exciting, in many of you, feelings of astonishment not unmixed with pain. But I must beg you to remember the nature of these lectures. We are here far from the calm retirement of the sanctuary, and from such words of solemn exhortation as flow from the lips of the religious teacher. I have introduced you to the ardent conflicts of contemporary thought, and into the midst of the clamors of the schools. The soul which is seeking to hold communion with God, and so from their fountain-head to be filled with strength and joy, has something better to do than to be listening to such discourses as these. Solitude, prayer, a calm activity pursued under the guidance of the conscience,— these are the best paths for such a soul, and the discussions in which we are now engaged are not perhaps altogether free from danger for one who has remained hitherto undisturbed in the first simplicity of his faith. But we are not masters of our own ways, and the circumstances of the present times impose upon us special duties. The barriers which separate the school and the world are everywhere thrown down. Everywhere shreds of philosophy, and very often of bad philosophy,—scattered fragments of theological science, and very often of a deplorable theological science,—are insinuating themselves into the current literature. There is not a literary review, there is scarcely a political journal, which does not speak on occasion, or without occasion, of the problems relating to our eternal interests. The most sacred beliefs are attacked every day in the organs of public opinion. At such a juncture, can men who preserve faith in their own soul remain like dumb dogs, or keep themselves shut up in the narrow limits of the schools? Assuredly not. We must descend to the common ground, and fight with equal weapons the great battles of thought. For this purpose it is necessary to make use of terms which may alarm some consciences, and to state questions which run the risk of startling sincerely religious persons. But there is no help for it, if we are to combat the adversaries on their own ground; and because it is thus only that, while we startle a few, we can prove to all that the torrent of negations is but a passing rush of waters, which, fret as they may in their channel, shall be found to have left not so much as a trace of their passage upon the Rock of Ages.

I now therefore resume my course of argument. God is neither an object of experience, nor yet of demonstration properly so called. In the view of science, as it is commonly understood, of science which follows out the chain of its deductions, without giving attention to the very foundations of all the work of the reason, — God, that chief of all realities for a believing heart, that experience of every hour, that evidence superior to all proof, God is an hypothesis. I grant it. Hence it is inferred that God has no place in science, for that hypothesis has no place in a science worthy of the name. But this I deny; and in support of this denial I proceed to show that the hypothesis which it is pretended to get quit of, is the generating principle of all human knowledge.

Whence does science proceed? Does it result from mere experience? No. What does experience teach us when quite alone? Nothing. Experience, separated from all element of reason, only reveals to us our own sensations. This, a Scotch philosopher, Hume, has proved to demonstration, — a demonstration which constitutes his glory. It is easy, without having even a smattering of philosophy, to understand quite well that science is formed by thought. Now, if we did not possess the faculty of thinking, it would not be given to us by experience. Thought does not enter by the eye or the ear. Imagine a living body not possessed of reason: its eye will reflect objects like a mirror, its tympanum will vibrate to the undulations of the air; but it will have no thoughts, and will know nothing.

Is science formed by pure reason? No. No one can say what pure reason is, for the exercise of our thought is connected indissolubly with experience. But, without pausing at this consideration, let us ask what pure reason can do, if deprived of all objects of experience? One thing only, namely, take cognizance of itself. Now the reason, in taking cognizance of itself, only creates logic, that is to say, the theory of the laws of knowledge. Some philosophers, to be sure, have undertaken to prove that reason, by dint of self-contemplation, might arrive at the knowledge of all things. They have maintained that all the secrets of the universe are contained in our thought, and that by just reasoning one may form the science of astronomy without looking at the stars, and write the history of the human race without taking the trouble to search laboriously into the annals of the past. But these attempts to *construct* facts, instead of observing them, have succeeded too ill to merit very serious attention.

Science does not proceed therefore either from pure experience or from pure reason; whence does it really come? From the encounter of experience and of reason. Man observes, and he ascertains that facts are governed according to intelligent design. He creates mathematics, and discovers that the phenomena of the heavens and the earth are ruled according to the laws of the calculus. His thought meets in the facts with traces of a thought similar to his own. If any one of you doubts this, I once more appeal to the almanac. Science, then, has birth only from a meeting of experience with reason; how is this meeting effected? The whole question of the origin of science is here. This encounter is not necessary; it does not result simply from perseverance in observation. The encounter of mind and of facts constitutes a discovery. The thought which has governed nature may remain long veiled from our mind. All at once perhaps the veil is lifted, and the thought of man meets and recognizes itself in the phenomena which it is contemplating. We encounter in this case the exercise of a special faculty, which is neither the faculty of observing nor the faculty of reasoning, but the faculty of discovering. When a man possesses it to a certain degree, we call him a man of genius. Genius, or the faculty of discovering, is the generating principle of science. Still, strange to say, this principle is scarcely pointed out by a great number of logicians. They develop at length the rules of observation and the rules of reasoning; and it seems that, in their idea, the conjunction of reason and experience is effected all alone and of necessity. I taught logic myself in this way for twenty years, until one day, thinking better upon the subject, I was obliged to say to myself (forgive me this rather trival quotation):

> Tu n' avais oublié qu' un point:
> C' était d' éclairer ta lanterne.*

---

* Thou hadst only forgotten one point,
And that was, to light thy lantern.

The meeting together of the understanding and of facts is a discovery; and discovery depends upon a faculty sung by poets, admired by mankind, and too little noticed by logicians — genius. Genius has for its characteristic a sudden illumination of the mind, a gratuitous gift and one which cannot be purchased. But let us hasten to supply a necessary explanation. Genius is a primitive fact, a gift; but the work of genius has conditions, or rather a condition — labor. Labor does not replace genius, but genius does not dispense with labor; nature only delivers up her secrets to those who observe her with long patience. Newton was asked one day how he had found out the system of the universe. He replied with a sublime *naïveté:* "By thinking continually about it." He so pointed out the condition of every great discovery; but he forgot the cause — the peculiar nature of his own intellect. It was necessary to be always pondering the motions of the stars; but it was necessary moreover to be Isaac Newton. So many had thought on the subject, as long perhaps as he, and had not made the discovery.

Labor, the condition of discoveries, should have as its effect to recognize the methods really appropriate to the nature of the inquiries, and to keep the mind well informed in existing science. In fact, every scientific discovery supposes a series of previous discoveries which have brought the mind to the point at which it is possible to see something new. For this reason it is that a discovery often presents itself to two or three minds at once, when there are found, at the same epoch, two or three minds endowed with the same power. They see all together because the onward progress of science has brought them to the same summit: this is the condition; and because they have the same power of vision: this is the cause. There is therefore a method for putting ourselves on the road to discovery, but no method for making the discovery itself. The man of genius sees where others do not see; and when he has seen, everybody sees after him. If, furnished with Gyges' ring, you could gain access to the studies of savants at the moment when a great discovery has just been made, you would see more than one of them striking his forehead and exclaiming: "Fool that I was! how could I help seeing it? it was so simple." Truth appears simple when it has been discovered.

Discovery therefore, which has labor for its condition, is the principle of the progress of science. Under what form does a discovery present itself to the mind of its author? As a supposition, or, which is the same thing, as an hypothesis. Hypothesis is the sole process by which progress in science is effected. If we supposed nothing, we should know nothing. In vain should we look at the sky and the earth to all eternity, our eye would never read the laws of astronomy in the stars of heaven, nor the laws of life upon the bark of trees or in the entrails of animals. This is true even of mathematics. The contemplation, prolonged indefinitely, of the series of numbers, or of the forms of space, would produce neither arithmetic nor geometry, if the human mind did not suppose relations between the numbers and the lines, which it can only demonstrate after it has supposed them. The conditions are very clearly seen which have prepared and made possible a fruitful supposition, but the hypothesis does not itself follow of any necessity. It appears like a flash of light passing suddenly through the mind.

The carpenter's saw opens a plank from end to end on the sole conditions of labor and time; but the discovery of truth preserves always a sudden and unforeseen character. Archimedes leaps from a bath and rushes through the streets of Syracuse, crying out, "I have found it!" Why? The flash of genius has visited him unexpectedly. Pythagoras discovers a geometrical theorem; and he offers, it is said, a sacrifice to the gods, in testimony of his gratitude. He thought therefore, according to the fine remark of Malebranche, that labor and attention are a silent prayer which we address to the Master of truth: the labor is a prayer, and the discovery is an answer granted to it.

When this wholly spontaneous character of discovery is not recognized, and when it is thought that the observation of facts naturally produces their explanation, it must needs be granted that a discovery is confirmed by the very fact that it is made. But this is by no means the case. Hypothesis does not carry on its brow, at the moment of its birth, the certain sign of its truth. A flash of light crosses the mind of the savant; but he must enter on a course, often a long course, of study, in order to know whether it is a true light, or a momentary glare. Every supposition suggested by observation must be confirmed by its agreement with the data of experience. Let us listen to a great discoverer — Kepler. He is giving an account of the discovery of one of the laws which have immortalized his name.

"After I had found the real dimensions of the orbits, thanks to the observations of Brahe and the sustained effort of a long course of labor, I at length discovered the proportion of the periodic times to the extent of these orbits. And if you would like to know the precise date of the discovery, — it was on the eighth day of March in this year 1618 that, — first of all conceived in my mind, then awkwardly essayed by calculations, rejected in consequence as false, then reproduced on the fifteenth of May with fresh energy, — it rose at last above the darkness of my understanding, so fully confirmed by my labor of seventeen years upon Brahe's observations, and by my own meditations perfectly agreeing with them, that I thought at first I was dreaming, and making some *petitio principii*; but there is no more doubt about it: it is a very certain and very exact proposition." *

All the logic of discoveries is laid down in these lines; and these lines are a testimony rendered by one of the most competent of witnesses. You see in them the conditions of a good hypoth-

* *Harmonices mundi libri quinque.*

esis: Kepler has long studied the phenomena of which he wishes to find the law; he has studied them by himself, and by means of the discoveries of his predecessor Brahe. The law has presented itself to his mind at a given moment, on the eighth of March, 1618. But he does not yet know whether it is a true light, or a deceptive gleam. He seeks the confirmation of his hypothesis; he does not find it, because he makes a mistake, and he rejects his idea as useless. The idea returns; a new course of labor confirms it; and so the hypothesis becomes a law, a certain proposition.

Such is the regular march of thought. An hypothesis has no right to be brought forward until it has passed into the condition of a law, by being duly confirmed. There are minds, however, endowed with a sort of divination, which feel as by instinct the truth of a discovery, even before it has been confirmed. It is told of Copernicus, that having discovered, or re-discovered, the true system of planetary motion, he encountered an opponent who said to him: "If your system were true, Venus would have phases like the moon; now she has none, and therefore your system is false. What have you to reply?"—"I have no reply to make," said Copernicus, (the objection was a serious one in fact); "but God will grant that the answer shall be found." * Galileo appeared, and by means of the telescope it was ascertained that Venus has phases like the moon; — the confidence of Copernicus was justified. The scientific career of M. Ampère, the illustrious natural philosopher, supplies an analogous fact. Trusting, like Copernicus, to a kind of intuition of truth, he read one day to the Academy of sciences the complete description of an experiment which he had never made. He made it subsequently, and the result answered completely to his anticipations. Genius is here raised to the second power, since it possesses at once the gift of discovery and the just presentiment of its confirmation; but these are exceptional cases, and in general we must say, with Mithridates, that—

> . . . . To be approved as true
> Such projects must be proved, and carried through.†

---

* The authenticity of this reply is disputed; M. Arago gives it in different terms; but the question is of small consequence here as one of historical criticism, my object being not to establish a fact, but to put an idea in a strong light by means of an example.

† . . . . Pour être approuvés
De semblables projets veulent être achevés.

We would encourage no one to attempt adventures so perilous, but would call to mind in a great example what is the regular march of science. Newton, after he had discovered the law which regulates the motions of the heavens, sought the confirmation of it in an immense series of calculations. A true ascetic of science, he imposed on himself a regimen as severe as that of a Trappist monk, in order that his life might be wholly concentrated upon the operations of the understanding; and it was not until after fifteen months of persistent labor that he exclaimed: "I have discovered it! My calculations have really encountered the march of the stars. Glory to God! who has permitted us to catch a glimpse of the skirts of His ways!" And astronomy, placed upon a wider and firmer basis, went forward with new energy.

It is thus that the human mind acquires knowledge. How then does hypothesis come to be made light of? How can it be seriously said that we have excluded hypothesis from the sphere of science, whereas the moment the faculty of supposing should cease to be in exercise, the march of science would be arrested; since, except a small number of principles the evidence of which is immediate, all the truths we possess are only suppositions confirmed by experiment? The reason is here: Our mind forms a thousand different suppositions at its own will and fancy; and it shrinks from that studious toil which alone puts it in a position to make fruitful suppositions. We are for ever tempted to be guessing, instead of setting ourselves, by patient observations, on the road to real discoveries. It is therefore with good reason that theories hastily built up have been condemned, and Lord Chancellor Bacon was right in thinking that the human mind requires lead to be attached to it, and not wings. Hence the inference has been drawn that the simplest plan would be to cut the wings of thought, without reflecting that thenceforward it would continue motionless. Because some had abused hypothesis, others must conclude that we could do without it altogether.

Trivial and premature suppositions have therefore discredited hypothesis, by encumbering science with a crowd of vain imaginations; but this encumbrance would have been of small importance but for the obstinacy with which false theories have too often been maintained against the evidence of facts. If Ampère had found his experiment fail, and had still continued to maintain his statements, he would not have given proof of a happy audacity, but of a ridiculous obstinacy. Genius itself makes mistakes, and experience alone distinguishes real laws from mere freaks of our thought. We have maintained the rights of reason in the spontaneous exercise of the faculty of discovery; but let us beware how we ignore the rights of experience. It alone prepares discoveries; it alone can confirm them. A system, however well put together, is convicted of error by the least fact which really contradicts it. A Greek philosopher was demonstrating by specious arguments that motion is impossible. Diogenes was one of his auditory, and he got up and began to walk: the answer was conclusive. You remember, if you have read Walter Scott, the learned demonstration of the antiquary who is settling the date of a Roman or Celtic ruin, I forget which; and the intervention of the beggar, who has no archæological system, but who has seen the edifice in question both built and fall to decay. Reason as much as you like; if your reasonings do not accord with facts, you will have woven spider's webs, of admirable fineness perhaps, but wanting in solidity.

It is time to sum up these lengthened considerations. Science does not originate solely from experiment, nor does it proceed solely from reason; it results from the meeting together of experience and reason. Experience prepares the discovery, genius makes it, experience confirms it. What distinguishes the sciences is not the process of invention, which is everywhere the same; but the process of control over supposed truths. A mathematical discovery is confirmed by pure reasoning. A physical discovery is confirmed by sensible observation joined with calculation. A discovery in the order of morals is confirmed by observation of the facts of consciousness. Therefore it is that between the physical and moral sciences there exists a broad line of demarcation. Moral facts have not less certainty than physical phenomena; but moral facts falling under the influence of liberty, all men cannot perceive them equally under all conditions. An optical experiment presents itself to the eyes, and all the spectators see it alike, if at least they have one and the same visual organization; but a case of moral experience has a personal character, and is only communicated to another person on condition that he puts faith in the testimony of his fellow. In this order of things a man can observe directly only what he concurs in producing. With this reservation, we may say that the control of moral truths is made by experience like that of physical truths. In all departments of knowledge, a thought may be held as true when it accounts for facts.

And so, Gentlemen, we conclude that every scientific truth is, in its origin, a supposition of the mind, the result of which is to produce the meeting together of experience and reason, and so to permit the rational reconstruction of the facts.

Every system is shown to be at fault by facts, if facts contradict it.

When a system explains the facts, we hold it as proved just to the extent to which it explains them. This accordance of our thought with the nature of things is the mark of what we call truth.

If you grant me these premises, my demonstration is completed, and it only remains for me to draw my conclusions.

It is said that the idea of God can have no place in a serious science, because this idea comes neither from experience nor from reason; that it is only an hypothesis, and that hypothesis has no place in science. I reply, grounding my answer on the preceding reasonings: No science is formed otherwise than by means of hypothesis. For the solution of the universal problem there exists in the world an hypothesis, proposed to all by tradition, and which bears in particular the names of Moses and of Jesus Christ. This hypothesis has the right to be examined. If it explains the facts, it must be held for true. The idea of God comes therefore within the regular compass of science; the attempt to exclude it is sophistical.

Let us separate the idea of God from the whole body of Christian doctrine of which it forms part, in order that we may give it particular consideration. What is this hypothesis which bears the names of Moses and Jesus Christ? It is that the principle of the universe is the Eternal and Infinite Being. His power is the cause of all that exists; the consciousness of His infinite power constitutes His infinite intelligence. In Himself, He is *He who is;* in His relation with the world, He is the absolute cause, the Creator. This explanation of the universe is not the privilege of a few savants; it is taught and proposed to all;

and this is no reason why we should despise it. If we further observe that this thought has renovated the world, that it upholds all our civilization, that thousands of our fellow-creatures raise their voice to tell us that it is only from this source they have drawn peace, light, and happiness, we shall understand perhaps that contempt would be foolish, and that everything on the contrary invites us to examine with the most serious attention an hypothesis which offers itself to us under conditions so exceptional.

The hypothesis is stated. We must now submit it to the test of facts. Where shall we find the elements of its confirmation? Everywhere, since it is the first cause of all things which is in question: we shall find them in nature and in humanity; in the motions of the stars as they sweep through the depths of space, and in the rising of the sap which nourishes a blade of grass; in the revolutions of empires, and in the simplest elements of the life of one individual. There is no science of God; but every science, every study must terminate at that sacred Name. I shall not undertake, therefore, to enumerate all the confirmations of the thought which makes of the Creator the principle of the universe: to recount all the proofs of the infinite Being would require an eternal discourse. We have stammered forth a few of the words of this endless discourse, by showing that, without God, the understanding, the conscience, and the heart lose their support and fall: this formed the subject of our second lecture. We saw further that reason makes fruitless attempts to find the universal principle in the objects of our experience — nature and humanity. Let us follow up, although we shall not be able to complete it, the study of this inexhaustible subject, by showing that the idea of the Creator alone answers to the demands of the philosophic reason.

Philosophy, in the highest acceptation of the term, is the search after a solution for the universal problem the terms of which may be stated as follows: Experience reveals to us that the world is composed of manifold and diverse beings; and, to come at once to the great division, there are in the world bodies which we are forced to suppose inert, and minds which we feel to be intelligent and free. The universe is made up of manifold existences; this is quite evident, and a matter of experience. Reason on the other hand forces us to seek for unity. To comprehend, is to reduce phenomena to their laws, to connect effects with their causes, consequences with their principles; it is to be always introducing unity into the diversity. All development of science would be at once arrested, if the mind could content itself with merely taking account of facts in the state of dispersion in which they are presented by experience. Each particular science gathers up a multitude of facts into a small number of formulæ; and, above and beyond particular sciences, reason searches for the connection of all things with one single cause. To determine the relation of all particular existences with one existence which is their common cause; such is the universal problem. This problem has been very well expressed by Pythagoras in a celebrated formula, that of the *Uni-multiple*. In order to understand the universe, we must rise to a unity which may account for the multiplicity of things and for their harmony, which is unity itself maintained in diversity.

If you well understand this thought, you will easily comprehend the source of the great errors which flow from too strong a disposition to systematize. Men of this mind attach themselves to inadequate conceptions, and look for unity where it does not exist. The barrier which we must oppose to this spirit of system is the careful enumeration of the facts which it forgets to notice. Materialism looks for unity in inert and unintelligent bodies; it suffices to oppose to it one fact — the reality of mind. Fatalism seeks unity in necessity. Point out to it that its destiny-god does not account for the fact of repentance, for example, which implies liberty, and it is enough. The worship of humanity forces you to exclaim with Pascal — A queer God, that! There is in the bitterness of this smile a sufficient condemnation of the doctrine. To seek for unity, is the foundation of all philosophy. To seek for unity too hastily and too low, is the source of the errors of absolute minds. Absolute minds, however great they may be in other respects, are weak minds, in that they do not succeed in preserving a clear view of the diversity of the facts to be explained. Take the problem of Pythagoras; keep hold of the two extremities of the chain; never allow yourselves to deny the diversity of things, for that diversity is plainly evidenced by human experience; beware of denying their unity, because it is the foundation of reason; then search and look through the histories of philosophy: you will find one hypothesis, and one only, which answers the requirements of the problem. It goes back, as I believe, to the origin of the world; it was glimpsed by Socrates, by Aristotle, and Plato; but, in its full light, it belongs only to men who have received the God of Moses, and who have studied in the school of Jesus Christ. If this hypothesis explains the facts, it is sound, for the property of truth is to explain, as the property of light is to enlighten.

The doctrine of the Creator can alone account to us for the universe, by bringing us back to its first cause. The first cause of unity cannot be matter which could never produce mind; the first cause of unity cannot be the human mind, which, from the moment that it desires to take itself for the absolute being, is dissolved and annihilated. The unity which alone can have in itself the source of multiplicity, is neither matter nor idea, but power; power the essential characteristic of mind, and infinite, that is to say, creative power. The Creator alone could produce divers beings, because He is Almighty, and maintain harmony between those beings, because He is One. Thus is manifested an essential agreement between the requirements of philosophy and the religious sentiment; for religion, as we said at the beginning of these lectures, rests upon the idea of Divine power. Reason and faith meet together upon the lofty heights of truth. But let us not enter too far into the difficulties of philosophy. Let us confine ourselves to considerations of a less abstruse order.

The Creator is the God of nature. All the visible universe is but the work of His power, the manifestation of His wisdom. The poet of the Hebrews invites to offer praise to the Most High, not only men of every age and of all nations, but the beasts of the field, the birds of the air, and the cedars of the forest, the rain and the wind, the hail and the tempest.* In the language of a modern poet:

> Thee, Lord, the wide world glorifies;
> The bird upon its nest replies;
> And for one little drop of rain
> Beings Thine eye doth not disdain
> Ten thousand more repeat the strain.†

And such thoughts are not vain freaks of the imagination. Man, the conscious representative of nature, the high-priest of the universe, feels

* Ps. cxlviii.

† Le monde entier te glorifie,
L' oiseau te chante sur son nid;
Et pour une goutte de pluie
Des milliers d' êtres t' ont beni.

himself urged by an impulse of his heart to translate the confused murmur of the creation into a hymn of praise to the Infinite Being, the absolute Source of life, — to Him who *is*, One, Eternal, — the first and absolute Cause of all existence.

The Creator is the God of spirits. He is not only the God of humankind; "the immense city of God contains, no doubt, nobler citizens than man, in reasoning power so weak, and in affections so poor." * But let us speak of what is known to us: He is the God of humankind. All nations shall one day render glory to Him. Mighty words have resounded through the world: "Henceforth there is no longer either Greek or barbarian or Jew; but one and the same God for all." The idols have begun to fall; the gods of the nations have been hurled from their pedestals; they have fallen, they are falling, they will fall, until the knowledge of the only and sovereign Creator shall cover the earth as the waters cover the sea.

The Creator shall one day be known of all His creatures; and in each of His creatures He will be the centre and the object of the whole soul; all

* Albert de Haller. *Lettres sur les vérités les plus importantes de la révélation.* Lettre 2.

the functions of the spiritual life lead on to Him. What is truth, beauty, good? We have already replied to the question, but we will repeat our answer.

To possess truth is to know God; it is to know Him in the work of His hands, and it is to know Him in His absolute power, as the eternal source of all that is, of all that can ever be, of all actual or possible truth in the mind of His creatures. Truth binds us to Him, "and all *science* is a hymn to His glory." *

He is the eternal source of beauty. He it is who gives to the bird its song, and to the brook its murmur. He it is who has established between nature and man those mysterious relations which give rise to noble joys. He it is who opens, above and beyond nature, the prolific sources of art; the ideal is a distant reflection of His splendor.

And goodness, again, is none other than He; it is His plan; it is His will in regard of spirits; it is the word addressed to the free creature, which says to it: Behold thy place in the universal harmony.

Thus a triple ray descends from the uncreated

* Et toute la *science* est un hymne à sa gloire.

light, and before that insufferable brightness I am dazzled and bewildered. There is no longer any distinction for me between profane and sacred; I no longer understand the difference of these terms. Wheresoever I meet with good, truth, beauty, be the man who brings them to me who he may, and come he whence he may, I feel that to despise in him that gleam, would be not only to be wanting to humanity, it would be to be wanting to my faith. If my prejudices or habits tend to shut up my heart or to narrow my mind, I hear a voice exclaiming to me: "Enlarge thy tent; lengthen thy cords; enlarge thy tent without measure. Be ye lift up, eternal gates, gates of the conscience and the heart! Let in the King of glory!" All truth, all beauty, all good is He. Where my God is, nothing is profane for me. To ignore any one of those rays would be to steal somewhat from His glory.

Oh! the happy liberty of the heart, when it rests on the Author of all good and of all truth. But if the heart is at liberty, how well is it guarded too! What is the most beautiful jewel (if we may venture to use such language) in the immortal crown of this King of glory? Powerful, He created power; free, He created liberty. And to the free creature, in the hour of its creation, He said: "Behold! thou art made in mine own image! my will is written in thy conscience; become a worker together with me, and realize the plans of my love." And that voice — I hear it within myself. Ah! I know that voice well, I know the secret attraction which, in spite of all my miseries, draws me towards that which is beautiful, pure, holy, and says to me: This is the will of thy Father. But I know other voices also which speak within me only too loudly: the voice of rebellion and of cowardice, the voice of baseness and ignominy. There is war in my soul. Enlightened by this inner spectacle, I cast my eyes once more over that world in which I have seen shining everywhere some divine rays; and I see that by a triple gate, lofty and wide, evil has entered thither, accompanied by error and deformity. Then I understand that all may become profane; I understand that there is an erring science, a corrupting art, a moral system full of immorality. But these words take for me a new meaning. There is no sacred evil, there is no profane good; there are no sacred errors and profane truths. Where God is, all is holy; where there is rebellion against God, all is evil. And so the God who is my light is my fortress also; my heart is strengthened while it is set at liberty, and I can join the ancient song of Israel:

Jehovah is our strength and tower.

Yes, Sirs, God is in all, because He is the universal principle of being; but He is not in all after the same manner. God is in the pure heart by the joy which He gives to it; He is in the frivolous heart by the void and the vexation which urge it to seek a better destiny; He is in the corrupt heart by that merciful remorse which does not permit it to wander, without warning, from the springs of life. God makes use of all for the good of His creatures. He is everywhere by the direct manifestation of His will, except in the acts of rebellious liberty, and in the shadow of pain which follows that evil light which leads astray from Him.

Having said that the idea of God the Creator alone satisfies the reason, and raises up, upon the basis of reason, man's conscience and heart, I should wish to show you, in conclusion, that this idea renders an account of the great systems of error which divide the human mind between them. Truth bears this lofty mark, that it never overthrows a doctrine without causing any portion of truth which it may have contained to pass into its own bosom.

What then, — apart from declared atheism, from the dualism which has almost disappeared, and from faith in God the Creator, — are the great systems which share the human mind between them? There are two: deism and pantheism.

What is deism? It is a doctrine which acknowledges that there is one God, the cause of the universe; but a God who is in a manner withdrawn from His own work, and who leaves it to go on alone. God has regulated things in the mass, but not in detail, or, to employ an expression of Jean-Jacques Rousseau (who came at a later period to entertain better opinions), "God is like a king who governs his kingdom, but who does not trouble himself to ascertain whether all the taverns in it are good ones." The idea of a general government of God which does not descend to details — such is the essence of deism.

What is pantheism, in the ordinary meaning of the word? We have already said: it is a doctrine which absorbs God in the universe, which confounds Him with nature, and makes of Him only the inert substance, the unconscious principle of the universe. These are the two great conceptions which wrestle, in the history of human thought, against the idea of the Creator. These two systems triumph easily one over the other, because each of them contains a portion of truth which is wanting to its antagonist. They cannot support themselves because each of them has in it a portion of error. This is what we must well understand.

Deism contains a portion of truth; for it maintains a Creator essentially distinct from the Creation, or, according to an expression which I translate from an ancient Indian poem: "One single act of His created the Universe, and He remained Himself whole and entire." This thought is true. What is the error of deism? It is that it makes a God like to a man who works upon matter existing previously to his action, and who puts in operation forces independent of himself, and which he does nothing but employ. In this way a watchmaker makes a watch which goes afterwards without him, because the watchmaker only sets to work forces which have an independent existence, and which continue to act when he has ceased his labor. We work upon matter foreign to us. The workman did not make matter, but only disposes of it, and he can never do more than modify the action of forces which do not proceed from his will, and have not been regulated by his understanding. But the Being who is the cause of all cannot dispose of foreign forces which act afterwards by themselves, since there exists in His work no principle of action other than those which He has Himself placed in it.

Deism results therefore from a confusion between the work of a creature placed in a preexisting world, and the work of the Supreme Will which is in itself the single and absolute cause of all. It contains an element of dualism: its God does not create; but organizes a world the being of which does not depend on him. Take what is true in deism — the existence of the only God; remember that the Creator is the absolute Cause of the universe; and the distinction between *ensemble* and detail will vanish, and you will understand that God is too great that there should be anything small in His eyes:

> God measures not our lot by line and square:
> The grass-suspended drop of morning dew
> Reflects a firmament as vast and fair
> As Ocean from his boundless field of blue.*

---

* Dieu ne mesure pas nos sorts à l'étendue.
La goutte de rosée à l' herbe suspendue
Y réfléchit un ciel aussi vaste, aussi pur
Que l' immense Océan dans ses plaines d' azur.

LAMARTINE.

In other words, take what is true in deism, and accept all the consequences of it, and you will arrive at the full doctrine of the creation.

Pantheism recognizes the omnipresence of God in the universe, or, if you like the terms of the school, the immanence of God; this is its portion of truth. When I open the Hindoos' songs of adoration, and find therein the unlimited enumeration of the manifestations of God in nature, I find nothing to complain of. But when, in those same hymns, I see liberty denied, the origin of evil attributed to the Holy One, and man cowering before Destiny, instead of turning his eyes freely towards the Heavenly Father, then I stand only more erect and say: You forget that if your God is the Cause of all, He is the Cause of liberty. If liberty exists, evil, the revolt of liberty, is not the work of the Creator. Your system contradicts itself. You make of God the universal Principle, and you are right; make of Him then the Author of free wills, so that He will be no longer the source of evil, and we shall be agreed.

Deism and pantheism therefore, pushed to their legitimate consequences, are transformed and united in the truth. And you see plainly that I am not making, for my part, an arbitrary selection in these systems. I am walking by one sole light, the light which has been given to us, and which serves me everywhere as a guiding clue:—The Lord is God, and there is no other God but He.

Such, Gentlemen, is the fundamental truth on which rests all religion, and all philosophy capable of accounting for facts. Such is the grand cause which claims all the efforts which we are wasting too often in barren conflicts—the cause of God. But do I say the truth? Is it the cause of God which is at stake? When a surgeon, by a successful operation, has restored sight to a blind man, we are not wont to say that he has rendered a service to the sun. This cause is our own; it is that of society at large, it is that of families, that of individuals; it is the cause which concerns our dignity, our happiness; it is the cause of all, even of those who attack it in words of which they do not calculate the import, and who, were they to succeed in banishing God from the public conscience, would, with us, recoil in terror at sight of the frightful abysses into which we all should fall together.

It is time to sum up these considerations.

Inert and unintelligent matter is not the cause of life and intelligence.

Human consciences would be plunged in irremediable misery, if ever they could be persuaded that there is nothing superior to man.

The universe is the work of wisdom and of power; it is the creation of the Infinite Mind. What can still be wanting to our hearts? The thought that God desires our good, — that He loves us. If it is so, we shall be able to understand that our cause is His, that He is not an impassible sun whose rays fall on us with indifference, but a Father who is moved at our sorrows, and who would have us find joy and peace in Him. This will be the subject of our next and concluding lecture.

LECTURE VII.

THE FATHER.

(At Geneva, 8th Dec. 1863. — At Lausanne, 1st Feb. 1864.)

GENTLEMEN,

We have proposed for solution the problem which includes all others whatsoever — the problem of the universe. What are the laws which govern the universe? They are those which are the objects of science, taking that word in its largest and most general meaning. What is the cause of the universe? The eternal power of the Infinite Mind. These are the two answers which we have hitherto obtained, but, as we have explained, a study is not complete if it confine itself to these two answers. When we know the law and the cause of an object submitted to our study, we further look for the end designed. This is no freak of our fancy, but the direct result of the constitution of our understanding. The universe is the creation of God. What is the design of the creation? I answer: the design of the creation is the happiness of spirits. Nature is made for the spiritual beings to which it offers the condition of their life and development; spiritual beings are made for felicity. The moving spring of infinite power is goodness: this is my thesis. If I succeed in establishing it, it will follow that we shall in imagination see issuing from the supreme unity of the Infinite Being three rays: the power which creates the being of things; the intelligence which orders them; and the love which conducts them to their destination. It will also follow that I shall have justified the title under which these Lectures were announced: Power and wisdom are attributes of the Creator; the Father reveals Himself in goodness.

What shall be our method? Can we enter into the counsels of God? By what means? To place our understanding in the midst of the Divine consciousness, there to behold the spring of the determinations of the Infinite Being, were an attempt so far exceeding our capacity, that it is impossible to point out any means whatever by which it could be made. This would be to conceive of God in His eternal essence, independently of His relation to the universe, to nature, and to our reason. I do not say merely that the attempt would be fruitless; I say that we have no means of attempting this metaphysical adventure. But might we not, in looking at the work of God, discern in it the evidence of its design? This is a process which we often follow in regard to our fellow-creatures. Do we wish to know the object which a man has in view in his labor? He may himself disclose that object to us directly in words, or we may endeavor to discover it. We watch him at work, and by observing the way in which he proceeds we sometimes come to know what his thoughts are, because we find ourselves in presence of the work of a mind, and we ourselves are mind. Can we in the same way, by looking at the universe, that grand work, succeed in discovering its end?

The way on which we are entering raises two objections, which proceed from the difficulties felt by two classes of men of opposite views; and our first business will be to rid ourselves of these preliminary difficulties.

You will never succeed, it has been said to me, in proving the goodness of God, because evil is in the world. I am not inventing, Gentlemen. A letter containing this challenge has been addressed to me by one of you. It is manifest, since we propose to ourselves to recognize in the work the intention of the Worker, and since our thesis is the goodness of the First Cause of the universe, that evil, in all its forms, sin, pain, imperfection, is the main objection which can be addressed to us. Evil is real; it is a sad and great reality; I am forward to acknowledge it. Any system which would prove that evil does not exist, or, which comes to the same thing, that evil is necessary, that good and evil in short are of the same nature, is an impossible, I had almost said a culpable, system. The strongest minds have worn themselves out in such attempts with no result whatever. The great Leibnitz attempted an enterprise of this nature. His system consisted in extenuating evil as far as possible, and in pronouncing that amount of evil, of which he could not dissemble the existence, to be necessary. He failed. The strong intellectual armor of one of the greatest geniuses the world has ever seen was completely transpierced by the sharp and brilliant shaft of Voltaire.

> Sad reckoners of the woes which men endure,
> Sharpening the pangs ye make pretence to cure,
> Poor comforters! in your attempts I see
> Nought but the pride which feigns unreal glee!
> O mortals, of such bliss how weak the spell!

Ye cry in doleful accents — "All is well!"—
And all things at the great deceit rebel.
Nay, if your minds to coin the flattery dare,
Your hearts as often lay the falsehood bare.
The gloomy truth admits of no disguise—
Evil is on the earth! *

For once, Gentlemen, we will not contradict our old neighbor of Ferney. Yes, evil is on the earth; and it constitutes, in the question which we are discussing, the greatest of problems, the most serious of difficulties. Let us listen to a modern poet:

Why then so great, O Sovereign Lord,
 Came evil from thy forming hand,
 That Reason, yea, and Virtue stand
Aghast before the sight abhorred?

And how can deeds so hideous glare
 Beneath the beams of holy light,
 That on the lips of hapless wight
Dies at their view the trembling prayer?

Why do the many parts agree
 So scantly in thy work sublime?

---

* Tristes calculateurs des misères humaines,
Ne me consolez point, vous aigrissez mes peines;
Et je ne vois en vous que l' effort impuissant
D' un fier infortuné qui feint d' être content.
Quel bonheur, O mortels, et faible et misérable.
Vous criez: "Tout est bien" d' une voix lamentable;
L' univers vous dément, et votre propre cœur
Cent fois de votre esprit a réfuté l' erreur.
Il le faut avouer, le mal est sur la terre.

DÉSASTRE DE LISBONNE.

And what is pestilence, or crime,
Or death, O righteous God, to Thee? *

We have only to put this poetry into common prose to obtain this argument, namely, — The presence of evil in the world is not compatible with the idea of the goodness of God. Here is the objection in all its force. And what is the answer? Simply this, that God did not create evil. It was not He who brought crime into the world. He created liberty, which is a good, and evil is the produce of created liberty in rebellion against the law of its being. I borrow from Jean-Jacques Rousseau the development of this thought. "If man," says he, "is a free agent, then he acts of himself; whatever he does freely

* Pourquoi donc, O Maître suprême,
As-tu créé le mal si grand
Que la raison, la vertu même
S' épouvantent en le voyant?

Comment, sous la sainte lumière,
Voit-on des actes si hideux,
Qu' ils font expirer la prière
Sur les lèvres du malheureux?

Pourquoi, dans ton œuvre céleste,
Tant d' él ments si peu d' accord?
A quoi bon le crime et la peste,
O Dieu juste! pourquoi la mort?

ALFRED DE MUSSET, *Espoir en Dieu.*

enters not into the ordained system of Providence, and cannot be imputed to it. The Creator does not will the evil which man does, in abusing the liberty which He gives him. He has made him free in order that he may do not evil but good by choice. To murmur because God does not hinder him from doing evil, is to murmur because He made him of an excellent nature, attached to his actions the moral character which ennobles them, and gave him a right to virtue. What! in order to prevent man from being wicked, must he needs be confined to instinct and made a mere brute? No; God of my soul, never will I reproach Thee with having made it in Thine image, in order that I might be free, good, and happy, like Thyself.

"It is the abuse of our faculties which renders us unhappy and wicked. Our vexations and our cares come to us from ourselves."

Such is Rousseau's answer to the objection drawn from the existence of evil. It is a good one. It is so good that it is impossible to find a better. If we are determined not to outrage the human conscience by denying the reality of evil; if God is the sovereign good, and if there is no other principle of things than He; evil cannot be accounted for otherwise than by the rebellion of the creature. But now, Rousseau's answer, excellent in itself and in the abstract, becomes profoundly inadequate, as the citizen of Geneva goes on to develop his theory. Evil comes from the creature; but each individual is not the exclusive source of the evils which he does and suffers. To attribute to each individual, not only the responsibility of his acts, but the origin of the evil germs which exist in his soul, is the untenable proposition of a desperate individualism. There is evidently among men a common property in evil; Rousseau sees it clearly enough, but he makes vain efforts to find in the organization of society and in the condition of civilization the causes of pain and of sin. When one has come to see clearly that the source of evil is in the creature, the close mutual connection of created wills and their relations with nature present a field for long and difficult study; and Rousseau has no sooner discerned the road to truth than he wanders away into byroads in which the solution of the problem escapes him. This problem, Gentlemen, I have the intention and desire of studying some day, if God permit, with those of you who may be willing to undertake it with me.

We shall then have to deal with an objection, or rather with a difficulty. But this difficulty, which we cannot now dispose of, must not hinder us from stating our thesis. In every well-conducted study, the propositions to be maintained must be laid down and supported before dealing with objections. If it were maintained that evil is the principle of things, it would be necessary first of all to endeavor to establish the thesis, in which the existence of good would be brought forward, and would constitute the objection. The objection would have to be answered — Why has good appeared in the world? And I would just say in passing, that our libraries are full of treatises upon the origin of evil, and I have never met with one upon the origin of good. It appears therefore that reason has always admitted, by a sort of instinct, the identity of good, and of the principle of being. Our thesis is that the principle of the universe is good. We are going to try to demonstrate it. Afterwards the difficulty, evil, will present itself, of which it will be necessary to seek the explanation. This will be the natural sequel, and the necessary complement of the course of lectures which we are concluding to-day.

I pass to another difficulty, another challenge which also has been addressed to me.

Your object, Christians have said to me, is to establish that the principle and ground of all things is goodness. This you will not be able to do without departing from your prescribed plan, and entering upon the domain of Christian faith properly so called. In your examination of the universe will you leave out of view Jesus Christ and His work? Do you not know that it is by means of this work that the idea of the love of God has been implanted in the world, and that it is thence you have taken it? Do you think to climb to the loftiest heights of thought, and to make the ascent by some other road than over the mountain of Nazareth and the hill of Calvary?

Gentlemen, I declared my whole mind on this subject at first starting. The complete idea of God demands, for its maintenance, the grand doctrinal foundations of our faith. Christian in its origin, firm faith in the love of God the Creator requires for its defence the armor of the Gospel. But before defending this belief, we must first establish it; we must show that it has natural roots in human nature. Christianity purifies and strengthens it, but it does not in an absolute sense create it. The mark of truth is that it does not strike us as something absolutely new, but that it finds an echo in the depths of our soul. When we meet with it, we seem to re-enter into the possession of our patrimony. The Cross of Jesus Christ is without all contradiction the most transcendent proof of the mercy of the Creator; but the Cross of Jesus Christ rather warrants the Christian in believing in the Divine love than gives him the idea of it. We must distinguish in the Gospel between the universal religion which it has restored, and the act itself of that restoration, which constitutes the Gospel in the special sense of the word. Now what I am here maintaining is the fact of the existence in modern society of the elements of the universal religion. I am far from sharing in the illusions of my fellow-countryman Rousseau, when he affirms that even if he had lived in a desert isle, and had never known a fellow-man, he would nevertheless have been able to write the *Profession de foi du Vicaire Savoyard*. I know very well that if I were a Brahmin, born at the foot of the Himalayas, or a Chinese mandarin, I should not be able to say all that I am saying respecting the goodness of God. The light which we have received — I know whence it radiates; but, by the help of that light, I seek its kindred rays everywhere, and everywhere I find them in humanity.

Let us endeavor, then, according to our plan, to recognize in the universe the marks of the Divine goodness. Let us first of all interrogate the human soul, which is certainly one of the essential elements of the world; and let us interrogate it with regard to the great fact of religion.

The universal religion presents to observation two principal forms of mental experience: the sense of the necessity for appeasing the Divine justice, and the sense of the necessity for obtaining the help of God.

The sense of the necessity for appeasing justice reveals itself in sacrifices. There are sacrifices which are merely offerings of gratitude, and free-will gifts of love. But when you see the blood of animals flowing in the temples, and not seldom human blood gushing forth upon the altars, you will be unable to escape the conviction that man, in presenting himself before the Deity, feels constrained to appease a justice which threatens him.

The sense of the need of help shows itself in prayer; and this must be the especial object of our study, because it is in the fact of religious invocation that we shall encounter the idea, obscure perhaps, but real, of the goodness of the First Cause of the universe.

Prayer is a fact of the universal religion. Whence is it that we derive a large part of what knowledge we have of the ancient civilizations of India and Egypt? From ruins: and the chief of these ruins are the ruins of temples, that is to say, of houses of prayer. Would we go further back than these monuments of stone? I interrogate those pioneers of science who are searching for the traces of antiquity in old languages, — in the ruins of speech. I inquire, for example, of my learned fellow-countryman, M. Adolphe Pictet: "You who have studied, with patient care, the first origins of our race — what have you discovered in the way of religion?" He replies: "When I have gone as far back as historical speculations can carry us by the aid of language, it appears to me that I no longer see temples built by the hand of man, but, beneath the open vault of heaven, I see our earliest ancestors sending up together the chant of prayer and the flame of sacrifice." *

And now, from this remote antiquity, I come

* *Les origines indo-européennes, ou les Aryas primitifs.* — The above is a *résumé*, not a verbatim quotation.

down to the paganism, in which modern civilization had its beginning. Tertullian teaches us that the pagans, seeming to forget their idols, and to offer a spontaneous testimony to the truth, were often wont to exclaim — Great God! Good God! What in their mind was the order of these two thoughts, the thought of greatness and that of goodness? The pediment of a temple at Rome bore this famous inscription, *Deo optimo maximo;* and Cicero explains to us that the God of the Capitol was by the Roman people named "very good" on account of the benefits conferred by him, and "very great" on account of his power.* It is the idea of goodness which here appears to be first. But let us go more directly to the root of the question: What do we gather from the universality of prayer? What is it to pray? To pray is to ask. Prayer may be mingled with thanksgivings, and with expressions of adoration, but in itself prayer is a petition. This petition rises to God: and when does it so rise? In distress, in anguish. It is misery, weakness, the heart cast down, the failing will, which unite to raise from

* Quocirca te, Capitoline, quem propter beneficia populus Romanus OPTIMUM, propter vim MAXIMUM nominavit. (*Pro domo sua*, LVII.)

earth to heaven that long cry which resounds across all the pages of history: Help! — I analyze this fact, and inquire what it means. A request is made, and for what? For strength, for tranquillity, for peace; for happiness under all its forms. And of whom is happiness asked? Of goodness. Justice is appeased, power is dreaded, but it is goodness which is invoked. It is so in human relations. The man who supplicates the fiercest tyrant only does so because he supposes that a fibre of goodness may still vibrate in that savage heart. Take from him that thought; persuade him that the last gleam of pity is extinct in the heart to which he appeals, and you will arrest the prayer on the lips of the suppliant. There will remain for him only the silence of despair, or the heroism of resignation.

To sum up: — Religion is a universal fact. "There is no religion without prayer," said Voltaire, and he never said better. There is no prayer without a confused, perhaps, but real, conviction of the goodness of the First Cause of the universe. If you could stifle in man's heart the feeling that the Principle of things is good, you would silence over the whole globe that voice of prayer which is ever rising to God. Thus humanity itself testifies to the truth for which I am contending. Humanity prays; it believes therefore in the goodness of God. This fact is an argument. The heart of man is organized to believe that God is good: it is the mark set by the Worker Himself upon His work.

Let us study now another of the elements of the universe. We have heard the answer of man's heart; let us ask for the answer of reason. Has reason nothing to tell us respecting the intentions of the Creator? Let us place it in presence of the idea of God — of the Infinite Being, and see what it will be able to teach us.

To attain my object, I must explain more particularly than as yet I have done, a word rendered frivolous by the levity of our heart, a word defiled by the disorder of our passions, and too often by the unworthiness, and worse, of poets and novelists, but which still, in its virgin purity, is ever protesting against the outrages to which it has been subjected: that word is *love*.

This word has two principal meanings. In the Platonic sense of it, it is the search after what is beautiful, great, noble, pure, — after what, as being of the very real nature of the soul, attracts, fills, and delights it. But there is another sort of love, which does not pursue greatness and beauty, but which gives itself; a love which seeks the wretched to enrich him, the poor to make him happy, the fallen to raise him up. These two kinds of love seem to follow different and even contrary laws. Here, for instance, is a description of what often occurs in a large city.* A man leaves his house in the evening in order to be present at performances in which I am willing to believe that everything bears the stamp of nobleness and grandeur, or at least of a pure and wholesome taste. He experiences keen enjoyment, and that of an elevated kind. The spectacle over, he returns to his dwelling, and at a still later hour he retires at length to his repose. He has not long extinguished his luxurious tapers, perhaps, when other men, who have slept while others were seeking amusement, rise before daylight, and, lighting their small lanterns, go forth to succor the unfortunate, without witnesses and without ostentation.

I have taken this example from Xavier de Maistre. Let me give you another from scenes more familiar to ourselves. You know those pure

* See the *Voyage autour de ma chambre* of Xavier de Maistre.

summer mornings, when one may truly say that the Alp smiles and that the mountain invites. A young man quits his dwelling at the first dawning of the day, in his hand the tourist's staff, and his countenance beaming with joy. He starts on a mountain excursion. All day long he quaffs the pure air with delight, revels in the freedom of the pasture-grounds, in the view of the lofty summits and of the distant horizons. He reposes in the shade of the forest, drinks at the spring from the rock, and when he has gazed on the Alpine chain resplendent in the radiance of the setting sun, he lingers still to see —

Twilight its farewell to the hills delaying.*

Noble enjoyments! This young man enjoys because he loves. The spectacle of the creation speaks to his heart and elevates his thoughts. He loves that enchanting nature, which blends in a marvellous union the impressions which in human relations are produced by the strong man's majesty and the maiden's sweetest smile.

On this same summer-day, another man has also risen before the sun. He is devoted to the assuaging of human miseries, and he has had

* *Le crépuscule aux monts prolonger ses adieux.*

much to do. He has mounted gloomy staircases; he has entered dark chambers; he has spent time in hospitals, in the midst of the pains of sickness; he has come, in prisons, to the relief of pains which are sadder still. Day, as it dawned, gilded the summits of the Alps, but he saw not that pure light of the morning. Day, as it advanced, penetrated into the valleys, but he did not notice its progress. The sun set in his glory, but he had no opportunity to admire either the bright reflection of the waters, or the rosy tint of the mountains. And yet he too is joyful because he loves. He loves the fulfilment of stern duty, he loves poverty solaced, and suffering alleviated.

Here are the two kinds of love. The disciple of Plato rises, far from the vulgarities of life, into the lofty regions of the ideal, and feeds on beauty. Vincent de Paul takes the place of a convict at the galleys that he may restore a father to his children. These two kinds of love seem to us to be contrary one to the other: the one seeks itself, and the other gives itself. Still they are both necessary to life, for in order to give we must receive. In the accomplishment of the works of goodness, the soul would be impoverished and would end by drying up in a purely mechanical exercise of beneficence, had it no spring from which to draw forth the living waters. Man must himself find joy in order to diffuse it amongst his fellows. But mark the incomparable marvel of the spiritual order of things! The love which gives itself is able to find its worthiest object and its purest satisfaction in the very act of kindness. There is joy in self-devotion; there is happiness in self-sacrifice: the fountain furnishes its own supplies. Thus are harmonized the two contrary tendencies of the heart of man. "It is more blessed to give than to receive;" words these, of Jesus Christ, which, forgotten by the Evangelists, have been recorded by the Apostle St. Paul. And since the thought is a beautiful one, it has adorned the strains of the poets: says Lamartine —

Dost thou happiness resign
To another? It is thine —
Larger for the largess — still! *

And Victor Hugo, personifying Charity, makes her speak as follows:

---

* Tout le bonheur tu cèdes
Accroît ta félicité.

Dear to every man that lives,
Joy I bring to him who gives,
Joy I leave with him who takes.*

And because this thought is profound as well as beautiful, it has been taken up by the philosophers. "To love," said Leibnitz, "is to place one's happiness in the happiness of another." Here is the connecting link between Platonic love and the love which is charity. Hear how a Christian orator comments upon these words: — "This sublime definition has no need of explanations: it is either understood at once, or it is not understood. The man who has loved understands it; and he who has not loved will never understand it. He who has loved knows that a shadow in the heart of the beloved one would darken his own: he knows that he would reckon no means too costly — watchings, labors, privations — by which to create a smile on the lips of the sorrowful; he knows that he would die to redeem a for-

* Chère à tout homme quel qu' il soit,
J' apporte la joie à qui donne
Et je la laisse à qui reçoit.

And Shakspeare —

" . . . . Mercy . . . is twice bless'd,
It blesseth him that gives, and him that takes."
Merchant of Venice. — [TR.]

feited life; he knows that he would be happy in another's welfare, happy in his graces, happy in his virtues, happy in his glory, happy in his happiness. The man who has loved knows all this; he who has not loved knows nothing of it: — I pity him!" *

But the great mistake, which seems peculiar to our nature, is that we are ever connecting happiness with the idea of receiving, and are always thinking of giving as of a loss to ourselves. We do not understand that selfishly to keep is to be impoverished, while freely to relinquish is to be enriched. Yet here is the grand discovery of the spiritual life; and once this discovery made, in order that the spiritual life may attain its object, it only remains to find the strength to put it into practice. Selfishness is wrong, no doubt, but it is not only wrong, it is ignorant, for it looks for happiness where it is not; and it is unhappy, for it wanders from the paths of peace.

Let us now apply these considerations to the Infinite Being, and to the problem of the end of the creation. Leaving ourselves to the guidance of the laws of our reason, let us ask what object we shall be able to attribute to the Creator in His

* Lacordaire. *Conférences de* 1848.

work? Will creation be the effect of a necessity? No, Sirs, for in that case everything in the world would be a matter of fate, and liberty would remain inexplicable. If a blind power were directing the Almighty Will, we should return to the worship of destiny. Will creation, then, be the carrying out of a design of which the motive is interest? But what conceivable interest can influence Him who is the plentitude of being? Or will creation be a duty? But whence should come the obligation for the Being who is in Himself the absolute law? Creation can only be conceived of as a work of love. But of what love? Of that which is the manifestation of absolute disinterestedness, of supreme liberty. Allow me to introduce into this discussion some eloquent words, uttered in the year 1848, in the midst of the revolutionary agitations of Paris. The problem which we are debating was treated then, in the presence of an excited crowd, by Père Lacordaire.* He is entering upon this question: What can have been the motive of the creation? And he distinguishes between love in the Platonic sense of it, for which he retains the name of love, and the love which gives itself, which he desig-

* *Conférences de* 1848, p. 78.

nates by the term—goodness. "Was it then love," he asks, "which impelled the Divine Will, and said to it unceasingly: Go and create? Is it love which we must thus regard as our first father? But, alas! love itself has a cause in the beauty of its object; and what beauty could that dead and icy shade possess before God, which preceded the universe, and to which we cannot give a name without betraying the truth? . . . . There remained something, Sirs, be very sure, more generous than self-interest, more elevated than duty, more powerful than love. Search your own hearts, and if you find it hard to understand me, if your own endowments are unknown to you, listen to Bossuet speaking of you:—'When God,' says he, 'made the heart of man, the first thing He planted there was goodness:' goodness; that is to say, that virtue which does not consult self-interest, which does not wait for the commands of duty, which needs not to be solicited by the attraction of the beautiful, but which stoops towards its object all the more, as it is poorer, more miserable, more abandoned, more worthy of contempt! It is true, Sirs, it is true: man possesses that adorable faculty. It is not genius, nor glory, nor love, which measures the elevation of his soul,—it is goodness.

This it is which gives to the human countenance its principal and most powerful charm; this it is which draws us together; this it is which brings into communication the good and the evil, and which is everywhere, from heaven to earth, the great mediating principle. See, at the foot of the Alps, yon miserable *crétin*, which, eyeless, smileless, tearless, is not even conscious of its own degradation, and which looks like an effort of nature to insult itself in the dishonor of the greatest of its own productions: but beware how you imagine that that wretched object has not found the road to any heart, or that his debasement has deprived him of the love of all the world. No: he is beloved; he has a mother, he has brothers and sisters; he has a place at the cottage-hearth; he has the best place and the most sacred of all, just because of all he may seem to have the least claim to any. The bosom which nursed him supports him still, and the superstition of love never speaks of him but as of a blessing sent of God. Such is man!

"But can I say, Such is man, without saying also, Such is God! From whom would man derive goodness, if God were not the primordial Ocean of goodness, and if, when He formed our heart, He had not first of all poured into it a drop from His own? Yes, God is good; yes, goodness is the attribute which includes in it all the rest; and it is not without reason that antiquity engraved on the pediment of its temples that famous inscription, in which goodness preceded greatness."

Now, to say nothing of the sparkling beauty of these words, let us pause at this definite idea: The Eternal, the first universal Cause of all things, independently of which nothing exists, could only create under the impelling motive of the goodness which gives, and not of the love which seeks requital. This proposition is as clear in the abstract as any theorem of geometry. But we have touched the threshold of the infinite; and we never touch the threshold of the infinite without falling into some degree of bewilderment. Clear as this thought is in the abstract, if we wish to analyze it in its real substance, our view is confused. You understand well that goodness increases in the proportion in which its object is diminished. We are by so much more good as we stoop to that which is poorer and more miserable. What then shall be the infinite goodness? In order to find it, we must infinitely diminish its object: and here we encounter mystery. To diminish an object infinitely is an operation impossible to our thought. This mystery is encountered even in the mathematical sciences. We take a quantity, halve it, and again halve this half, and so on without end, but we shall never obtain the infinity of smallness; for the quantity indefinitely divided will always remain indefinitely divisible. At whatever degree of division we may have arrived, between what remains and nothingness there extends always the abyss of the infinite. So I seek for the object of infinite goodness: that object must be infinitely destitute. I diminish accordingly the existence of the universe: I extinguish all the rays of its beauty; I take from it order, life, measure, color, light; I reduce it until it is nothing but formless matter, a something — I know not what — which has no longer a name. Vain attempt! This nameless something, so long as it is anything, will not be *nothing*. Between it and nothing there will always be the infinite. If the goodness of God is applied to any object which was existing independently of Him, however poor and abject that object be conceived to have been, then God is no longer the unique, the absolute Creator. If imagination will cross the abyss, we shall come of necessity to say —

what? that the object of infinite love must have been non-existence. This is what the orator already quoted has done:—"All perfection supposes an object to which to apply itself. The divine goodness therefore requires an object as vast and profound as itself. God discovered it. From the bosom of His own fulness He saw that being without beauty, without form, without life, without name, that being without being which we call non-existence: He heard the cry of worlds which were not, the cry of a measureless destitution calling to a measureless goodness. Eternity was troubled, she said to Time: Begin!"

This, Gentlemen, is eloquence. The thought in itself does not bear a rigorous analysis; but do not think that the lustrous beauty of the language is only a brilliant veil to what in itself is absurd. We have arrived at darkness, but it is at darkness visible; the cloud is lighted up by the ray that issues from it. Our goodness, finite creatures as we are, is so much the greater as the object on which it is bestowed is less. Infinite goodness must create for itself an object. It does not love nothingness, but a creature which is nothing in itself, a creature simply possible, which, before owing to it the blessings of existence, shall owe to it that existence itself. The only being that we can represent to ourselves, by a sublime image, as stooping towards nothingness, is He whose look gives life. The creature is willed for itself, or, — to quote the words of Professor Secrétan, addressed to you last year, — the foundation of nature is grace.* We ask: What can have been the object of creation? Our reason answers: The Infinite Being can only act from goodness, He can have no other object than the happiness of His creatures.

And now I recapitulate. We ask what is the object of creation; and whereas we cannot transport ourselves into the inaccessible light of the Divine consciousness, we question the work of God in order to discern the intentions of the Creator. From the fact that humanity prays, we gather the reply that man has a spontaneous belief in the goodness of the First Cause of the universe. We place reason in presence of the

* *La raison et le Christianisme:* twelve lectures on the existence of God, one vol. 12mo. In the *Philosophie de la liberté* (2 vols. 8vo.) M. Secrétan has set forth, in a severely scientific form, the arguments of which the reader has just seen the oratorical expression from the pen of Père Lacordaire. This agreement is worth notice, the dates showing that no communication was possible.

idea of the Infinite Being; reason declares to us that He who is the plenitude of Being could not have created except from the motive of love. We understand that God has made all for His own glory, and that His glory consists in the manifestation of His goodness. These thoughts, in their full light, belong to the Gospel revelation, but they appear, under a veil, in the conceptions which lie at the basis of pagan religions. Without entering the temple of idols, we may bow the knee before the pediment of the ancient sanctuary, and, beneath the open vault of heaven, adore, with the Roman people, that God whose goodness takes precedence of His greatness.

The direct consequence of the principles which we have just laid down is that happiness is the object of our existence. Created by goodness, we can have no other end than blessedness.

But beware of supposing that we can take for our guide our desire of happiness, and ourselves calculate its conditions. Happiness is our end; it is the will of our Father; but we must let ourselves be conducted into it. If, shutting our ears to the voice which lays upon us commands and obligations, we would take our destinies into our own hands; if we made the search after happiness our rule, understanding happiness in our own way, we should be taking for light fantastic gleams which would lead us into abysses of ruin. The unruly propensities of our heart would lead ns to make ourselves the centre of the world. To "live for self" is the motto of selfishness, and the watchword of unhappiness. To live for God is the way to happiness. To live to God, that is to say, over the ruins of our shattered selfishness, to enter into order, to take our place in the spiritual edifice of charity, and to share in the joy which God allots to all His children — this is the end of our creation. Once lifted to the height of this thought, we are able to understand the great struggle which rent the conscience of the ancients, because in their times the light of truth illumined only at intervals the clouds of error which covered the world.

There are in man two voices; the one leading him to happiness, the other calling him to holiness. The first impulse of his nature is to start in eager pursuit of mere enjoyment; but ere long the second voice is heard, the voice of conscience, striving to arrest him in his course. If man do not obey her call, conscience becomes his chastiser. Hence arises a painful struggle of conflicting feelings, and the human mind is the subject of a strong temptation to pacify itself by silencing one of the two voices. It is the history of antiquity. Socrates, the wise Socrates, had indeed cried aloud: Woe! woe to the man who separates the just from the useful; and had warned men that happiness may be found apart from what is right and good. Cicero put into beautiful Latin the lessons of the Grecian sage; but the torn heart of man was not long in tearing the mantle of the philosopher. From the thought, full and complete as it is, of Socrates issued two celebrated sects, one of which wished to establish man's life on the basis of duty without reference to happiness; and the other on the basis of happiness without reference to duty.

The Stoics attached themselves to duty; but the need of happiness asserted itself in spite of them, and sought satisfaction in the gloomy pleasure of isolation, and in the savage joy of pride. The sage of these philosophers sets himself free, not only from all the cares of earth, but from all the bonds of the heart, from all natural affection. Finally, by a consequence, at once sad and odd, of the same doctrine, the highest point of self-possession is to prove that man is master of himself, by the emancipation of suicide and in the liberty of death. The Stoic philosopher declares himself insensible to the ills of life; he denies that pain is an evil; and, on the other hand, he claims the right to kill himself in order to escape from the ills of existence! So ended this famous school. At the same period, the herd of Epicurus' followers, giving themselves over to weak and shameful indulgences, were thus in fact laboring with all their might (this is Montesquieu's opinion) to prepare that enormous corruption under which were to sink together the glory of Rome and the civilization of the ancient world.

This struggle which rent the ancient conscience, and which still rends the modern conscience wherever the goodness of God continues veiled — this great conflict is appeased when we have come to understand that goodness is the first principle of things, that happiness is our end, and that the stern voice of conscience is a friendly voice which warns us to shun those paths of error in which we should encounter wretchedness. The conscience is the voice of the Master; and the same authority which, speaking in the name of duty, bids us — "Be good," adds, in the gentle accents of hope — "and thou shalt be happy." Happiness, duty, — these are the two aspects of the Divine Will. Love is the solution of the universal enigma. Therefore, surprising as the thought may be, it is our duty to be happy. Our profession of faith, when we look above, must be: "I believe in goodness;" and when we enter again into ourselves, our profession of faith should be: "I believe in happiness." And we do not believe in it. Not to believe in happiness is the root of our ills; it is the original misery which includes all our miseries. Triflers that we are, we give ourselves up to pleasure because we do not believe in joy: frivolous, we run after giddy excitement because we do not believe in peace: with hearts corrupt, we abandon ourselves to the devouring flame of the passions, because we do not believe in the serene light of true felicity. But the more the thought of God's love enters our mind, the more will faith in happiness issue from our soul as a blessed flower. Happiness is the end of our being; it is the will of the Father. To each one of us are these words addressed: God loves thee; be happy! If therefore (and I address myself more particularly to the younger of my hearers), if in the depth of your soul you are conscious of a sudden aspiration after true felicity, ah! do not suffer the holy flame to be extinguished, do not talk of illusions; do not, I pray you, resign yourselves to the prose of life; to a dreary and gloomy contentedness with a destiny which has no ideal. Your nature does not deceive you; it is you who deceive yourselves, if you seek your own welfare in the world of foolish or guilty chimeras. Listen to all the voices which speak to you of comfort; be attentive to all the words of peace. Seek, labor, pray, till you are able to utter, in quiet confidence, those words of the Psalmist:

In peace I lay me down to rest;
No fears of evil haunt my breast:
In peace I sleep till dawn of day,
For God, my God, is near alway:
On Him in faith my cares I roll;
He never sleeps who guards my soul.*

God in the heart — this it is which adds zest to our enjoyments, sanctifies our affections, calms our

* Je me couche sans peur,
Je m' endors sans frayeur,
Sans crainte je m' éveille.
Dieu qui soutient ma foi
Est toujours près de moi,
Et jamais ne sommeille.

griefs, and which, amidst the struggles, the sorrows, and the harrowing afflictions of life, suffers to rise from the heart to the countenance that sublime smile which can shine brightly even through tears.

THE END.

Cambridge: Printed by John Wilson and Son.

www.ingramcontent.com/pod-product-compliance
Lightning Source LLC
LaVergne TN
LVHW020121110826
845151LV00001B/233

9781425541897